THE ISRAELI-PALESTINIAN CONFLICT
WHAT EVERYONE NEEDS TO KNOW®

THE ISRAELI-PALESTINIAN CONFLICT

WHAT EVERYONE NEEDS TO KNOW®

DOV WAXMAN

OXFORD

UNIVERSITY PRESS

OXFORD
UNIVERSITY PRESS

Oxford University Press is a department of the University of Oxford. It furthers
the University's objective of excellence in research, scholarship, and education
by publishing worldwide. Oxford is a registered trade mark of Oxford University
Press in the UK and certain other countries.

"What Everyone Needs to Know" is a registered trademark of
Oxford University Press.

Published in the United States of America by Oxford University Press
198 Madison Avenue, New York, NY 10016, United States of America.

Library of Congress Cataloging-in-Publication Data
Names: Waxman, Dov, author.
Title: The Israeli-Palestinian conflict : what everyone needs to know /
Dov Waxman.
Description: New York, NY : Oxford University Press, 2019. |
Series: What everyone needs to know | Includes index.
Identifiers: LCCN 2018057081| ISBN 9780190625337 (pbk. : alk. paper) |
ISBN 9780190625320 (hardback : alk. paper) |
ISBN 9780190625344 (Universal PDF) |
ISBN 9780190625351 (electronic publication)
Subjects: LCSH: Arab-Israeli conflict. | Palestinian Arabs—Politics and
government. | Arab-Israeli conflict—Peace.
Classification: LCC DS119.7 .W39935 2019 | DDC 956.04—dc23
LC record available at https://lccn.loc.gov/2018057081

Paperback printed by Sheridan Books, Inc., United States of America
Hardback printed by Bridgeport National Bindery, Inc., United States of America

This book is dedicated to my father, Denis Waxman, who first introduced me to the subject, and dedicated to my wife, Stephanie, who made it possible for me to write this book.

CONTENTS

5 The Occupied Territories   155

Conclusion: The Long Path to Peace   212

PREFACE

The Israeli-Palestinian conflict is not the world's deadliest conflict, nor is it the most destabilizing—the war in Syria has killed vastly more people and wreaked more havoc in just a few years than the Israeli-Palestinian conflict has in decades. But the dispute between Israel and the Palestinians is one of the longest-running conflicts in the world and possibly the most intractable. Despite numerous diplomatic efforts and many years of intermittent peace talks, the Israeli-Palestinian conflict remains stubbornly unresolved, fueling violence on an almost daily basis and intense animosity on both sides. Indeed, to many people, including many Israelis and Palestinians, the Israeli-Palestinian conflict seems interminable and insoluble.

Not only is the Israeli-Palestinian conflict perhaps the world's most intractable conflict, it is also by far the most controversial. No other conflict in the world attracts as much attention, stirs as intense passions, and generates as many news headlines as the Israeli-Palestinian conflict. It is an issue that animates and often angers people who are far removed from the conflict itself. The Israeli-Palestinian conflict is a topic of lively debates in parliaments around the world and in international organizations, of heated arguments on college campuses, and even of bitter disagreements between friends and family members. The high degree of interest in the conflict around the world and the controversy surrounding it is even more remarkable given the fact that the conflict is over a relatively small piece of land and directly involves a relatively small number of people. Many other conflicts of much greater scale and severity receive far less attention.

For whatever reason, the Israeli-Palestinian conflict has captured the world's attention. But despite, or perhaps even because of this interest, the conflict is still poorly understood. This is partially due to the fact that it has become so highly politicized. Instead of trying to understand the conflict in all its complexity, there is a common tendency to take sides. Thus many people adopt a one-sided, simplified view of the conflict, sometimes seeing it as a kind of morality play between good and evil. Such a view obscures the nuances of the conflict and detracts from understanding the perspectives, narratives, and experiences of both sides in the conflict. It's impossible to think about the Israeli-Palestinian conflict completely objectively as we all inevitably bring our own personal backgrounds, beliefs, and biases to the subject, but we can try to shed our preconceptions and prejudices, reevaluate our personal opinions, and even set aside our political, religious, and social allegiances to achieve a reasonably fair, relatively impartial understanding of the conflict. It has undoubtedly become more difficult to do so at a time of increasing political partisanship and polarization, but it is even more necessary.

Another reason why there is so much misunderstanding about the conflict is that most people rely upon the media to inform them about it. The problem with this is not that the media is biased, although it might be, but that it is generally superficial and focused on contemporary events. The context and background to these events, including the long history preceding them, is often missing in media reporting and commentary about the conflict. Consequently, most people only focus on the conflict today and know little, if anything, about its origins and history. All too often, they think the main issue is simply Israeli settlements, Palestinian terrorism, or whatever else is in the news. Finally, if people do seek a deeper understanding of the conflict, and a less biased one, they can quickly become overwhelmed with learning about all the events, issues, and personalities involved. The long duration and sheer complexity of the conflict deter many people who might be interested to learn more about it. The controversial nature of the conflict also means that people are sometimes too wary or intimidated to even ask questions about it.

For all these reasons, there is an acute need for a book that answers the questions many people might have about the Israeli-Palestinian conflict and helps them to make sense of the issue. After years of teaching university students about the conflict and giving public lectures on the topic, I have collected the questions I've been asked most frequently and tried to provide clear, concise answers to them in this book. By answering the most commonly asked questions about the conflict, the purpose of this book is to provide the reader with a helpful guide to what is a highly charged and complex issue. The book aims to provide the reader with important facts and knowledge about the conflict and offer some basic insights. It also seeks to clear up popular misunderstandings and misconceptions about the conflict and its protagonists so that people can have a more accurate and factual understanding about it. The question-and-answer format of this book also enables readers to find it easily accessible. The book thus allows readers with no background knowledge of the subject to have their questions about the conflict answered, and it can serve as a quick reference guide for those who already have some knowledge. It can be read from start to finish or by "dipping in" and picking whichever questions and answers are of interest.

The chapters in this book cover the evolution of the conflict from the rise of the Zionist movement in the late nineteenth century, through the various Arab-Israeli wars and the peace process, and up to the present day. In covering the history of the conflict, rather than provide a detailed description of all its events and developments, as traditional narrative histories of the conflict try to do, this book focuses on explaining the major events and the impacts they have had upon the conflict. Since Israelis and Palestinians often view these events very differently, the book also highlights these contrasting popular narratives because they not only play a key role in shaping their collective beliefs about the conflict but also fuel the conflict itself. What matters, in other words, is not simply what happened and why, but also how it is collectively interpreted and remembered by Israelis and Palestinians. In addition to analyzing the critical events and accompanying narratives that have shaped the Israeli-Palestinian conflict, the book will also examine the major issues that must be resolved to peacefully end the conflict. In doing so, it will try to explain why the conflict has been so hard to resolve. This book, however, cannot cover the entirety of the conflict or examine every facet of it. By necessity, it concentrates only on the major events and issues and omits a lot of detail. I do not offer a comprehensive history of the conflict—there are already many such books available—nor an in-depth study of the many issues at stake in the conflict.

Through its selectivity and brevity in covering the conflict, this book may be subject to criticism over what is omitted or given little attention. Such criticism is especially likely since the subject of the book is so controversial. Indeed, writing a book about the Israeli-Palestinian conflict, let alone one that proclaims to offer "what everyone needs to know" about it, is a daunting task. Partisans of both sides are bound to take issue with some of my answers, and accusations of unfairness or bias are almost inevitable. Although I've attempted to be as impartial as possible, the book is unavoidably informed by my own views and values and shaped by my upbringing, education, and experiences. Even my choice of words and terminology is inherently political (for instance, my use of the term "West Bank" rather than the biblical name for the area, "Judea and Samaria"). Nevertheless, throughout the book, I've tried to present the different perspectives and narratives of Israelis and Palestinians and avoid "playing the blame game." I have done so not only because this book is meant to be a primer, not a polemic, but also because I believe there is enough blame to go around. Neither side is wholly innocent or completely guilty, and both sides have legitimate rights and needs. As the recently deceased Israeli novelist Amos Oz once put it, "The Israeli-Palestinian conflict is a tragedy; it is a clash between right and right. And therefore it's not black and white. Sometimes, recently it is indeed a clash between wrong and wrong." Fundamentally, I hope this book will enable readers to better understand this ongoing tragedy and that greater understanding can help finally end the conflict.

MAPS

Map 1 Present-day map of Israel and its neighbors

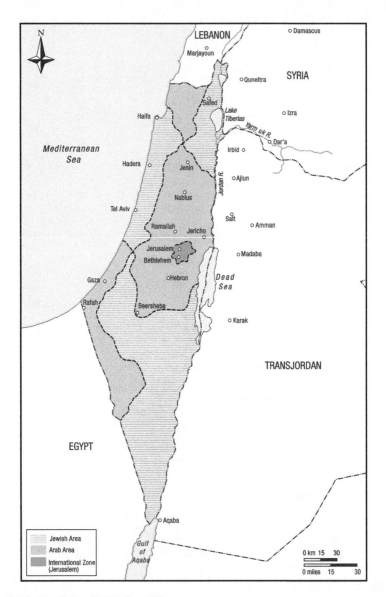

Map 2 United Nations Partition Plan, 1947

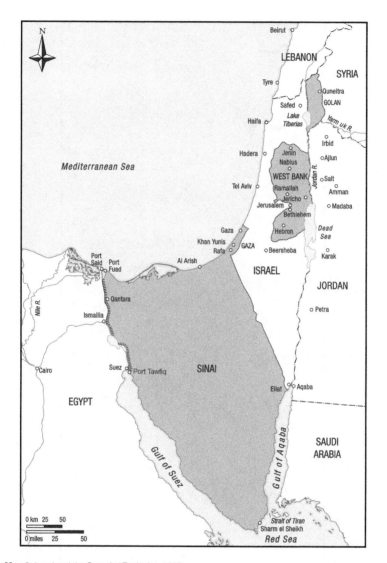

Map 3 Israel and the Occupied Territories, 1967

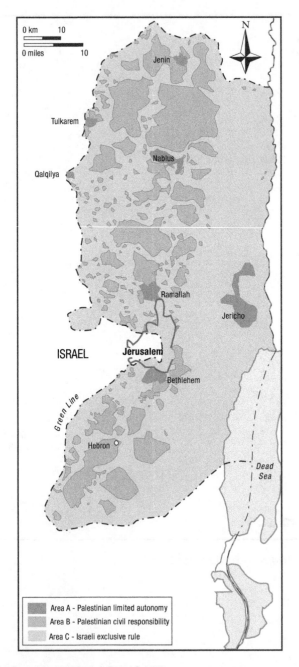

Map 4 West Bank divided into Areas A, B, and C, 1995

1

THE BASICS

Who is the conflict between?

To understand any conflict, the first and most basic task is to accurately identify the parties involved. When it comes to the Israeli-Palestinian conflict, this is not as straightforward as it might seem. As with so much about the conflict, there is disagreement over who are the main protagonists. Is it just a conflict between Israelis and Palestinians, or is it a broader conflict between Israel and the Arab world or even between Jews and Muslims worldwide? How you answer this question shapes not only how you perceive the conflict but also whom you might sympathize with. Many people tend to instinctively sympathize with the supposed underdog, just as they root for the underdog in a sports match. If Israel is perceived as a tiny state in the Middle East up against the combined might of the Arab world, consisting of twenty-two Arab states and over three hundred million Arabs, then it appears to be the underdog in need of support. This is how most Israelis have generally viewed the conflict along with many of their supporters around the world. Conversely, if the conflict is seen as simply pitting Israel against the Palestinians, then sympathy shifts toward the Palestinians as they are the weaker party. Most Palestinians and their supporters tend to see it this way, especially in recent decades.

So who's right? Well, to some extent they both are because there are actually two distinct conflicts that are overlapping and interrelated. These two conflicts are often confused or sometimes deliberately conflated. The first conflict—which is the main focus of this book—is between Israelis (primarily Israeli Jews) and Palestinians. This is the principal and most enduring conflict. It started around a century ago as an intercommunal conflict between Arabs and Zionist Jews living in the territory then known as Palestine. Fundamentally, it was a conflict between two communities whose dominant nationalist movements both claimed the right to exercise national self-determination and assume sovereignty over the same piece of land. After the Zionists succeeded in establishing their state in 1948, what was initially a conflict between two groups competing for statehood developed into a conflict between the State of Israel and Palestinians, who remained stateless. That dynamic continues to this day as Palestinians still aspire to national self-determination, although the conflict for control over land, resources, and religious sites now largely focuses on a much smaller geographic area than pre-1948 Palestine, consisting of the West Bank, East Jerusalem, and the Gaza Strip—areas that Israel captured in the 1967 Arab-Israeli war (the "Six-Day War").

In addition to the Israeli-Palestinian conflict, there is a second conflict, separate but interconnected with the first, which can be designated as the "Arab-Israeli conflict." This is an interstate conflict between Israel and the Arab states of the Middle East. The broader Arab-Israeli conflict began immediately after Israel's founding in 1948, and for the next three decades it overshadowed and even eclipsed the narrower Israeli-Palestinian conflict. For many years, the Arab states categorically rejected Israel's right to exist, and they called for the elimination of what they referred to as the "Zionist entity" from their midst. This arose partly from a genuine sense of solidarity with the Palestinians, whose cause resonates widely in the Arab world, but also because Arab regimes, though authoritarian, were (and are) sensitive to domestic public opinion, which is strongly pro-Palestinian. The Arab states' opposition to Israel has also been motivated by Arab nationalist ideology, including pan-Arabism, which views the creation of Israel as another attempt by Western powers to colonize Arab land and weaken and divide the Arab world. Israel's very existence, therefore, was seen as an affront to Arab dignity and a major impediment to Arab unity and power.

Although the Arab states have often claimed to be acting on behalf of the Palestinians, their actions have been primarily determined by their own national interests (as defined by their regimes).

Despite their solidarity with the Palestinians and their rhetoric of Arab unity, in practice each of the Arab states has pursued their own policies vis-à-vis Israel, and some have been much more combative and aggressive than others. All the Arab states have lent varying degrees of support to the Palestinian cause, and for decades they collectively boycotted Israel, but not all of them have actually fought against it. Just a few Arab states have engaged in full warfare against Israel—its immediate neighbors, Egypt, Syria, and Jordan—while others have contributed troops on occasion, if only token amounts (Lebanon, Iraq, Algeria, Morocco, Yemen, and Saudi Arabia). The most common forms of support the Arab states have given to the Palestinians have been diplomatic and financial. The wealthy, oil-rich Arab states of the Gulf have been the biggest benefactors of the Palestinians. Saudi Arabia has provided the most aid, amounting to many billions of dollars over the years. This largesse is motivated by Saudi Arabia's commitment to Arab and Islamic causes, which is one of the foundations of the Saudi royal family's domestic legitimacy and their alliance with the country's Wahhabi religious establishment. But it also serves Saudi Arabia's strategic interests and desire to lead the Sunni Muslim world since it is the birthplace of Islam and home of its two holiest mosques (in Mecca and Medina).

While the Saudis continue to donate a lot of money to the Palestinians, their attitude toward Israel has shifted over time—from completely rejecting its existence to proposing its own peace initiative in 2002 (which was subsequently adopted by the Arab League and endorsed by the Organization of Islamic Cooperation). This proposal, now known as the "Arab Peace Initiative," promised to end the Arab-Israeli conflict and establish full diplomatic relations with Israel if it withdrew from all the territory it occupied, accepted the establishment of a Palestinian state, and reached a "just solution to the Palestinian refugee problem." The Arab Peace Initiative made clear that the Arab world was ready to make peace with Israel if it resolved its conflict with the Palestinians and its territorial disputes with Syria and Lebanon. Although the Israeli government at the time dismissed the proposal, it remains on the table to this day.

Not only has Saudi Arabia offered to make peace with Israel and encouraged the rest of the Arab world to do the same, in recent years it has surreptitiously developed relations with the Jewish state, despite still not officially recognizing it. This is largely because it shares

Israel's antipathy toward Iran (in accordance with the old proverb, "the enemy of my enemy is my friend"). Their mutual hostility toward Iran has produced a thaw in relations between the Saudi and Israeli governments, and even raised some hopes of a new anti-Iranian alliance that would transcend the Arab-Israeli conflict and possibly reshape the strategic landscape of the Middle East. As long as the Israeli-Palestinian conflict remains unresolved, such hopes are probably premature at best. Nevertheless, the burgeoning relationship between Israel and Saudi Arabia and some other Arab Gulf states (particularly the United Arab Emirates and Oman) clearly demonstrates the diminishing importance of the Arab-Israeli conflict in the region's affairs. It is no longer the greatest source of tension or instability in the Middle East, as it once was. In fact, since the late 1970s the Arab-Israeli conflict has been winding down, though it has not entirely abated. Egypt and Jordan have made peace with Israel (in 1979 and 1994 respectively), leaving only Syria and Lebanon as the so-called frontline Arab states still officially at war with Israel. Most other Arab states have, however reluctantly, come to terms with Israel's existence in the region, and a few now maintain discreet diplomatic, commercial, and even security relationships with Israel. Yet, though the Arab-Israeli conflict has waned, popular sentiment across the Arab world remains strongly supportive of the Palestinians and hostile to Israel.

While Israel's relations with Arab states have, in most cases, gradually improved over the past four decades (not without some serious setbacks), its relationship with Iran has severely deteriorated. They were once allies, but after the Iranian revolution in 1979 that overthrew the Pahlavi monarchy and established an Islamic Republic, the Iranian regime made hostility to Israel and support for the Palestinians a core tenet of its radical ideology and a central pillar of its foreign policy (this has been a way for the regime to shore up its domestic support, increase its popularity across the Muslim world, and bolster its regional ambitions). The Iranian regime has demonized Israel in its official discourse (referring to it as "little Satan"), rejected its right to exist, and repeatedly called for its destruction. The Islamic Republic of Iran's strident opposition to Israel has been more than merely rhetorical. It has funneled large sums of money and weapons to militant Islamist groups fighting against Israel—most notably, the Lebanese group Hezbollah and the Palestinian group Hamas—and to Syria, Israel's main Arab adversary. The so-called Axis of Resistance that Iran has forged with Syria, Hezbollah, and Hamas has become Israel's primary threat. Indeed, the Israeli government and most Israelis are currently more preoccupied with this threat than with Israel's ongoing conflict with the Palestinians. Iran is now their biggest concern, not the Palestinians or the Arab states.

Who are the Israelis?

Israelis are citizens of the State of Israel. Israeli citizenship is granted to anyone with an Israeli parent, whether or not they are born in Israel; to anyone born in Israel if they apply for citizenship between the ages of 18 and 25 and have been living there for five consecutive years; and to any Jew who immigrates to Israel under the Law of Return (passed in 1950). A 1970 amendment to the Law of Return also grants the children and grandchildren of any Jew, as well as their spouses, the right to immigrate to Israel and receive citizenship. This has enabled hundreds of thousands of non-Jews (by the criteria of Orthodox Judaism) to immigrate to Israel, most of them from the former Soviet Union (FSU)—part of a wave of emigration to Israel from the USSR that began in the 1970s and accelerated in the 1990s after the end of the Cold War and the collapse of the Soviet Union.

Today, there are around 1.2 million "Russian" Israelis (immigrants from the FSU and its successor states), comprising almost 15 percent of Israel's total population of 8.9 million citizens (this figure includes Israelis living in the West Bank). They constitute the largest immigrant community in Israel and the third-largest Russian-speaking community in the world living outside the FSU. Though integrated into Israeli society, they maintain a separate subculture in Israel with their own Russian-language newspapers and television stations. They also have their own political party, Yisrael Beiteinu ("Israel Is Our Home"), whose right-wing secular nationalist orientation regarding the Israeli-Palestinian conflict has made it both a political ally and an electoral competitor with Israel's dominant right-wing party, Likud. Most members of Israel's large Russian-speaking community are politically on the right—largely because they tend to favor a hawkish approach to the Israeli-Palestinian conflict and oppose making territorial concessions to the Palestinians. Hence this community wields considerable political clout and has had a significant role in moving the Israeli electorate to the right over the past decade.

In addition to immigrants from the former Soviet Union, there are also sizable, but smaller, communities of Israelis from Ethiopia (approximately 125,000), India (approximately 80,000), and dozens of other countries. Indeed, Israel's population is a mosaic of different ethnicities—much more diverse than the popular image of Israelis as mostly European in origin. While this was once true—when Israel was founded in 1948, the vast majority of its Jewish citizens were of European origin—over time, due largely to immigration, Israel's population has significantly grown and diversified. It is now more than ten times larger than it was in 1948, and more than half of the country's Jewish population is of at least partial Middle Eastern or North African origin.

Nowadays, Israeli Jews are roughly divided between those of European descent (*Ashkenazim*) and those of Middle Eastern or North African descent (*Mizrahim*, i.e., "Eastern" Jews, sometimes also called *Sephardim*). Due to increasing intermarriage between the two ethnic groups, many younger Israeli Jews are of mixed Mizrahi-Ashkenazi ancestry. This is one way in which the longstanding ethnic divide between Ashkenazim and Mizrahim in Israel—with the former occupying the upper echelon of Israeli society and traditionally dominating Israeli politics—has gradually narrowed over the years, although it has not entirely disappeared (Mizrahi Jews still tend to be less affluent and proportionally less well represented than Ashkenazi Jews in the Israeli political and cultural establishment).

Another major change in Israel's population over the years is the growing number of native-born Israelis (called *Sabras* in Hebrew). When the state was established, most of its citizens were foreign-born, with only 35 percent of its Jewish citizens actually born there. In 2017, by contrast, around three-quarters of Israelis were born in Israel, more than half of them to parents who were also born in Israel. Israeli society, therefore, is no longer the predominantly immigrant society it once was. Successive waves of mass Jewish immigration from around the world transformed Israeli society, beginning in the immediate aftermath of the state's founding when the population more than doubled with the arrival of roughly 700,000 Jews from war-torn Europe, most of them Holocaust survivors, and Jews from

Libya, Yemen, and Iraq. This was followed by the immigration of Jews from other Arab countries (mainly, Morocco, Tunisia, and Egypt) in the 1950s and 1960s, and later Jews came from Ethiopia and the FSU. Although Jews still immigrate to Israel, their numbers have significantly declined, despite ongoing efforts by the Israeli government, and some nongovernmental organizations, to incentivize Jewish immigration (while immigration has declined, so too has emigration).

The demographic makeup of Israeli society has, therefore, changed considerably over the past seven decades of Israel's existence. Who Israelis are, in other words, is quite different today than who they once were. They used to be mostly European immigrants; now they are mostly Israeli-born and ethnically mixed. What has not changed, however, is the fact that most Israelis are Jewish (75 percent), whether or not they are religious. Although the proportion of Israel's population that is not Jewish has increased from less than one in five Israeli citizens in the past to one in four today, the state still has a large, and fairly stable, Jewish majority (maintaining this majority has always been one of its central objectives). Israel's Jewish majority is politically, economically, and culturally dominant—so much so, in fact, that the term "Israeli" is basically synonymous with being Jewish in common Israeli discourse.

Around 21 percent of Israeli citizens are Arab (1.8 million people in total). Israel's Arab population, like its Jewish population, is diverse. It is composed of different religious and ethnic groups—principally, Muslims, Christians, Druzes, and Bedouins—each with its own distinct sense of identity. Muslims are the largest group, making up more than three-quarters of the Arab population. Bedouins (once seminomadic shepherds) are a subgroup within the Muslim population, numbering around 170,000, and mostly residing in the southern Negev (*Naqab*) desert region of the country and northern Galilee. Christian Arabs, about 9 percent of the total Arab population, are themselves divided into many different sects. Finally, the Druzes (also roughly 9 percent of the Arab population) are the most distinct group, generally having quite different attitudes than the rest of the Arab minority. Unlike other Arab citizens of Israel, Druzes are conscripted into the Israeli military (like Jews), something that has alienated them from other Arabs in Israel (a very small minority of whom—mostly Bedouins—volunteer for military service).

Israel's Arab population has grown in size and confidence over the years. They have also grown more politically assertive, defending their individual rights as citizens of Israel, demanding their collective rights as a minority, and increasingly calling for the abolition of Israel's self-definition as a Jewish state. Many "Israeli Arabs" (as Israeli governments and Israeli Jews generally refer to them), perhaps most, have embraced Palestinian nationalism and prefer to identify themselves as Palestinian Israelis or simply as Palestinian citizens of Israel. Their close identification with Palestinians living in the West Bank, the Gaza Strip, and East Jerusalem (who are not citizens of Israel), and their support for the Palestinian national cause, has been a source of growing tension with Israeli Jews, who tend to regard this as disloyal and threatening. Relations between Israel's Jewish majority and Arab minority have never been good, with high levels of fear and mistrust on both sides. But they have become even worse in recent years as Arabs have become more successful, more visible, and more outspoken. This has provoked a backlash from many Israeli Jews who perceive them as a demographic and security threat, a potential "fifth column" in Israel's ongoing conflict with the Palestinians.

Arab citizens of Israel have the same democratic rights as Israeli Jews—for instance, they can vote for and are elected to the Knesset, they serve as mayors and judges, and they freely express their views and practice their own religion—but they have suffered from discrimination and neglect by the state (as recognized in a groundbreaking report issued in 2003 by the Orr Commission, an Israeli government-appointed body headed by a former Supreme Court judge). To be sure, in some respects Arab citizens of Israel have undoubtedly benefited from living there. Their living standards have dramatically improved since Israel's establishment, and their health, education, and income have greatly increased (their life expectancy, for instance, has risen by thirty years). Yet, despite this progress, there is still systematic inequality between Arabs and Jews in most aspects of life. While Arabs are no longer the completely ghettoized minority they were during the first two decades of Israel's existence when most lived under repressive military rule, they remain a self-conscious, often stigmatized minority, still subject to the suspicion and at times outright hostility of members of the Jewish majority. They are largely excluded from Israeli policymaking and marginalized in Israeli society and politics. To this day, Jews and Arabs in Israel generally reside in different areas, attend different schools, and rarely socialize. Indeed, the divide between Jewish and Arab citizens of Israel is the deepest social cleavage within the country. There are many divisions in Israeli society (such as that between secular and religious Jews), but the social and political divide between the Jewish majority and the Arab minority is the biggest. Whether Arabs can be truly accepted as Israelis, with full equality, and completely identify as Israelis is still an open question.

What's the difference between Israelis and Jews?

It is essential to clearly distinguish between Israelis and Jews as these terms are frequently confused (in popular Palestinian discourse, for example, Israelis are often referred to as Jews). The term "Israeli" denotes a person's citizenship, whereas the term "Jew" describes a person's religion and/or ethnic background.

While the definition of a Jew is contested among Jews themselves, especially now that intermarriage between Jews and non-Jews is common, there is a general consensus that a Jew is someone who practices Judaism (there is no agreement on the version of Judaism practiced) or someone who is born to a Jewish mother (or a Jewish father, according to more progressive streams of Judaism, like the Reform and Reconstructionist movements). It is thus possible, and indeed quite common, for a Jew to be completely secular and still consider themselves, and be considered by other Jews, to be Jewish. Jews are defined not only by religion but also by descent. Hence, Jews are an ethno-religious group that shares a common religious and cultural heritage and a belief in their common ancestry (i.e., the ancient Israelites). Jews are not, however, a race (contrary to racial antisemitism and Nazi ideology). Whether Jews are a nation has been a topic of prolonged Jewish debate for more than two hundred years, since the advent of modern nationalism. Some Jews, especially those in Israel, claim that Jews are a nation—modern Zionism is based upon this fundamental claim—but others believe that while Jews are a people, they are not really a nation.

Based on this brief definition of who Jews are, it should be clear that they are not the same as Israelis. There are Israelis who are not Jewish, and there are Jews who are not Israeli. Most Israelis are

Jewish, but a significant minority of them, about a quarter, are not. While there are nearly 6.6 million Jews living in Israel, there are even more living in other countries. The total Jewish population in the world is estimated to be between fourteen and fifteen million (just 0.2 percent of the world's population). More than 80 percent of world Jewry is concentrated in Israel and the United States. Israel's share of the world's Jewish population has skyrocketed since the country's founding, from 6 percent in 1948 to 45 percent in 2018. Even so, to this day most Jews in the world still do not live in Israel. Instead, they remain in what is called the "diaspora" (a term derived from the Greek word meaning "to scatter about"). There is also now a growing Israeli diaspora, with estimates of its size varying widely from around three hundred thousand people to more than a million, most of them living in the United States, Russia, Canada, the United Kingdom, and Germany.

The Jewish diaspora has existed for more than 2,600 years since its beginnings during the Greek and Roman empires. During this long history, Jewish communities of varying sizes have been established all over the world. Today, there are Jewish communities in around a hundred different countries, some numbering just a few dozen Jews (or even less) and others hundreds of thousands (the largest Jewish communities are in North America and Western Europe). By far the biggest Jewish community in the diaspora is the American Jewish community, comprising roughly six to seven million Jews, which is about 40 percent of world Jewry and almost 70 percent of diaspora Jewry. Given the diversity of the Jewish diaspora, it is impossible to generalize about its relationship with Israel. Different Jewish communities have different relationships with Israel. Some are close—marked by a strong emotional attachment to Israel, a high volume and frequency of visits to Israel, and a lot of political and financial support for the country—while others are more distant. The kind of relationship that exists depends upon many factors, such as the size, location, and demographics of the community, its history, and its relationship with the society and state in which it is based. In states that are hostile to Israel, for example, it is difficult and sometimes dangerous for members of the local Jewish community to maintain active relations with Israel (the Soviet Union once contained the third-largest Jewish community in the world, but until the late 1980s, Jews there were forbidden from maintaining any kind of relations with Israel).

It would be remiss, therefore, to assume that all diaspora Jews identify with Israel or support it. Many do, but not all, and there are also many who are ambivalent, alienated, or just apathetic. Although there is widespread support for Israel in the Jewish diaspora, there is also growing criticism of its government's policies, especially regarding Palestinians. This is particularly the case among American Jews, who are becoming increasingly divided over Israel. Compared with their counterparts in Israel, American Jews are, on average, more liberal politically, religiously, and socially. Growing numbers of them are married to non-Jews or are the offspring of mixed marriages (in Israel, by contrast, Jews cannot legally marry non-Jews). The practice of Judaism in the United States also tends to differ from that in Israel, where an Orthodox rabbinical establishment wields control over most aspects of Jewish religious life. These differences mean that Jews in Israel and the United States do not necessarily share the same political opinions, cultural values, religious beliefs, or even Jewish identities. Nor do Jews elsewhere (which is one reason why antisemitic stereotypes are false). Hence, not only is it essential to distinguish between Israelis and Jews, it is also crucial to distinguish between Jews in Israel and Jews living in other countries.

Who are the Palestinians?

There are few nations in the world as misunderstood and maligned as the Palestinians. For decades, their very existence was doubted and denied, not only by Israeli Jews who long believed, as Israel's prime minister Golda Meir famously put it in an interview in 1969, "there was no such thing as Palestinians," but also by many Americans and Europeans who only saw Palestinians as Arabs, not as a distinct nation. Once Israelis, Americans, and Europeans finally began to recognize the existence of a Palestinian nation (it was not until 1978 that Israel officially acknowledged Palestinian nationhood), Palestinians were often perceived, and depicted in the media and popular culture, solely as terrorists and fanatics. This common stereotype of Palestinians still appears in the media, and it prevails in the imagination of many Israeli Jews and their supporters abroad. Needless to say, it is both inaccurate—only a tiny percentage of Palestinians have ever engaged in terrorism (although many have supported it at times)—and demeaning.

To begin with, then, it is necessary to dispel the belief that Palestinians are not really a nation. It is impossible to understand the Israeli-Palestinian conflict without recognizing the simple fact that Palestinians see themselves as a nation. Unlike many nations, the Palestinians do not have a state of their own. Their collective demand for statehood is one of the driving forces of the conflict, but this does not mean that they lack a national identity. Palestinian national identity has developed despite the fact that Palestinians are stateless and geographically dispersed. In fact, the condition of statelessness, dispersal, and exile has been central to the formation and definition of Palestinian national identity. In this respect, Palestinian identity is like Jewish identity, which has also been shaped by the experience of exile, dispersion, and statelessness. A massive tragedy and collective trauma is also central to the definition of Palestinian identity and modern Jewish identity. For Palestinians, it is what they call *Al-Nakba* ("the catastrophe" in Arabic), referring to the forced displacement and dispossession of Palestinians in 1948; for Jews, it is the Holocaust (*Ha-Shoah* in Hebrew, which actually also means "the catastrophe"). But unlike Jewish identity, which is millennia old, Palestinian identity is comparatively new. It is a modern identity, not an ancient one. Before the twentieth century, there was no Palestinian national identity, which is why some people continue to dispute the existence of a Palestinian nation.

The modernity of Palestinian nationalism does not discredit it. Nationalism itself is a modern cultural and political phenomenon, dating back to the end of the eighteenth century. Before then, there were no "nations" as we identify them today (although scholars of nationalism have argued that some modern nations grew from premodern ethnic groups). It was not until the nineteenth century that people began to think of themselves and others as members of different nations. In many parts of the world, this didn't happen until even more recently, as new states were formed from the rubble of European empires. Most of the states and nationalities of the Middle East (such as Syrians, Lebanese, Jordanians, and Iraqis) emerged during the first half of the twentieth century, as products of, and in reaction to, British and French colonialism in the region. The same was true for Palestinians, although their nationalism arose in response to the emergence of other local Arab nationalisms as well as in resistance to Zionism and British colonialism (the extent to which Palestinian nationalism was a reaction to Zionism is a subject of scholarly debate).

While it is possible to date the first stirrings of Palestinian nationalism back to the mid-nineteenth century—when the local population in Palestine rebelled in 1834 against the occupying Egyptian army that had invaded the region a few years earlier—the population did not identify as Palestinians throughout the nineteenth century. Instead, they had local identities (based upon which cities or villages they lived in), tribal identities, religious identities, and perhaps a weak sense of Ottoman identity (since the area had been under Ottoman rule for hundreds of years). Toward the end of the nineteenth century, they also developed an Arab identity due to the rise of Arab nationalism. This started as a form of cultural nationalism celebrating Arabic language and literature and the Arabs' seminal contribution to Islamic civilization, and then it grew into a political nationalism largely in reaction to the increasing centralization of political and administrative power in the Ottoman Empire and the "Turkification" policies of its rulers (especially after 1908 under the regime of the Young Turks).

Arab nationalism historically preceded Palestinian nationalism. The first time that a distinct Palestinian identity was articulated was in the pages of Arabic-language newspapers published in Ottoman Palestine in the years immediately before World War I (one such newspaper, founded in 1911, was called *Filastin* [Palestine]). Palestinian nationalist organizations were formed during the war, and once it ended and the Ottoman Empire collapsed, the first Palestinian-Arab Congress took place in Jerusalem in 1919. The participants at that historic conference, however, did not call for an independent Palestinian state. Rather, they wanted to be part of a Greater Syria, issuing the following resolution: "We consider Palestine as part of Arab Syria, as it has never been separated from it at any time. We are connected with it by national, religious, linguistic, natural, economic and geographical bonds." It was only later, during the interwar years under British rule, that Palestinian nationalists sought a separate Palestinian state. Palestinian national consciousness gradually spread beyond the urban, upper and middle classes to the masses (partly due to the influence of the Arabic press and increasing literacy).

Thus, the Palestinian nation, like many nations, is a modern creation. This should not call into question its legitimacy or authenticity. It exists simply because large numbers of people identify as Palestinians. To be a Palestinian today, one does not have to be a resident of the Palestinian territories (the West Bank and Gaza Strip), nor does one need to be born in historic Palestine (including present-day Israel) or even to have set foot there. There are many Palestinians living in the West who have never been to Palestine and don't even speak Arabic, yet they proudly identify themselves as Palestinian. Their Palestinian identity is based upon their heritage (if one or both parents, or even grandparents, are Palestinian) and their attachment to the Palestinian collective memory and national narrative.

Only around half of the estimated 12.5 million Palestinians in the world today live in historic Palestine—Israel, the West Bank, and the Gaza Strip (12 percent live in Israel and 38 percent in the West Bank and Gaza Strip). The West Bank is home to the highest concentration of Palestinians—2.9 million according to the Palestinian Central Bureau of Statistics (a figure that some claim is inflated). There are 1.9 million Palestinians crowded into the Gaza Strip and another 1.8 million or so Palestinians who are citizens of Israel (comprising roughly 20 percent of Israel's population). While there are deep and extensive ties between these three groups of Palestinians, especially since the West Bank and Gaza came under Israeli control in 1967, their geographical fragmentation has created significant, and growing, differences. Palestinians with Israeli citizenship enjoy much more freedom and opportunity than do Palestinians in the West Bank and Gaza Strip, although many still feel like second-class citizens in Israel. For more than a decade now, Palestinians in the West Bank have lived under a different regime than those in the Gaza Strip, and they have generally been better off. Finally, the approximately 370,000 Palestinians in East Jerusalem—which Israel has annexed—also have a different status since they are entitled to work in Israel and have access to its welfare system as residents (but not citizens) of Israel. These differences, along with others, mean that even in their homeland, Palestinians are divided—geographically, politically, legally, and socially.

The Palestinian diaspora (comprising about 6 million people) is also far from monolithic. Although almost all identify as refugees and share a collective narrative of displacement, dispossession, and exile, Palestinians in the diaspora have varied experiences and different rights. Even in the Arab countries where most Palestinian refugees live, their predicaments differ. The largest number of Palestinians in the diaspora, more than two million, live in Jordan, where most, but not all, have full citizenship. Until the outbreak of the Syrian civil war in 2011, the second-largest population of Palestinian refugees (around half a million) was in Syria. Since then, many have fled or been driven out to Lebanon, which also has a large population of Palestinian refugees (approximately 450,000). Palestinian refugees in Lebanon (an estimated 10 percent of the country's total population) have been particularly disadvantaged—they are not allowed to work in many professions, they cannot own property, and they cannot use the state's health services or attend its public schools—with a majority living in refugee camps run by the United Nations and many in severe poverty. Further afield, beyond the Arab world, there are sizable Palestinian communities in Central and South America, the United States, and Western Europe.

Finally, it should be noted that not all Palestinians are Muslim, although the vast majority, more than 90 percent, are (overwhelmingly, Sunni Muslim). Around 6 to 7 percent of Palestinians worldwide are Christians (Orthodox, Catholic, and various Protestant denominations), a majority of them living in the diaspora. Less than 3 percent of Palestinians in the West Bank and Gaza Strip are Christian, a figure that has declined over the years primarily due to the rapid growth of the Muslim population, which has a much higher birth rate than Christian Palestinians, but also because of emigration.

What's the difference between Palestinians and Arabs?

A major reason why people doubt or deny the existence of a Palestinian nation is because they are unable, or unwilling, to recognize the difference between Palestinians and other Arabs. They perceive Palestinians simply as Arabs, or perhaps as a subgroup of a wider Arab nation, but not as a distinct nation themselves. This misperception, in turn, can spur skepticism or even suspicion toward the Palestinian demand for national self-determination. Why, people often wonder, should the Palestinians have a state of their own when there are already so many Arab states? Why can't they live in one of those states if they want to run their own affairs? Since "the Arabs" already have twenty-two states, extending from Morocco in the west to Oman in the east, why are they so opposed to allowing a single, small Jewish state in their midst? What ulterior motive might they have? Right-wing Israeli Jews (and their supporters abroad) have been raising these questions for decades, particularly those who suspect that Palestinian nationalism is a stalking horse, deliberately designed to delegitimize Israel internationally and disguise the Arabs' real ambition to destroy Israel.

Besides propaganda, it is easy to understand popular confusion about Palestinians and Arabs and why the two are sometimes conflated. Palestinians are indeed Arabs, culturally and linguistically. They speak Arabic—a defining feature of Arab identity—and they share a similar culture with other Arabs, especially with those in the surrounding states. But however much Palestinians have in common with other Arabs, they are not identical. Palestinians speak a distinct dialect of Arabic, and they have their own traditions, folklore, customs, and cuisine. Above all, they have developed their own distinct sense of national identity, just as Egyptians, Syrians, Lebanese, and others have done. As with these other cases, Palestinian national identity is not at odds with Arab identity—both identities generally coexist as people can define themselves as both Palestinian and Arab. Nowadays, the term "Arab" refers to people whose first language is Arabic and who identify with Arab culture (the term originally referred to the nomadic inhabitants of the Arabian Peninsula). The Arabs are not a nation, although, like Jews, they do consider themselves a people. Arabs are united by culture and history but not by religion (while most Arabs are Muslims, there are millions of Arabs—about nine million in the Middle East and thirty to thirty-five million worldwide—who are Christian, and even some who are Jewish). Nor are Arabs a race, but they can be loosely defined as an ethnic group or, more accurately, as an ethnolinguistic group. Today, there are more than 350 million Arabs living in the Middle East and North Africa, where they constitute a majority in most states. In the wider Muslim world, however, Arabs are a minority—only about 20 percent of the world's estimated 1.6 billion Muslims are Arab.

Thus, the Palestinians are a distinct nation within a much larger transnational Arab community that is composed of many different nationalities. To be sure, this was not always the case. A century ago, when Palestinian nationalism was just emerging, most Palestinians did not think of themselves as a separate nation but as members of an Arab nation. Arab nationalism was initially much stronger than Palestinian nationalism and has at different times subsumed it (especially during the heyday of pan-Arabism in the late 1950s and early 1960s). Gradually though, Palestinian nationalism has replaced Arab nationalism in the hearts and minds of most Palestinians, especially since 1967. As a result, Palestinians today have their own national identity and their own national aspirations—aspirations that remain unfulfilled. Acknowledging these aspirations is crucial to understanding what motivates the Palestinians and why they are in conflict with Israel.

What are Palestinians and Israelis fighting about?

The simplest way to explain the conflict between Palestinians and Israelis (more precisely Israeli Jews) is that they both lay claim to the same piece of land. Jews call this place the Land of Israel (*Eretz Yisrael* in Hebrew) and Arabs call it Palestine (*Filastin* in Arabic). Both sides insist that this land belongs to them, and both claim the right to exercise sovereignty over it. Palestinians believe that the land is rightfully theirs because they have inhabited it for centuries, and because they constituted a large majority of the local population until Israel's establishment in 1948. Israeli Jews, on the other hand, claim that their ancestors lived there first and once ruled parts of it until they were forcibly driven into exile, during which they longed to return to their original homeland. Moreover, they argue that the virulent antisemitism European Jews faced in the late nineteenth and early twentieth centuries, which culminated in the Holocaust, necessitated a mass resettlement of Jews in what was then Palestine, and the restoration of Jewish political sovereignty there so that Jews could be guaranteed a safe haven. Religious Israeli Jews also believe, based upon various passages in the Bible in which God makes promises to Abraham, Isaac, and Jacob (the three Jewish patriarchs), that God gave the Land of Israel—"the Promised Land"—to the Jewish people for all eternity.

At its core, then, the Israeli-Palestinian conflict is a struggle between two peoples over who gets to rule the land and the population living there. But it is not only about territorial control. To reduce the Israeli-Palestinian conflict to just a territorial dispute downplays what is at stake for both parties and ignores other dimensions of the conflict. Israelis and Palestinians believe that controlling this land, or at least a significant part of it, is essential to fulfilling their national aspirations and even securing their national survival. Both nations want exclusive control over their own affairs (national self-determination), as most nations do since the advent of nationalism, and both believe that their continued existence ultimately depends upon this control. Since both sides are convinced that exercising sovereignty over territory is essential to their future survival, Israelis and Palestinians believe that they are engaged in an existential conflict as well as a territorial conflict. It is also perceived to be an existential conflict because both sides suspect that the other is intent on destroying them. The deep-seated mutual fear and distrust that has developed over the duration of the conflict means that most Israelis and Palestinians have come to regard each other as implacable enemies, with whom long-term peaceful coexistence is impossible (whether this is true is beside the point—it is the perception that matters). Hence, as far as most Israelis and Palestinians are concerned, they are fighting for their lives and for the lives of future generations.

What started as a territorial conflict, therefore, has become, in the minds of its protagonists, an existential conflict—a struggle for survival. The Israeli-Palestinian conflict has also evolved into what scholars in the field of conflict studies term an "identity conflict." This means that the conflict is about the collective identities and narratives of both parties and not just a struggle for material resources (land, water, etc.). During the course of the conflict, both sides have rejected not only the other's territorial claims but also their very existence as a nation. Each has dismissed the other's nationhood as false and invented and denounced the other's national narrative as myths and lies. As a result of this mutual denial, the conflict has become a contest over national identities and the competing historical narratives that shape and sustain them. It is about the past as much as the present and the future. It is important to recognize these abstract, intangible elements of the Israeli-Palestinian conflict in order to understand its intensity and intractability. Unlike, for example, a border dispute between two states, or a civil war between two ethnic groups fighting for material resources or political power, the ongoing battle between Israelis and Palestinians is driven by the collective psychological needs and desires of both sides. It is much harder to reconcile, let alone satisfy, these needs and desires than it is to draw a border on a map, divide land, or share power.

In sum, while the competing claims of two nations to the same piece of land has always been at the heart of the Israeli-Palestinian conflict, it has gained other dimensions over the years, further complicating and prolonging it. In addition to territory, Israelis and Palestinians have been fighting for their security and identity. This has raised the stakes for both sides and made the conflict more difficult to resolve. The salience of these different aspects of the conflict, however, has changed over time. For instance, as Israel's military might has grown, its survival is no longer really in jeopardy (although many Israeli Jews still perceive it to be at risk). Nowadays, the conflict is more about where Israel's final borders should be than it is about Israel's existence (but its right to exist as a specifically Jewish state is still bitterly contested). Similarly, as the existence of the Palestinian nation has been widely recognized, including by Israel (albeit not by all Israelis), the conflict today is less about whether the Palestinians should have statehood and more about the size, location, and prerogatives of a future Palestinian state. But that is not what many ordinary Palestinians living in the West Bank and Gaza care most about nowadays. Above all else, they are fighting for their freedom and dignity. For them, Palestinian statehood is now less of a goal than a means to free themselves from Israeli control and military rule and no longer suffer the hardships and indignities of life under occupation. The average Israeli today—having already achieved statehood—seeks security more than anything else. Reconciling the Palestinians' need for freedom with the Israelis' need for security has, therefore, become the key to resolving this protracted conflict.

What role does religion play in the conflict?

Perhaps the most common misconception about the Israeli-Palestinian conflict is that it is a religious conflict. It is easy to understand why this is such a popular misconception. After all, it is a conflict between two nations with different religions, and it takes place in the "Holy Land," the land of the Bible, the birthplace of Christianity and Judaism—a place that continues to hold immense religious significance for Christians, Muslims, and Jews around the world. Yet, the widespread perception that the Israeli-Palestinian conflict is some kind of religious war is wrong or, at best, grossly oversimplified.

Fundamentally, the conflict is not over religion. It is not about which religion is right or superior, and religious disagreements have not been the main source of strife. In fact, Judaism and Islam have a lot in common, and both religions accept the validity of the other as monotheistic faiths. Although Islam regards itself as the final successor to Judaism and Christianity, holding that everyone should convert to Islam (Judaism, by contrast, is nonproselytizing), the Quran and subsequent Islamic tradition describe Jews and Christians as "People of the Book." As such, they were afforded the status of *dhimmi* (protected people) under Muslim rule, a lesser status than Muslims, but one that allowed Jews and Christians to practice their religion, relatively freely. Historically, Muslims have generally been more tolerant of Jews than Christians have, and large Jewish communities have existed, and even flourished, in Muslim states and Islamic empires (most of these communities have now disappeared largely as a result of emigration, voluntary and forced, to Israel, but some small ones still remain).

Religion, then, is not the cause of the Israeli-Palestinian conflict, but it is inextricably bound up with it. Although it is not primarily a religious conflict, the conflict does have a religious dimension along with its other dimensions. This is most clearly the case with regard to the struggle for sovereignty over the city of Jerusalem (*Yerushalayim* in Hebrew, *Al-Quds* in Arabic), and for control over the many holy sites located in and around its walled Old City (among them the Temple Mount, Western Wall, Dome of the Rock, Al-Aqsa Mosque, and Church of the Holy Sepulchre). Jerusalem's religious importance to Jews, Muslims, and Christians worldwide has always made it a focal point of the conflict. It could even be described as its epicenter. No other place has provoked as much passion and blood-shed throughout the conflict (and, in fact, since long before it began).

Jerusalem is the holiest place in the world for Jews. It is where, according to the Bible, King David established his capital three thou-sand years ago, and where the First Temple (built by King Solomon) and Second Temple (built by King Herod) once stood, the succes-sive centers of Jewish ritual for around a thousand years (there is historical and archaeological evidence confirming the existence of the Second Temple). To this day, the Western Wall, an outer rem-nant from the Second Temple, and the Temple Mount above it are the holiest places in Judaism. This area is also sacred to Muslims, who call it the "Noble Sanctuary" (*al-Haram al-Sharif*). Considered to be the third-holiest place after Mecca and Medina, it is the site of the Al-Aqsa Mosque and the Dome of the Rock (built in the late seventh century by one of the early caliphs). It is where, according to Islam, the prophet Muhammad miraculously ascended to heaven on his winged horse, when he met Allah and received the Islamic commandment to pray five times a day (Jerusalem was actually the first direction of prayer for Muslims before it was changed to Mecca). The sanctity of the Temple Mount/Noble Sanctuary to Jews and Muslims means that both want guaranteed access to it for reli-gious reasons, so control over the area is highly contested. From the earliest days of the conflict until now, the area has been a flashpoint for protests and violence. In fact, the first incidence of large-scale violence between Jews and Arabs occurred in 1929 over a dispute about Jewish activities at the Western Wall. To this day, any sort of change to this area, including archaeological work or even construc-tion designed to improve physical access to it, is fiercely resisted. Compromising over its future status—whether it will be under Israeli or Palestinian sovereignty or neither—has, so far, proven to be impossible for both sides. Indeed, it is perhaps the hardest issue to resolve in the entire conflict.

Religion has thus always played a role in the conflict, but to varying degrees at different points in time. Historically, it has mainly played a supporting or secondary role. From the outset, the conflict has been driven by ideology—Zionism and Palestinian nationalism—much more than by theology. Both nationalisms are motivated by secular political aspirations (above all, national self-determination), not theological ones. Still, from the beginning of the conflict, the Zionist movement and the Palestinian national movement have used religion to promote their interests. Both national movements selectively drew upon religion to mobilize popular support, and both have employed religious concepts, language, and imagery in the service of the nationalist cause, as many other nationalist movements have done.

The instrumental use of religion to serve secular, nationalist goals was most apparent in the case of Zionism. While the Zionist movement always included religious groups and parties within it, it was overwhelmingly a secular movement. Many early Zionist leaders were actually antireligious and stridently opposed to Judaism, regarding it, at best, as simply a means to preserve Jewish identity in the diaspora that would become redundant once Jews returned en masse to their "homeland." In the homeland, they wanted to create a secular society. Yet, ironically, the homeland had immense religious significance as the land that Jews traditionally believed had been given to them by God and to which diaspora Jews had always prayed to eventually return to. The Land of Israel had an emotional appeal for Jews that no other territory had, so the Zionist movement relied upon a religiously sacred territory to achieve its secular, nationalist ambitions. To spur mass Jewish emigration, the leaders of the Zionist movement chose the Land of Israel (Palestine) as the territory for settlement. Even the Hebrew word for immigration to Palestine (and now Israel)—*aliyah* ("to ascend")—carried a religious connotation. Furthermore, when it came to justifying the Zionist movement's claim to Palestine, secular Zionist leaders also drew upon religion, presenting the Bible as an ancient national history of the Jewish people and proof that the land belonged to the Jews.

Religion has played an even greater role in Palestinian nationalism. Unlike their secular Zionist counterparts, the early Palestinian leaders were themselves religious. The Palestinian national movement was initially led by a cleric, Hajj Amin al-Husseini; and a religious preacher, Izz al-Din al-Qassam, launched the first Palestinian armed struggle against the Zionists. Palestinian nationalist leaders have regularly employed Islamic rhetoric and symbols to mobilize the Palestinian masses in support of the national cause. In the 1920s and 1930s, for example, Husseini frequently tried to stir up popular sentiment against the Zionists by alleging a Jewish threat to Muslim holy sites, especially the Al-Aqsa Mosque in Jerusalem (a tactic also employed more recently by Palestinian leaders). Later Palestinian leaders, most notably Yasser Arafat (the longtime chairman of the Palestine Liberation Organization [PLO]) have also tried to harness popular religious sentiment among Palestinians to further their nationalist ambitions. Arafat often quoted from the Quran and used Islamic terms and references in his speeches, and the name of the group that he founded and led, Fatah (meaning "conquest" in Arabic), which has dominated Palestinian politics since the early 1960s, has Islamic connotations associated with it (referring to the expansion of the early Islamic empire in the seventh century).

While religion has always impacted the conflict, at times fanning the flames of violence, its role has increased in recent decades, becoming much more pronounced. This is largely due to the growing influence of religious nationalism on both sides. On the Israeli side, religious nationalism has principally taken the form of messianic religious Zionism, whose adherents have spearheaded the Israeli settler movement in the West Bank (or Judea and Samaria, according to its biblical names) and the Gaza Strip. On the Palestinian side, the Hamas movement has been the main exponent of religious nationalism, as it has fused Islamism and Palestinian nationalism. Both messianic religious Zionism and Islamism are varieties of religious fundamentalism. The growing popularity of messianic religious Zionism and Islamism among Israeli Jews and Palestinian Muslims, respectively, has paralleled the global rise of religious fundamentalism. Just as religious fundamentalism has fueled conflict in many places around the world, it has exacerbated the Israeli-Palestinian conflict and made it much harder to resolve. Both messianic religious Zionists and Palestinian Islamists sanctify the territory in dispute (Hamas considers all of historic Palestine to be an Islamic *wakf*, a religious endowment or trust). Both claim exclusive rights to this sacred territory and believe that their religion forbids them from ceding control over any inch of it. Messianic religious Zionists also consider it their religious duty to settle in all parts of the Land of Israel (even in the midst of areas densely populated by Palestinians). For messianic religious Zionists and Palestinian Islamists, therefore, the holy status of the land means that any kind of territorial compromise is a violation of their religious beliefs, and hence something that they are categorically opposed to. This opposition has had a major impact on efforts to make peace between Israel and the Palestinians. In the 1990s, Hamas and the Jewish settler movement were the most determined and powerful opponents of the Oslo peace process. To this day, they continue to form the hardcore opposition to peacemaking, and their significant domestic political power (boosted by support from some of their coreligionists overseas) is a major obstacle to a resolution of the conflict.

Not only has religious extremism on both sides made it much more difficult to make peace, it has also motivated many acts of violence by Palestinians and Israelis and been used to justify and condone many more. Hamas, Palestinian Islamic Jihad, and other Palestinian militant groups, have used Islam to legitimize their use of suicide terrorism against Israelis. Although suicide is forbidden in Islam, Palestinian militant groups justify suicide attacks against Israeli targets by describing it as "martyrdom" rather than suicide. They glorify martyrdom and praise it as an act of supreme religious devotion (dying for the sake of God), one that will be richly rewarded in the afterlife when martyrs will go straight to heaven. The belief that becoming a martyr (*shaheed* in Arabic) is the fulfillment of a religious command has inspired many Palestinian attacks against Israelis. Although religion has by no means been the only motivation for these attacks, it has been an important influence upon many of the attackers.

Militant Islamist groups like Hamas are not the only actors who have carried out political violence in the name of religion and used—or, more accurately, abused—religion to justify such violence. Militant Jewish groups and individuals have also carried out and supported religiously motivated violence, albeit on a lesser scale. Radical Israeli settlers motivated by messianic religious Zionism have perpetrated many acts of violence, including terrorism against Palestinian civilians (some even plotted in 1984 to blow up the Dome of the Rock). The worst instance of violence by a messianic religious Zionist occurred in the early days of the Oslo peace process in February 1994, when a Jewish settler gunned down twenty-nine Palestinians while they prayed in the Ibrahimi Mosque in Hebron (the Muslim site within the Cave of the Patriarchs). To this day, radical settlers glorify this massacre and revere its slain perpetrator as a martyr.

As long as the Israeli-Palestinian conflict continues, religion is likely to play an even greater role in it due to the growing political power of religious Zionists and Palestinian Islamists, and more broadly, the increasing influence that religion is having upon Zionism and Palestinian nationalism. For Palestinians in particular, the Israeli-Palestinian conflict is increasingly portrayed and perceived to be, at least partly, a struggle between Islam and Judaism; and Palestinian political rhetoric has become more anti-Jewish rather than just anti-Israeli in character (in contemporary Palestinian discourse, Jews—and not only Israelis—are frequently denounced, and antisemitic beliefs and themes are widely invoked). If the conflict does eventually become a clash between Muslims and Jews, and between Islam and Judaism, it will become even harder to peacefully resolve, since a conflict over religion is less amenable to compromises and concessions.

What is the size of the territory?

The territory's religious significance is not the only reason why it is so fiercely contested and fought over. Another reason is the simple fact that it is very small. The total land area of Israel, the West Bank, and the Gaza Strip is only about 10,162 square miles (26,320 square kilometers). Outside observers of the Israeli-Palestinian conflict (especially Americans) might find it hard to grasp just how small an area this is. It is smaller than the state of Massachusetts and slightly bigger than Vermont. Not only is the tract of land at stake so small, it is also scarce in natural resources, particularly water. Much of it is desert and inhospitable to humans. The lack of fertile land and water means that these resources are at a premium, and it is hard for Israelis or Palestinians to give them up. Every patch of land and every drop of water counts. This contributes to the conflict's intensity and makes it more difficult to resolve, since it is hard to share or divide the land.

The small size of the territory also means that Israelis and Palestinians live in close proximity (though nowadays they hardly ever meet or interact in person, except at Israeli military checkpoints in the West Bank). The distances between Israeli and Palestinian population centers are very short. Jerusalem, the most populous city in Israel, is less than 20 miles away (about 30 kilometers) from

Hebron, the most populous city in the West Bank. The city of Tel Aviv, which is Israel's commercial and cultural capital, is just 28 miles (45 kilometers) from Ramallah, the political and commercial center of the West Bank. On a clear day, it is possible to stand on a hilltop deep inside the West Bank and see the shimmering coastline of Tel Aviv to the west. In the south, the Israeli city of Sderot is less than a mile (1 kilometer) from the Gaza Strip, which has made it a prime target in recent years for rocket attacks by Palestinian militants in Gaza. Though Sderot is an extreme example, it underlines the security challenges posed by the proximity between Israeli and Palestinian communities. Put simply, it is hard for Israelis and Palestinians to feel safe when their enemies are so near.

For Israelis, it is not only Palestinians who are too close for comfort. They are acutely aware of the fact that Syria, Lebanon, Jordan, and Egypt are next-door and not far away (for instance, it is less than 100 miles from Damascus and Beirut to the Israeli city of Haifa). It could take little time for an invading army to cross Israel's borders and reach its demographic and economic heartland, and even less time for missiles to land. Israel's lack of "strategic depth," and thus vulnerability to external attack, is a fundamental security challenge that has determined its military posture and strategic doctrine from the state's establishment until the present day.

If Israel itself is a small country—about the size of New Jersey—then the West Bank and Gaza Strip are tiny. The West Bank is roughly the same size as the state of Delaware, while the Gaza Strip is approximately the same size as the city of Detroit. Given this, it is hardly surprising that Palestinians are determined to retain all of this land for their state and strongly oppose Israeli territorial demands in the West Bank. In their eyes, every Israeli settlement built in the West Bank eats up a little bit more of their already meager territory. Moreover, as far as Palestinians are concerned, the West Bank and Gaza are just a small fraction of the land of historic Palestine that rightfully belongs to them.

The size of what was once Palestine, however, is not so clear. "Palestine" did not exist as a distinct territorial unit until the twentieth century. Before then, it had different names and vague, shifting boundaries. For four hundred years (1517–1917), it was merely a province of the Ottoman Empire, ruled from Constantinople (today, Istanbul) and divided into different administrative districts.

Palestine was never an independent state. It was only after the British conquered the area from the Ottomans in World War I that Palestine actually became a geopolitical entity. Britain and its wartime ally France first drew up the rough borders of what became Palestine in an agreement that they secretly hatched during the war to divide up the territory of the Ottoman Empire (the 1916 Sykes-Picot Agreement). After the war ended, the newly created League of Nations gave the British permission to rule Palestine in the form of a Mandate. In 1922, after lots of diplomatic haggling, the borders of the British Mandate in Palestine were demarcated, somewhat arbitrarily, and resulted in the large desert area east of the Jordan River that was initially included in the British Mandate being separated and becoming Transjordan (now called Jordan). Palestine was thus defined as the area between the Jordan River and the Mediterranean Sea. This area is what Palestinians have come to call "Palestine" and what Jews call the "Land of Israel" (although its boundaries are fuzzy since it was defined in the Bible in different ways).

Who was there first?

At the heart of the Israeli-Palestinian conflict are the competing claims of two peoples to the same small piece of land. Each side justifies its claim at least partly on the grounds of prior residence in the disputed territory—insisting that they are indigenous to the land, that they lived there first, and that the other is essentially a foreign intruder. Both sides selectively draw upon history, ancient and modern, to construct their own national narratives to support these claims and to counter the other side's claim. These narratives contradict each other in various ways, and there are endless arguments over which side's historical narrative is closer to the truth. Thus, the conflict between Israelis and Palestinians and their foreign supporters has become, among other things, a highly charged intellectual and emotional battle over clashing historical narratives.

The Palestinian narrative begins in the latter half of the nineteenth century, when the territory was under Ottoman rule and Arabs constituted the vast majority of the population (more than 90 percent). The sudden arrival of masses of European Jews beginning in the 1880s and continuing over subsequent decades is presented in this narrative as an unwelcome, foreign intrusion. The European

Jewish immigrants are described as Zionist settlers or colonists and depicted as hostile interlopers, no different than other European colonialists of the time who were busy stealing land and resources from native populations and often violently subjugating them. In this narrative, then, the Palestinian Arabs are the local, indigenous population—and hence the rightful owners of the land—and the Jews are foreigners with no right to be there.

In stark contrast to the Palestinian narrative, the mainstream Israeli-Jewish narrative presents the Jewish people as the indigenous population and the Arabs as the foreign invaders. This narrative begins about three thousand years before the Palestinian narrative, going all the way back to when the ancient Israelites (also known as the Hebrews)—who are supposedly the descendants of the patriarchs Abraham, Isaac, and Jacob and the ancestors of today's Jews—conquered the land of Canaan, a land that they believed had been divinely promised to them. After establishing a series of kingdoms (initially ruled by King Saul, then by King David, followed by King Solomon), the Israelites were conquered by the Assyrian Empire (which destroyed the northern kingdom of Israel in 722 BCE) and then by the Babylonian Empire (which destroyed the remaining southern kingdom of Judea in 586 BCE). More empires came and went—the Persians, the Greeks, and the Romans—until eventually the remaining Jewish population of Judea was massacred and expelled by the Romans in 135 CE after a second failed revolt against Roman rule. The name of the territory was changed to "Palaestina" (from which the modern name of Palestine is derived), and the Jews, now scattered across the Roman Empire and beyond, began their long exile, throughout which they longed to some day return to their homeland. Thus, when large numbers of Jewish immigrants began settling in Palestine from the 1880s onward, they were, according to this narrative, returning home.

Neither of these narratives is simply false, but both are one-sided and selective (as national narratives tend to be). There is plenty of evidence that Arabs largely populated the land for many centuries, since an influx of Arab tribes from the Arabian Peninsula settled in the area during and after the Muslim conquest in the mid-seventh century. There is also textual, archaeological, and even genetic evidence to support Jewish roots in the area, dating back over thousands of years. It is impossible to definitively know who was there first since both sides claim to be the descendants of peoples who inhabited the region in antiquity. While Jews claim to be the descendants of the Israelites, Palestinians have claimed to be descendants of the Canaanites or sometimes the Jebusites or the Philistines (by claiming kinship with these groups, Palestinians assert a historical claim to the land that predates that of the Jews). Both Jews and Palestinians may, in fact, be partially descended from the Canaanites, who are the earliest known inhabitants of the area, entering it around 3000 BCE (some scholars now argue that the Israelites were originally a group of Canaanites who rebelled against the Canaanite urban elite). Indeed, recent genetic studies have found a substantial genetic overlap between most Jews and Palestinians, suggesting that they are genetically related.

Over the course of three millennia since the time of the Canaanites, control over the land, or parts of it, has passed through many hands, from city-states to kingdoms, dynasties, empires, and modern states. There has been a dizzying succession of rulers: Canaanites and Egyptians (circa 3300–1000 BCE), Israelites (circa 1000–722 BCE), Assyrians (722–609 BCE), Babylonians (612–539 BCE), Persians (539–332 BCE), Greeks (332–67 BCE), Hasmoneans (166–37 BCE), Romans (67 BCE–330 CE), Byzantines (330–638), Arabs (638–1071), Turks/Seljuks (1071–1098), Fatimids (1098–1099), Crusaders (1099–1291), Mamluks (1291–1517), Ottomans (1517–1917), Egyptians (1831–1840), British (1917–1948), and Israelis (1948–). Given this long history of invasion and occupation, of settlement and displacement, and the mixing of populations that accompanied it, it is hard to say who is really a native and to whom the land belongs. In any case, it is ultimately beside the point—what matters is that both sides genuinely believe they are entitled to the land.

2

THE BEGINNING OF THE CONFLICT

When did the conflict begin?

By far the most enduring popular myth about the Israeli-Palestinian conflict is that it is an age-old conflict. All too often, one hears the claim that the conflict has been going on for thousands of years. Some even believe that it dates all the way back to the sibling rivalry between Abraham's two sons, Ishmael (his firstborn son with Hagar, his wife's handmaiden, from whom the Arabs are supposedly descended) and Isaac (the son of Abraham's wife Sarah, from whom, according to religious belief, the Jews are descended). Claiming that the conflict has such ancient roots not only suggests that it is driven by some kind of primordial ethnic antagonism between Arabs and Jews but also that it is eternal and, hence, irresolvable. But this assertion has absolutely no factual basis. The Israeli-Palestinian conflict is not the product of a biblical family feud or the culmination of an inherent, ancient hatred. While biblical stories and ancient history are often invoked in the conflict, it did not begin in antiquity. It is, in fact, a modern conflict—about a century old, not millennia old. This still makes it a comparatively long conflict, but not nearly as long as many people believe.

Unlike wars that tend to commence on a specific date, the Israeli-Palestinian conflict has no clear beginning. It slowly developed over time as tensions emerged between Jews and Arabs in Ottoman Palestine. The tensions gradually escalated and led to mounting intercommunal violence under British rule, and finally to all-out hostility, culminating in a vicious war. This process occurred over roughly six decades and was the result of numerous events, developments, decisions, and social forces. There was nothing inevitable or preordained about it. In fact, Jews and Arabs had been coexisting for centuries in the Ottoman Empire (masses of Jews were expelled from Spain and Portugal in 1492, during the Inquisition, and welcomed into the Ottoman Empire). The Jews who lived in Ottoman Palestine—a small fraction of the empire's Jewish subjects—were mostly religious, devoting themselves to the study of Jewish religious texts and depending on the charity of world Jewry for their subsistence. They were mainly concentrated in four cities of religious significance to Jews—Jerusalem, Hebron, Safed, and Tiberias—where they lived peacefully alongside Muslim and Christian Arabs, who comprised the vast majority of the population. At the time, nobody could have imagined that there would be a violent conflict between Jews and Arabs in Palestine.

What triggered this conflict was an event thousands of miles away in Saint Petersburg, the capital of the Russian Empire (which then included the Baltic states and most of Poland and was home to more than half of the world's Jewish population). On March 1, 1881, Tsar Alexander II was assassinated by a group of young Russian revolutionaries. He was succeeded by his son, Tsar Alexander III, who immediately suppressed civil liberties and rolled back many of the domestic reforms his father had initiated. Deeply antisemitic, the tsar blamed Jews for the assassination (only one of the assassins was Jewish) and turned Russia's large Jewish population into a scapegoat for domestic discontent. A wave of anti-Jewish riots and violence, known as "pogroms," took place, and the limited freedoms that Russian Jews had been granted were rescinded. For the Jews of Russia, this was a devastating turn of events, especially since they had experienced an improvement in their material conditions and social and economic rights during the previous two decades or so. This sudden reversal of fortune, and the pogroms, persecution, and poverty that accompanied it, led growing numbers of Russian Jews to conclude that they had no future in the Russian Empire and that they had to leave if they could. Consequently, a mass exodus of Russian Jews began in 1882 and continued until the outbreak of World War I. During this period, more than 2.5 million Jewish refugees fled the Russian Empire. Most went to the United States, others to Western Europe (particularly Germany, France, and

Britain), and some traveled as far as Argentina, South Africa, and Australia. A tiny minority, less than 3 percent of the total (about 70,000 Jews), immigrated to Palestine.

It was the arrival of these Jewish immigrants in Palestine from 1882 onward that sowed the seeds of what eventually became the Israeli-Palestinian conflict. The influx of European Jews into Palestine changed the demographic makeup of the area, which led to growing tension between the newcomers and the local Arab population. In 1882, Jews accounted for no more than 8 percent of the population of Ottoman Palestine. By 1922 (with the establishment of the British Mandate for Palestine), Jews constituted 11 percent of the population. By 1931, they had increased to 17 percent, and just five years later, in 1936, this figure had jumped to 28 percent. By 1946, Jews made up 30 percent of the country's population. Over this entire period (1882–1946), the total number of Jews living in Palestine skyrocketed from 24,000 to 543,000, mostly due to immigration. This single fact explains the origins of the conflict better than any ancient history.

The conflict did not happen overnight. At first, the Jewish immigrants were too few in number to arouse much opposition from the local Arab population. The early encounters between these Jewish immigrants and local Arabs were mixed: often wary (partly because of xenophobia), occasionally violent (due to property disputes and the displacement of Arab tenant farmers), but sometimes even friendly (particularly when new Jewish agricultural settlements employed Arab peasants, which they later stopped doing). As the number of Jewish immigrants swelled, and as their intentions became clearer to the Arab population, tensions grew and relations steadily worsened. Once it became apparent that these Jewish immigrants hoped to establish an autonomous and self-sufficient Jewish colony in Palestine (one that excluded Arab workers), and maybe even their own state, Arab opposition intensified. It also took time for the Jewish immigrants to recognize the depth and extent of Arab opposition, as they initially hoped that the Arab inhabitants of Palestine would welcome or at least accept their presence—a hope born out of ignorance, arrogance, and idealism.

The first organized Arab protest against the influx of Jewish settlers occurred on June 24, 1891, when some five hundred Arab notables from Jerusalem sent a petition to the Ottoman government in Constantinople, requesting that no more Russian Jews be allowed to enter Palestine and that they should be barred from buying land there. Although the government complied and banned Jewish immigration and land sales to Jews, it was too weak to enforce this. Jewish immigration and land acquisition continued under Ottoman and then British rule, provoking growing alarm and anger among Arabs, constant protests, occasional outbursts of violence (in 1920, 1921, and 1929), and eventually an armed uprising (known as the Arab revolt, which lasted from 1936 to 1939). By the 1930s, Jews and Arabs (who increasingly identified as Palestinian Arabs) were locked in a bitter and progressively more violent conflict.

Why did many European Jews move to Palestine in the late nineteenth and early twentieth centuries?

The surge of Jewish immigration from Europe to Palestine in the late 1800s and early 1900s must first be placed in the broader context of the mass migration of Eastern European Jewry during this period (which was itself part of a global migration trend as millions of Europeans and Asians left their homes and moved to other countries and continents). Approximately three-quarters of the world's Jewish population at the time lived in Eastern Europe (which was largely under the control of the Russian Empire and the Austro-Hungarian Empire until the end of World War I). Between 1870 and the early 1920s, almost three million Jews left Eastern Europe. More than two million moved to the United States, completely changing the face of American Jewry and turning the United States from a backwater of Jewish life into a major center (the Jewish community in New York City, for example, grew from just 60,000 Jews in 1880 to more than a million by 1925). Many others moved to countries in Western Europe and South America, rapidly swelling the size of existing Jewish communities or creating new ones.

Why, then, did masses of Eastern European Jews relocate? The simplest answer is that they could. The availability of cheaper and quicker methods of transportation (railways and transatlantic ocean liners) made international travel much easier and more affordable than ever before. Not only did more and more Eastern European Jews have the ability to move abroad, they also had a strong incentive to do so. Like all migrants, they were motivated by some combination of "push" and "pull" factors. The "push" for most was to escape poverty, pogroms, and persecution at home, which worsened as antisemitism became more virulent in the late nineteenth century. The "pull" for most was primarily economic opportunity (especially in the United States—popularly described in Yiddish at the time as the *goldene medina*, or golden country)—but also social and political freedoms. The promise of a better life, of riches and opportunities, is what enticed most Eastern European Jews to migrate.

A very small minority, however, were attracted by loftier goals. Instead of simply seeking security and wealth for themselves, they wanted to lead more authentic Jewish lives in the Land of Israel, to reinvent themselves as Jews, and to transform not merely their own fortunes but also the condition of the entire Jewish people. Generally young, relatively well educated, and idealistic, these were the Eastern European Jewish immigrants who chose to settle in Palestine rather than elsewhere. They were motivated by a religiously infused romantic nationalism, which came to be known as Zionism (the term was coined in 1890 by Nathan Birnbaum, a Viennese-born Jewish journalist and writer).

The first wave of about 30,000 Jewish immigrants to Palestine during 1882–1903 (known as the "First Aliyah") fled Czarist Russia in the wake of the pogroms in 1881–1882. They were members of two newly established Zionist movements, *Bilu* and *Hibbat Zion*. Those who arrived during a second, larger wave of Jewish immigration to Palestine (the "Second Aliyah") during 1904–1914, about forty thousand people in total, tended to be even more ideological. Most were secular and socialist, and they were all fervent Zionists (many of Israel's early leaders, including David Ben-Gurion, were among this group). Inspired by a Zionism that championed physical labor and self-reliance, these immigrants drained swamps, cultivated the land, established cooperative rural settlements (called *kibbutzim* and *moshavim*), and built new urban centers (Tel Aviv in 1909). They also turned Hebrew, an ancient scriptural language, into a modern vernacular and the basis for a vibrant, secular culture. In short, they laid the foundations for Jewish statehood, although this was just a dream to most of them at the time. They also unintentionally provoked a conflict with the local Arab population that has now dragged on for more than a century.

What is Zionism?

"Zionism" means different things to different people. It encompasses a wide range of beliefs, both secular and religious, and it has been infused by a variety of ideologies (nationalism, socialism, liberalism, even fascism). Hence, there is no singular "Zionism," but many "Zionisms," most notably political Zionism, cultural Zionism, labor Zionism, revisionist Zionism, liberal Zionism, religious Zionism, messianic religious Zionism, and Christian Zionism. The latter, for example, is different from Jewish Zionism, whether in its form in the nineteenth century or today. Given the many versions of Zionism, it would be reductionist to characterize it as a single ideology or belief system. Probably the only belief that all Zionists have in common is that Jews should live in their ancestral homeland, the Land of Israel. There is no agreement among Zionists, however, about whether all Jews should live in the Land of Israel, why they should live there, and what they should actually do there—all these questions are still topics of ongoing debate.

Nevertheless, for Jews, at least, Zionism can be defined as a type, or subset, of Jewish nationalism, based upon four fundamental claims: (1) Jews are a nation; (2) all nations have a right to national self-determination (i.e., to govern themselves); (3) Jews should exercise their right to national self-determination in the Land of Israel, their national homeland; and (4) to achieve this, Jews in the diaspora (or in "exile" in classic Zionist terminology) should return en masse to the Land of Israel ("ingathering of the exiles").

None of these claims were (or are) self-evident or incontestable. In fact, there was widespread Jewish opposition to Zionism until the Holocaust convinced most Jews of its necessity. Most pious Jews opposed Zionism because they regarded it as a heresy for Jews to collectively return to the Land of Israel before the coming of the Messiah, which could only be brought about by God. Many secular Jews were anti-Zionist because they opposed nationalism in general and believed that socialism or communism was the best remedy to the problems facing Jews and humanity at large. Other Jews were anti-Zionist because they did not see the Jews as a separate nation, but solely as followers of a religion (Reform Jews initially held this view). And many Jews living in Western liberal democracies like the United States, Britain, and France opposed Zionism because they feared that it could call into question their loyalty to the states in which they lived and thus endanger their acceptance and integration. There was even opposition to Zionism among Jewish nationalists. Some insisted that it was more practical or desirable to achieve Jewish self-determination in places where Jews already lived in large numbers (this was the view of Autonomists, including supporters of the once-popular Jewish socialist Bund Party). Others argued that it should happen wherever Jews could easily find available territory (this was the position of Territorialists, who considered mass Jewish colonization in various places in Africa, Asia, and the Americas).

Zionists argued that Jews were a nation (even if they may have lacked national consciousness, which needed to be instilled); that the antisemitic persecution they faced was because they lived as a vulnerable minority in countries that belonged to other nations; and that the survival of the Jewish nation, physically and culturally, could only be secured if Jews lived in their own national homeland (the Land of Israel). Despite the awkward fact that another population already lived in this territory, Zionists insisted that Jews were also entitled to live there because it was their ancient homeland from which they were expelled and that they had never stopped hoping to eventually return there. It was also the only place where large numbers of Jews could be encouraged to move to, making it a practical necessity as well as the realization of a millennia-old aspiration. Hence, at a minimum, Zionists wanted to encourage Jews in the diaspora to immigrate to the Land of Israel or at least to support and strengthen the Jewish community that lived there.

Whether, and by what means, the growing Jewish community in what was then Palestine should seek statehood was the subject of a long-running debate among Zionists, which only ended during World War II (when the Zionist movement officially called for the establishment of a Jewish state). Jewish political self-determination, in the form of statehood, was the ultimate objective for "political Zionists," most notably Theodor Herzl, who founded the Zionist Organization in 1897. Providing Jews with a state of their own was seen as the best response to antisemitism in Europe. Some political Zionists optimistically believed it would also eradicate antisemitism since Jews would become more "normal" and just like other nations. For "cultural Zionists" such as Asher Ginsberg (whose pen name was Ahad Ha'am), Herzl's brand of political Zionism was insufficient. Ginsberg argued that the greatest threat to the Jewish people was not antisemitism but assimilation, and having a state of their own would not necessarily remove that threat. It was more important for Jews to create a flourishing modern, national Jewish culture in their homeland, one based upon the Hebrew language. While political Zionists focused on achieving Jewish political independence, cultural Zionists also wanted to revitalize and modernize Jewish culture and build a model Jewish society, which they hoped would inspire Jews around the world and even fulfill the Jews' unique ethical and spiritual mission to be a "light unto the nations." Over the course of time, political and cultural Zionists merged their ambitions so that the Zionist movement in which both participated developed three central objectives: first, to return Jews to the Land of Israel; second, to exercise Jewish sovereignty there; and third, to revive and promote Jewish culture and the Hebrew language and build an exemplary Jewish society. Before Israel's establishment in 1948, therefore, Zionism was not just a nationalist movement aimed at realizing the Jewish nation's right to national self-determination but also a revolutionary cultural project aimed at refashioning Jewish culture and reinventing the Jewish people.

Since 1948, the meaning of Zionism has changed, both in Israel and in the Jewish diaspora. For many Jews, it has now simply come to mean support for Israel's continued existence as a Jewish state (although what that actually entails is fiercely contested). Zionism has also gradually taken on a more religious character, especially since the 1967 war. It was once an avowedly secular ideological movement (though some religious Jews participated in it). While early Zionists appropriated many words, symbols, and themes from the Jewish religious tradition, most of them were staunchly secular in their beliefs and lifestyle and often dismissive of Judaism. In recent decades, by contrast, religious Jews in Israel and the diaspora have become the most vocal and energetic adherents of Zionism, and their fusion of Zionism and Orthodox Judaism has become increasingly influential, both politically and culturally. For many of these religious Zionists, particularly those who subscribe to messianic religious Zionism, Zionism is now primarily about settling Jews throughout the Land of Israel, especially in the region of Judea and Samaria (the West Bank), where most of the stories of the Bible took place. For them,

Zionism today is less about Jewish self-determination and more about fulfilling God's commandments and wishes.

In sum, Zionism is a diverse and dynamic set of beliefs. It has been adapted to different contexts and redefined in different eras. This helps explain not only why Zionists frequently disagree among themselves but also why Zionism has endured and been so successful.

What gave rise to Zionism?

Zionism is often seen by its adherents as a natural and inevitable outcome of Jewish history—the expression of an age-old Jewish yearning to return to their ancient, biblical homeland. In reality, however, Zionism is a modern phenomenon, the product of specific historical circumstances and currents of intellectual thought. It was born in nineteenth-century Europe in response to the two major challenges facing European Jewry at the time: antisemitism and assimilation. The former threatened the physical survival of Jews, while the latter threatened their cultural survival. Zionism claimed to be a solution to both of these threats, and it was embraced by growing numbers of Jews for this reason (although only a small minority of Jews became Zionists before World War II).

The rise of Zionism was the result of a confluence of three big "isms": antisemitism, nationalism, and secularism. Antisemitism was the immediate impetus. It was hardly a new threat to Jews, but the antisemitism that emerged and escalated in late nineteenth-century Europe posed an unprecedented challenge to European Jews. Antisemitism persisted and intensified not only in the Russian Empire but also in the Austro-Hungarian Empire, and even in supposedly progressive, "enlightened" countries in Western Europe (where Jews had integrated into intellectual, cultural, and professional life). The persistence of antisemitism dashed Jewish hopes that their emancipation (which began in France in 1791), along with the gradual spread of the values of the Enlightenment, would make it a thing of the past. Nor was antisemitism diminished by Jewish efforts to integrate or assimilate into European societies—in fact, it seemed that such efforts might only exacerbate it. Unlike antisemitism in the past, which was largely based upon religion, a new, racial antisemitism—which defined and denigrated Jews in terms of their alleged racial inferiority—became increasingly popular toward the end of the nineteenth century. Even the most assimilated Jew could not escape it, as the sensational 1894 trial and conviction of the French Jewish army captain Alfred Dreyfus—who was deliberately framed for treason—made shockingly evident.

Zionism offered a clear explanation and solution to modern antisemitism. The reason antisemitism persisted, Zionist thinkers argued, was because the Jewish nation was an anomaly, scattered among other nations, and dependent upon their hospitality and goodwill—which, they believed, would always be short-lived. Once Jews lived in their own national homeland, they would no longer be at risk of antisemitism, and they would become a "nation like other nations," as Herzl famously put it. What made this proposed solution to antisemitism compelling to many Jews was that it captured the nationalist spirit of the time. During a period in which many ethnic and linguistic groups were asserting their nationhood and seeking self-determination (and, in many cases, insisting that Jews did not and could not belong in their nation-states), it is hardly surprising that Jews would also embrace their own brand of nationalism. The idea of a Jewish nation-state, however far-fetched it seemed, was perfectly suited to an age of nationalism, particularly ethnic nationalism. For Jews who were unable or unwilling to adopt the nationalism of the European society in which they lived, Zionism became an attractive alternative. Many Eastern European Jews, who were generally less assimilated and more attached to Jewish culture and tradition than their counterparts in Western Europe, also saw in Zionism a way to preserve and modernize Jewishness. For them, a Jewish homeland could be more than just a refuge from antisemitic persecution, desperately needed though that was. It could also foster a vibrant Jewish culture and a new kind of Jewish identity, thereby preventing the assimilation of Jews and their ultimate disappearance.

Zionism was not only a response to the increasing secularization of European Jews but also a product of it. Although it drew upon the traditional Jewish aspiration to eventually return to Jerusalem ("Zion"), and invoked Jewish religious themes (such as exile and return) and language (such as "redemption"), Zionism was initially a secular ideology with a rebellious attitude toward Judaism and the Jewish past. No longer content to pray and wait for divine deliverance, as religious Jews had always done, Zionists took it upon themselves to change the course of Jewish history and save or "redeem" the Jewish people by returning them to their ancestral homeland. They also disdained religious Jews for their passivity and dismissed Judaism itself as anachronistic and unhelpful. This attitude would once have been completely unacceptable, if not unthinkable, to most Jews. By the end of the nineteenth century, after decades of secularization, it had become commonplace among Jews, albeit still controversial.

Thus, while virulent antisemitism was the catalyst for the rise of Zionism, widespread nationalism inspired Zionism and gave it credence, and secularism made it possible. Without antisemitism, nationalism, and secularism in nineteenth-century Europe, there would probably be no Zionism.

Who was Theodor Herzl?

Theodor Herzl is often described as the father of modern Zionism. This is not because Herzl was the first Zionist thinker or activist. Jews and Christians had already articulated Zionist ideas and proposals many years before Herzl, and young Zionists from Eastern Europe had already begun "returning" to Palestine. But Herzl popularized Zionism, turned it into a mass movement, and brought it to the world's attention. No less importantly, he created the organizational framework for advancing Zionist goals. Herzl's charisma, literary skills, dramatic flair, restless energy, and vaunting ambition transformed Zionism from an esoteric pipe dream to a popular plan of action. Although he never lived to see it, Herzl was the visionary architect of the Jewish state.

Herzl was an unlikely Jewish hero. Born in 1860 in Budapest, Hungary, he had a completely secular, middle-class upbringing and grew up to be the embodiment of a bourgeois European. He studied law at university in Vienna, wrote plays, and became a successful journalist writing for the *Neue Freie Presse*, then the most influential newspaper in Central Europe. Nevertheless, Herzl personally encountered antisemitism. He witnessed it on a large scale in Paris while covering the Dreyfus trial in 1894, and in Vienna when an antisemitic populist was elected mayor in 1895. As he grew increasingly worried about "the Jewish problem," Herzl contemplated various potential solutions to it, including a socialist revolution and a mass Jewish conversion to Christianity, before concluding that only by leaving Europe and establishing their own homeland could Jews escape antisemitism (this homeland did not have to be in Palestine, as far as Herzl was concerned, and he initially considered Argentina and then later part of East Africa as possible locations). Although Leon Pinsker, a Russian Jewish physician, had already made this argument in a pamphlet titled "Auto-Emancipation" in 1882, Herzl himself was unaware of this. In 1895, he wrote his own Zionist manifesto, *Der Judenstaat* ("The Jewish State"), which garnered a lot of attention and controversy when it was published the following year. It helped spread Zionism among Jews, especially in Eastern Europe, and attracted the interest of non-Jews. Capitalizing on this, Herzl organized a conference for Zionist activists in Basel in 1897, which became the first Zionist Congress. The two hundred or so attendees established the Zionist Organization, whose mission was "to create for the Jewish people a home in Palestine secured by public law." Herzl was elected its president.

Herzl believed that in order for the Zionist project to succeed it needed diplomatic backing from a great power. In the space of just a few years before his early death in 1904 (at the age of 44), Herzl frantically traveled across Europe, desperately trying to gain international support for a Jewish homeland. He met with the German kaiser, the Ottoman sultan, and Russian and British government ministers, largely to no avail. Only the British government was prepared to help, offering an area in British-ruled East Africa for Jewish settlement. This was known as the Uganda proposal (although the area was actually in what is today Kenya), and Herzl presented it to the delegates at the Sixth Zionist Congress in 1903, sparking bitter disagreement within the Zionist movement. Herzl died in the wake of this controversy, which only ended a year after his death when the Uganda proposal was voted down at the Seventh Zionist Congress in 1905. From that point on, Zionists were united in seeking a Jewish homeland in Palestine. Herzl, more than any other individual, was responsible for making that aspiration seem possible. As he famously put it in his utopian novel *Altneuland* ("Old-New Land," published in 1902): "If you will it, it is no dream."

Was Zionism a form of colonialism?

The most persistent, and perhaps most common, criticism of Zionism is that it is another instance of European colonialism. Palestinian and Arab nationalists have continually leveled this charge against Zionism, and many supporters of the Palestinian cause around the world have echoed it. Indeed in left-wing circles in Western societies, and especially on university campuses and in academia, it has become not only fashionable, but almost taken for granted, to view Zionism as synonymous with colonialism.

The equation of Zionism with colonialism is not merely a way of historically characterizing it or theoretically conceptualizing it. It also generally implies a moral condemnation of Zionism since colonialism has been delegitimized in our era. Colonialism is now associated with violent conquest, the subjugation and exploitation of indigenous populations, and the theft of their land and other resources. In many people's minds, it is also associated with imperialism and racism. Thus, if Zionism is a form of colonialism, then Zionism must also be illegitimate and, by extension, so too is its product: the State of Israel. Needless to say, supporters of Israel reject this view. For most Jews, in particular, Zionism is regarded as the antithesis of colonialism. They see it as a movement of national liberation for an oppressed people, more like the anticolonial independence movements that evicted European colonial powers in the years after World War II.

As with many of the competing claims made about the Israeli-Palestinian conflict, there is some truth to both of these readings of Zionism. In theory, Zionism was akin to a national liberation movement for Jews, who were undoubtedly oppressed in Europe. It also had to contend with imperial powers, initially the Ottoman Empire and then the British Empire. But unlike other national liberation movements, or nationalist movements in general, Zionism required the mass relocation and resettlement of Jews to an area (Palestine) that was inhabited by another population (Arabs). In doing so, Zionists had to justify their presence and overcome the resistance of the indigenous population, who saw them as intruders. In this respect, the Zionist project was similar to colonial projects undertaken by European settlers in North America, Australia, New Zealand, Algeria, Brazil, and South Africa. In these cases of what scholars term "settler-colonialism," European settlers established colonies and built new societies, largely modeled on the ones they had left behind. Although they frequently claimed that the "natives" would benefit from their presence since they brought progress and "civilization" to them, in reality the indigenous population ended up being dispossessed of its land, and socially and politically marginalized at best (at worst, they were simply killed off).

Like these cases of settler-colonialism, Jewish settlers came to Palestine from Europe and established a colony there (they were even financially assisted by the Jewish Colonial Trust, established by the Zionist movement in 1899). Rather than integrating with the local population, they created their own society. They tended to view their Arab neighbors with a mix of condescension, contempt, and benevolent paternalism, typical of European attitudes at the time. They harbored the same cultural prejudices as other Europeans of their era, assuming both the superiority of European civilization and the benefits it would inevitably bring to the more "primitive," "backward" Arabs. They were not oblivious to the presence of Arabs, as some critics of Zionism have claimed—largely because of the early Zionist slogan "a land without a people for a people without a land"—at least not after they arrived in Palestine. However, most of them did not recognize Arabs as cultural or political equals or view them as a distinct people with any territorial or national rights.

While Zionism shares some similarities with European colonialism, it differs in important ways, the biggest being its motives. European colonialism was generally motivated by imperialism. European states established colonies to enhance their national power, extend their cultural influence, exploit the local labor force, and extract the territory's resources. The territory targeted for colonization was selected based upon the strategic and economic interests of the colonizing state (the "mother country"). When the colonizing state took over this territory, often through military conquest, it set up its own political and economic system (serving its own interests). In the case of settler-colonialism, it usually brought members of its own population to live there, either ruling over or replacing the indigenous population. These settler-colonists typically sought to recreate the "old country" in the new, using its language, importing its culture, and sometimes imposing its customs on the reluctant natives, often under the guise of a "civilizing mission." The colonizing state itself tried to rule over its colony, directly or indirectly, at least for some time.

Zionism, by contrast, was not driven by imperialism. It was not motivated by the political, economic, or strategic interests of any European state (although it received support from some, who had their own motives). Jewish settlers were not sent to Palestine by any imperial power—in fact, they were fleeing the Russian and Austro-Hungarian empires—nor were they acting on behalf of any imperial power. They did not even come from a single country. They chose to settle in Palestine not because of its strategic value or natural resources but solely because of its historic, religious, and cultural value to Jews. In fact, Zionist settlement in Palestine was expensive and unprofitable. Rather than conquering or stealing the land, before 1948 the Zionist movement legally purchased it, often at exorbitant prices, from its owners, who were mostly absentee Arab landowners (but only about 7 percent of the land in Palestine was purchased by the Zionist movement before 1948). Nor did the Zionist movement in its early years seek to eliminate, subjugate, or exploit the native population. Zionists even tried not to employ Arabs because they wanted to be self-reliant and ensure that Jewish immigrants could find work (this was, however, discriminatory and materially harmful to the Arab population). Crucially, Zionist settlers saw themselves as the indigenous people of the land, who were returning to it after a long, forced exile. Instead of trying to recreate the societies and cultures they left behind in Europe, they wanted to create a new kind of Jewish society focused on Hebrew culture.

The Zionist settlement project, therefore, significantly differed in its intentions and its practices from the kind of colonial projects carried out by the British, Dutch, French, Spanish, Portuguese, Germans, and Italians. Though European in origin, and influenced by the same cultural prejudices and blind spots that prevailed in Europe at the time and inspired European colonialism, Zionist settlers were not European colonialists. They engaged in "colonization," not "colonialism." Nevertheless, from the perspective of the local Arab population, there was no difference between Zionist colonization and European colonialism, especially after the British gave their support to the Zionist movement and conquered Palestine. In the eyes of the Arabs, the Jewish settlers were just the latest in a long

line of foreign invaders, and their arrival was part of the same process of European imperialism that had been occurring in the Middle
East throughout the nineteenth and early twentieth centuries. Such
a view, though inaccurate, is completely understandable in the context of that time.

What role did Britain play in the beginning of the conflict?

Zionism was not the same as European colonialism, but it certainly
benefited from it. Were it not for the support of European colonial
powers, especially Great Britain, the Zionist mission to achieve the
mass return of Jews to the Land of Israel and the restoration of Jewish
political sovereignty there would not have succeeded. British colonialism played a key role in the success of Zionism—so much so that
it is fair to say that the State of Israel is partly a product of British
colonialism (although British policymakers and colonial officials
did not intend to create a Jewish state). Britain not only endorsed
Zionism and helped legitimize it but also fostered the development
of a Jewish national home in Palestine during its three-decade rule
over the territory from 1917 to 1948. To be sure, British policy toward Palestine was driven less by pro-Zionist sentiment and more
by Britain's strategic interest in the eastern Mediterranean region,
which was primarily to protect the overland and shipping routes to
India (after its opening in 1869, the Suez Canal in Egypt became a
critical artery for the British Empire and guarding it became a major
concern).

British colonialism in Palestine, as in many other parts of the
world, left a lasting legacy. Although the roughly thirty years of
British rule in Palestine was comparatively brief, it was instrumental
in shaping the country and the relations between its Arab and Jewish
inhabitants. Britain made Palestine a country (it was previously not
a distinct political unit), gave it an official name (reviving the ancient Roman name "Palaestina"), drew up its borders (separating
it from the territory east of the Jordan River that became Jordan),
established its legal system, and designated Jerusalem as its capital
city. The British also presided over a period in which Jewish–Arab
relations in Palestine became increasingly antagonistic and violent,
eventually culminating in all-out civil war. As the governing power
in Palestine, Britain not only failed to prevent a violent conflict

between Jews and Arabs, it actually exacerbated it. Hence, to this day, many Palestinians still harbor resentment toward Britain for its seminal role in the conflict's early years, while Israelis feel much the same way, despite the fact that Israel's creation owes a lot to British assistance. Both sides bitterly accuse Britain of having favored the other side. What, then, did the British do to have caused such lasting resentment? How did they manage to anger and alienate both Arabs and Jews in Palestine and inflame the conflict between them?

The Balfour Declaration

The Balfour Declaration of November 2, 1917, was Britain's most famous (or notorious, depending upon your point of view) contribution to the incipient Arab–Jewish conflict in Palestine and ultimately to the creation of Israel. It was a public letter from the British foreign secretary, Arthur James Balfour, to Lord Lionel Walter Rothschild, a prominent British Jew and scion of the famous banking family who was then the president of the Zionist Federation of Great Britain and Ireland. The letter stated:

> His Majesty's Government view with favor the establishment in Palestine of a national home for the Jewish people, and will use their best endeavours to facilitate the achievement of this object, it being clearly understood that nothing shall be done which may prejudice the civil and religious rights of existing non-Jewish communities in Palestine, or the rights and political status enjoyed by Jews in any other country.

There are many explanations for why the British government issued the Balfour Declaration in the midst of World War I, after much debate within the British cabinet—the only Jewish member of the cabinet, Edwin Samuel Montagu, argued against it—and despite the objections of some British military and foreign office officials. The main reason was a misguided belief that, by expressing support for Zionism, Britain would instantly win the backing of world Jewry (especially the large Jewish communities in Russia, Germany, and the United States), thereby helping to simultaneously cement its wartime alliances with Russia and the United States and undermine its German enemy. Implicit in this belief was a false conflation of Jews with Zionists—most Jews at the time were not Zionists—and a hugely exaggerated notion of Jewish power (which echoed antisemitic conspiracy theories, particularly the "Protocols of the Learned Elders of Zion"). The Balfour Declaration was not only driven by wartime desperation; supporting a Jewish homeland in Palestine was also seen as a way for Britain to ensure its long-term presence in an area adjacent to the strategically vital Suez Canal and to keep away its rival, France. Some members of the British cabinet, most notably the Prime Minister David Lloyd George and Balfour himself, were also deeply influenced by Christian Zionism—a biblically inspired desire to "restore" the Jewish nation to the Holy Land as a precursor to the Second Coming of Jesus.

Motivated by this mix of pragmatism and piety, the Balfour Declaration constituted an endorsement of Zionism by the most powerful state in the world at that time, boosting its legitimacy and credibility among Jews and non-Jews alike. Although deliberately ambiguous and somewhat qualified—referring only to a "national home" (not a state) "in Palestine" (not of Palestine)—it gave the Zionist movement the diplomatic backing it had sought since Herzl's failed attempts to secure an international charter. In doing so, it suddenly turned the idea of a Jewish homeland in Palestine from an unrealistic dream into a serious possibility. Britain was not the only great power to publicly support Zionism at the time—French and American leaders also expressed support for it—but it was by far the most important because the British were poised to conquer Palestine from the Ottoman Empire, which they were fighting against in World War I.

Britain's Mandate in Palestine

On December 9, 1917, just weeks after the Balfour Declaration was issued, British soldiers under the command of General Edmund Allenby triumphantly marched into Jerusalem. The British conquest of Palestine put it in a unique position to translate its words of support for Zionism into concrete actions, although British officials gave little, if any, consideration as to what these actions should be, or how they could be done, without affecting "the civil and religious rights of existing non-Jewish communities in Palestine" (especially its majority Arab population, who were not even named in the Balfour Declaration). This lack of foresight proved to be highly problematic for British rule in Palestine, particularly since the Balfour Declaration was incorporated into the terms of the Mandate for Palestine that Britain was given at the 1920 San Remo peace conference following the end of World War I (the Mandate was then officially approved by the newly established League of Nations in 1922). As the Mandatory power, Britain became legally responsible for implementing the Balfour Declaration, while also preparing the population of Palestine for self-rule and independence (which they were deemed to be not yet ready for).

The problem was that Arabs constituted the vast majority of the local population in Palestine, and their leaders opposed the British Mandate and the Balfour Declaration. They regarded both as a betrayal of Britain's wartime promise to support the establishment of an independent Arab state in return for an Arab rebellion against the Ottoman Empire (which broke out in 1916 and was assisted by the legendary British intelligence officer T. E. Lawrence). This promise had been conveyed in an exchange of letters between the British High Commissioner in Egypt, Sir Henry McMahon, and Sharif Hussein bin Ali, the emir of Mecca and head of the Hashemite tribe. Although Palestine was never specifically mentioned in the letters, and the British later insisted that it was not meant to have been included in the area designated for Arab independence, Arab nationalists were bitterly disappointed by Britain's failure to fulfill its commitment to Arab independence in the aftermath of World War I and angered by its apparent duplicity and double-dealing (in 1916, Britain had also secretly hatched a plan with its wartime ally France—known as the Sykes-Picot Agreement—to dismember the Ottoman Empire after its defeat and divide it up into their own "spheres of influence").

From its inception, therefore, the British Mandate in Palestine was beset with a fundamental, if not insurmountable, challenge: to prepare the country for independence, while simultaneously helping to establish within it a Jewish national home that the vast majority of the population strongly opposed. British officials initially hoped that this opposition would diminish as Arabs came to benefit economically from a growing Jewish presence in Palestine (a reassuring and self-serving belief that they shared with Zionists). But as the intensity of Arab opposition to Zionism gradually became apparent to them, they realized how difficult it was to reconcile Jewish and Arab demands for self-determination in Palestine. Once this realization had fully set in by the end of the 1920s—after a major outbreak of Arab rioting and mob violence in 1929 during which 133 Jews and 116 Arabs were killed (the latter mostly by British troops and police)—British colonial officials in London and Jerusalem spent the remaining years of their turbulent rule in Palestine repeatedly trying to back away from their commitment to the Zionist cause without renouncing it altogether, which they could not formally do. This did not appease the Arabs, who still distrusted and resented the British, and it disappointed and increasingly angered the Jews, who felt that Britain broke its promise to support the creation of a Jewish homeland. Worse, it did so at a time when Jews most desperately needed a safe haven—just as Nazism and fascism were sweeping across Europe, and the United States was no longer admitting Jewish refugees.

In retrospect, it seems clear that the British Mandate in Palestine was doomed to end in failure, acrimony, and conflict. However hard they tried, the British simply could not fulfill their conflicting obligations to the Zionist movement and to the local, mostly Arab, population in Palestine, who overwhelmingly opposed it. But this was less clear at the time because the fragmented leadership of the Arab community was not uniformly or categorically opposed to any accommodation with Zionism. Nor was the Zionist leadership completely unwilling to compromise with the British and the Arabs or, for that matter, unambiguous in expressing their ultimate political ambition to achieve Jewish statehood (some leading Zionists, in fact, were not yet commited to having a Jewish state).

Britain wanted to establish a state in Palestine in which Arabs and Jews would share political power. This aspiration was not completely detached from reality. Arabs and Jews did coexist in British Mandatory Palestine (albeit often uneasily), and there were even some friendships and cooperation between them, particularly in certain industries and locales. If the first British High Commissioner in Palestine, Sir Herbert Samuel (who was himself Jewish and a Zionist), had succeeded in his efforts in the 1920s to create an elected parliament or even just an advisory council representing both communities, it is possible that Arabs and Jews in Palestine could have learned to share power and might even have developed a shared civic identity (as Palestinians). Britain's failure to create governing institutions in which both Arabs and Jews could democratically participate—a failure that stemmed from the adamant refusal of Arab leaders to accept the terms of the British Mandate and, by extension, to implicitly accept and legitimize the Balfour Declaration—played a decisive role in shaping the course of the Zionist-Palestinian conflict. From that point on, the Arab and Jewish communities in Palestine developed separately and largely autonomously, with their own political leaderships dealing directly with the British Mandate government.

This proved to be much more beneficial for the Jewish community (which called itself the "Yishuv") than it was for the Arab community. The Jewish Agency for Palestine, which the British established as a liaison with the Jewish community, became a proto-government for the Yishuv (it was headed after 1935 by David Ben-Gurion, the leader of Mapai [the Land of Israel Workers' Party], which became the ruling party once Israel was established). The British gave the Jewish Agency a lot of authority over the Yishuv, enabling it to become a state-in-the-making, thereby paving the way for the subsequent formation of a Jewish state. Along with the Jewish Agency, the Yishuv also had its own trade union, welfare and healthcare provider (the Histadrut), educational system (including the Hebrew University of Jerusalem), and an armed militia (the Haganah, which later became the Israel Defense Forces). The Arab community, by contrast, lacked strong central institutions and was less organized, largely because their traditional leadership, consisting of Arab notables from prominent families and clans, was riven with internal rivalries (which Britain exploited with its well-honed colonial tactic of "divide and rule," playing Arab notables off against each other).

By allowing, however reluctantly, the Arab and Jewish communities in Palestine to develop as separate societies, the British created the conditions for a nationalist conflict to take place between them (some scholars contend that this was actually intentional since it gave the British an excuse to stay in Palestine on the grounds of keeping control). It is, of course, impossible to know whether a violent conflict between Arabs and Jews in Palestine would have happened regardless. There had been growing tension and occasional violence under Ottoman rule. Nonetheless, had the Ottoman

Empire survived World War I, the Zionist movement would not have been able to bring sufficient numbers of Jews to Palestine or buy nearly enough land there to build a Jewish homeland, let alone a Jewish state. Whereas the Ottoman government generally tried to prevent Jewish immigration and land purchases—the two most pressing and worrying issues for the Arab inhabitants of Palestine— the British government, in accordance with the Balfour Declaration, permitted both (although it regulated and limited Jewish immigration to Palestine, especially after 1939). Consequently, nearly a quarter of a million Jews—mostly refugees fleeing first Poland and then Germany and Austria—came to Palestine between 1932 and 1939.

Arab resistance to Zionist settlement and British rule

The Arab community vigorously, and at times violently, objected to British assistance to the Zionist enterprise during this period, be-cause continued Jewish immigration threatened to erode their ma-jority status in Palestine and their goal of national self-determination. Whenever Jewish immigration to Palestine increased, it was accompanied by mounting Arab protests, rioting, and violence, which the British forcefully suppressed. Sporadic protests and vi-olence occurred throughout the 1920s and 1930s, culminating in an Arab General Strike in 1936 and a mass uprising against British rule and Zionist settlement that became known as the "Great Revolt," lasting from 1936 to 1939. This was a turning point in the history of the Palestinians and the history of the Israeli-Palestinian conflict more generally—a kind of "coming-of-age" for Palestinian nation-alism and for organized, armed resistance to Zionism. Any slim hope for Arab–Jewish rapprochement was lost in the bloodshed of those years, as enmity hardened on both sides and outright war increasingly appeared inevitable. The British eventually managed to crush the nationalist uprising, using brutal counterinsurgency tactics (including mass arrests, torture, executions, deportations, and demolitions of homes) with the assistance of Zionist militias. Thousands of Arabs were killed and most of their leaders were imprisoned or went into exile (leaving a leadership vacuum that afflicted the Palestinians a decade later when a civil war eventually broke out between Jews and Palestinians).

In response to the Arab revolt, as Palestine became increasingly ungovernable, in 1937 Britain proposed a partition of the country into an Arab state (which would be united with Transjordan) and a much smaller Jewish state, with some areas of strategic interest remaining under British control (this was the recommendation made by the Peel Commission that had been appointed to investigate the causes of the Arab revolt). The Zionist leadership provisionally accepted the proposal, although they objected to the proposed borders of the Jewish state. But the Arab leadership rejected the proposal because they opposed partition in principle and also objected to specifics of the Peel Commission's plan, which envisaged the "transfer" of more than 200,000 Arabs who were then living in the territory earmarked for the Jewish state.

Two years later, in 1939, with a war against Germany looming, Britain rescinded its partition plan and instead issued a White Paper (an official policy document) proposing a single, Arab-majority state after a ten-year transitional period. In the meantime, there would be severe restrictions on Jewish land purchases and a strict quota for Jewish immigration for five years (just fifteen thousand a year), after which the Arab community would have to approve further Jewish immigration. The White Paper amounted to a repudiation of the Balfour Declaration (although Britain had by then gone a long way toward fulfilling its promise to the Zionist movement). Like the Balfour Declaration, the White Paper was born out of pressing wartime considerations, only this time the British were desperately trying to curry favor with Arabs rather than Jews (Britain wanted to safeguard its access to Arab oil and ensure that Arab states did not ally with Nazi Germany, whereas Jews, for obvious reasons, could be counted on to oppose the Nazis). Now it was the turn of the Zionists to feel betrayed by the British, and given the desperate plight of Jews in Nazi Europe, their sense of betrayal was acute and enduring. But while alienating the Jews, the British failed to win over the Arabs, whose leadership (principally Hajj Amin al-Husseini, who had emerged as the dominant leader of the Palestinian national movement) rejected the White Paper because it still allowed for some Jewish immigration and set too long a timetable for an independent Palestinian state. This rejection turned out to have dire consequences for the Palestinians (and they never got a better offer than the one made by the British government in 1939).

The Jewish revolt and British retreat from Palestine

Although both Jews and Arabs opposed it, the 1939 White Paper guided British policy toward Palestine during and after World War II, despite the horrors of the Holocaust. In its effort to strictly limit Jewish immigration to Palestine in order to maintain its Arab alliances, Britain forcibly prevented Jewish refugees fleeing Nazi-occupied Europe from illegally entering Palestine (thus sending them back to their deaths). After the war ended, Britain turned away boatloads of Holocaust survivors—most famously, the Haganah's ship *Exodus*, which in 1947 arrived in the port of Haifa with 4,500 Jewish refugees and was forced to return to Europe. In response to what they perceived (not unreasonably) as the British government's callousness and cruelty, Zionist militias in Palestine launched a revolt against British rule. Right-wing underground paramilitary groups (the Irgun and Lehi) were the first to do this, starting in 1944, attacking British soldiers and policemen and even assassinating the top British official in the Middle East, Lord Moyne. After initially helping the British to combat these groups, the Haganah (the main Zionist paramilitary group) joined the fight against the British in October 1945. From November 1945 to July 1946, approximately twenty British personnel were killed and more than a hundred wounded. The deadliest attack against the British occurred on July 22, 1946, when the Irgun, led by a young Polish Jew, Menachem Begin, blew up a wing of the King David Hotel in Jerusalem that housed the British military and civilian headquarters in Palestine, killing ninety-one people, including Arabs and Jews. (Whether this constituted a terrorist attack has been much debated since its perpetrators claimed that the hotel was a legitimate military target and that they had given advance warnings to evacuate the hotel, which were ignored.)

The bombings, shootings, and sabotage carried out by Zionist groups against the British in Palestine undoubtedly contributed to Britain's decision in 1947 to turn the "Palestine problem" over to the newly created United Nations (UN), which was the successor to the League of Nations. Despite stationing almost 100,000 troops in Palestine and imposing martial law, the British were struggling to maintain control, and back home the war-weary British public increasingly regarded British rule in Palestine as a costly, bloody, and futile endeavor. At a time when Britain was financially depleted and thoroughly exhausted after winning World War II, and shedding its draining imperial responsibilities, the British Mandate in Palestine became one more burden to get rid of, whatever the consequences for its inhabitants. The fact that Anglo–American relations were also being strained by Britain's rule in Palestine, especially by its obstinate refusal to admit more Jewish Holocaust survivors—who were left languishing in displaced persons camps in Europe or confined to British detention camps in Cyprus—was another impetus behind Britain's decision to withdraw from Palestine. As far as the British government was concerned, it was now up to the international community, especially the United States, to figure out what to do about Palestine and its bitterly divided Arab and Jewish communities. On May 15, 1948, the last British soldiers in Palestine went home, leaving Jews and Arabs to battle it out between themselves.

Who was Hajj Amin Al-Husseini?

Mohammed Amin Al-Husseini was the preeminent political and religious leader of the Arab community in Palestine in the interwar years, during the British Mandate. Husseini was born in Jerusalem in the 1890s into a prominent family (his father was the Mufti of Jerusalem, a leading Sunni Muslim official), which was part of the prestigious and powerful Husseini clan. He received a secular and Islamic education in Jerusalem, Istanbul, and Cairo. As a young man, he served as an officer in the Ottoman army during World War I, and then switched sides to join the Arab revolt against the Ottomans led by Faisal bin Hussein, the son of Sharif Hussein bin Ali (who wanted to have an independent Arab state, and the British had promised to support this goal).

Husseini embraced Arab nationalism and supported Faisal's attempt to establish an Arab Kingdom of Syria, based in Damascus, which sought to rule over all of what was called Greater Syria (an area encompassing the entire Levant or Fertile Crescent region, including what is today Syria, Lebanon, Jordan, Israel, and the Palestinian territories). After France defeated Faisal's army and occupied Damascus in a brief war in 1920, Husseini, like other Palestinian Arab nationalists at the time, went from supporting pan-Arabism (aspiring to unify all Arabs under a single Arab state) to

Palestinian nationalism (seeking an independent state in Palestine), although his pan-Arab inclinations never entirely disappeared. In the following decades leading up to the first Arab-Israeli war in 1948, Husseini emerged as the leading champion of Palestinian nationalism and the most powerful figure within Palestinian Arab society.

Although Husseini originally opposed British rule in Palestine, it was the British colonial administration there that helped him become the dominant leader of the fractious Palestinian nationalist movement. Despite being convicted of incitement by the British authorities for his role in violent anti-Jewish Arab rioting that occurred in Jerusalem in April 1920, the British High Commissioner in Palestine pardoned Husseini and appointed him Mufti of Jerusalem, putting him in charge of the city's Islamic holy places, including the Al-Aqsa Mosque. In 1922, Husseini was elected president of the Supreme Muslim Council, a body created by the British to administer the religious affairs of Palestine's Muslim population (who made up most of the country's inhabitants at the time). Using his religious authority, the funds available to him, and the extensive powers of patronage at his disposal, Husseini gradually came to exert more and more influence on Palestinian politics, outmaneuvering, delegitimizing, and even occasionally killing off his rivals and critics (of which there were many).

Whereas some Palestinian leaders were willing, however reluctantly, to compromise with the Zionist movement, Husseini was an implacable opponent. He vociferously denounced any attempt to reach a compromise with the Zionists, any recognition of Jewish national rights, or even any sign of Arab-Jewish cooperation in Palestine. While initially working with the British Mandatory government, he adamantly objected to its support for the establishment of a Jewish national home in Palestine. As far as he was concerned, Jews had no right to such a home and those in Europe should stay there, regardless of the increasingly dire circumstances they faced. He was a relentless opponent of Jewish immigration to Palestine (before, during, and after the Holocaust) and of Jewish land purchases in Palestine (Arabs who sold land to Jews were vilified as traitors). For these reasons, Husseini categorically rejected both of Britain's proposals for the future of Palestine—the Peel Commission's partition proposal in 1937 and the White Paper of 1939. Most controversially, he rejected the UN's partition plan, which was approved by the UN General Assembly in November 1947. In doing so, Husseini, more than any other Palestinian leader, bears some responsibility for the collective disaster that befell the Palestinians in the wake of the UN vote, when war broke out and most of the Palestinian community fled or was expelled by the triumphant Zionist, and later Israeli, military forces.

In addition to his uncompromising and ultimately disastrous stance on Zionism, Husseini also severely damaged the Palestinian national cause by allying himself with Nazi Germany and Fascist Italy. After fleeing Palestine in 1937 to avoid arrest by the British for his role in the Arab uprising, he went to Lebanon and then Iraq (where he helped instigate a 1941 military coup against the British-supported regime). Eventually he ended up in Berlin, where he spent the remainder of World War II. While there, he met with Adolf Hitler on November 28, 1941, a notorious meeting that some claim significantly influenced Hitler's decision to exterminate European Jewry. Most historians, however, do not believe that Husseini influenced Hitler's decision to carry out the "Final Solution." This decision had, in fact, already been made, and the record of the meeting does not show that Husseini suggested the mass murder of Europe's Jews, but that he asked for a declaration of support from Nazi Germany for "the independence and unity of Palestine, Syria, and Iraq" under Arab rule. While Husseini cannot be blamed for the Holocaust, he played a role in it, helping to recruit Bosnian Muslims into the SS who participated in the killing of Jews in Bosnia, Croatia, and Hungary. He also played a key role in Nazi Germany's Arabic-language propaganda aimed at Arabs in North Africa and the Middle East. His broadcasts on Radio Berlin were laced with virulent antisemitism, which helped to spread European antisemitism across the Arab world with lasting consequences.

Having discredited the Palestinian cause in the eyes of the world due to his wartime collaboration with Nazism, Husseini's stature and influence among Palestinians steadily declined after World War II. However, his outspoken opposition to the UN partition plan was decisive. He also played a part in the first Arab-Israeli war and in the short-lived Palestinian government-in-exile in the Gaza Strip when it came under Egyptian control. He eventually moved to Beirut, where he died in 1974, having lost his de facto leadership of the Palestinian national movement to Yasser Arafat, the leader of the Palestine Liberation Organization (PLO). Unlike Arafat, who is still widely revered by Palestinians, Husseini remains a controversial figure among Palestinians.

Was Israel created because of the Holocaust?

Exactly three years and one week after the defeat of Nazi Germany in World War II, the establishment of the State of Israel was declared on May 14, 1948. In the short time period between these two events, the world learned, to its horror, about the fate of European Jewry—two-thirds of them, about six million people, had been systematically killed in what became known as the Holocaust. The chronological proximity of the Holocaust and Israel's establishment has led many people to assume that the two events are causally connected and that Israel was created because of the Holocaust. Contrary to this popular belief, however, a Jewish state would probably have emerged in Palestine, sooner or later, with or without the Holocaust. After all, modern political Zionists like Herzl made the case for Jewish statehood decades before the mass murder of European Jewry took place, and the Zionist movement had spent many years actively building in Palestine the political and economic infrastructure for an eventual Jewish state. Zionists, in Palestine and elsewhere, did not need the Holocaust to convince them of the Jews' existential need for statehood, although it did make them even more determined, and less patient, to achieve this long-held objective. Indeed, in May 1942, shortly after receiving the first reports of the ongoing extermination of European Jews, the Zionist Organization officially called for the establishment of a Jewish state in Palestine in its "Biltmore Program," named after the New York hotel where its meeting took place.

Most diaspora Jews, who had previously been opposed to Zionism or largely indifferent toward it, were convinced of the need for Jewish statehood upon learning about the near-annihilation of European Jewry and the desperate plight of those who managed to survive. In the wake of the Holocaust, Zionism became the dominant ideology across the Jewish world. The Holocaust seemed to vindicate the Zionist argument that Jews needed a state of their own to protect, rescue, and shelter them from their enemies. This led many diaspora Jews, especially those in the United States, to become vocal and energetic advocates for the creation of a Jewish state in Palestine. American Jews also provided much-needed money and arms to Jews in Palestine to help them develop and defend such a state. The mass mobilization of American Jewry in support of Jewish statehood after World War II undoubtedly played a role in persuading the U.S. government to vote in favour of the partitioning Palestine in the pivotal UN vote in November 1947, and then to immediately recognize the State of Israel after it was declared. Historians continue to debate how much this support was a factor in the Truman administration's decision-making at the time. President Harry Truman was concerned about winning the influential Jewish vote in the presidential election of November 1948, and he was subjected to intense lobbying by American Jewish Zionists (he later described it as the most "pressure and propaganda" he encountered during his presidency). But it is by no means clear that these were the main reasons why Truman supported the partition of Palestine and recognized the State of Israel, going against the advice of his own State Department.

American public opinion was deeply affected by the Holocaust, and consequently the United States became more supportive of Jewish statehood in its aftermath. This certainly influenced U.S. foreign policy, as did President Truman's genuine sympathy for Jewish suffering in the Holocaust and for the plight of Jewish Holocaust survivors (shortly after he became president at the end of World War II, for instance, Truman asked the British government, unsuccessfully, to admit 100,000 Holocaust survivors into Palestine). None of these factors, however, outweighed the influence of pragmatic considerations in determining U.S. foreign policy regarding the future of Palestine. Above all, it was driven by the pressing need to resettle up to 250,000 Jewish refugees and displaced persons in Europe (many of whom were unwilling to return to their countries of origin), and by an equally important desire to avoid a war in Palestine that might destabilize the Middle East and be exploited by the Soviet Union. Some American policymakers, including Truman himself, also expected a Jewish state to be democratic and pro-Western, thereby helping to contain the spread of Soviet influence in the region. In the context of the emerging Cold War with the Soviets, U.S. strategic interests shaped American foreign policy more than humanitarian concerns for Jewish survivors of the Holocaust. A belief that Jews should be compensated for their suffering in the Holocaust and morally deserved to have their own state was, at most, a secondary factor.

Other states, particularly Great Britain and the Soviet Union, were even more motivated by realpolitik than by sympathy for the Holocaust in their stances toward the creation of a Jewish state in Palestine. The British opposed Jewish statehood largely out of a desire to maintain good relations with Arab states (whose plentiful oil supplies they needed). The Soviets, on the other hand, supported Jewish statehood because they wanted to get the British out of Palestine and hoped that a Jewish state, led by the socialist-oriented Mapai Party, would have good relations with the USSR. Although there was certainly widespread international sympathy for the victims and survivors of the Holocaust, this sympathy was transient, and it did not automatically translate into popular support for the creation of a Jewish state. Nor was the public support that did exist the main reason why the UN General Assembly voted to divide Palestine into a Jewish state and an Arab state. The vote primarily reflected the wishes of Washington and Moscow—which, for once, happened to be aligned—and the perceived national interests of the UN member states (some were heavily pressured to vote for partition).

The Holocaust, therefore, was not nearly as much of a factor in Israel's creation as many people think. Though it has generated popular support for Israel's existence, particularly in some Western countries, it was not the cause of Israel's establishment. The Holocaust has, however, had a profound impact upon Israel, shaping the culture and collective identity of Israeli-Jewish society and the ethos of the Israeli state. It is impossible to summarize this in just a few sentences—whole books have been written about it—but two major consequences of the Holocaust for Israel must be highlighted. First, the destruction of the majority of European Jewry meant that Israel lost a large share of its pool of potential immigrants. Modern Zionism originated and spread primarily among European Jews, especially Eastern European Jews, and it was mainly directed toward them. They were the intended inhabitants of a future Jewish state, but, tragically, by the time that state finally came into being, most European Jews had been killed. Hence, it was mostly Jews from

North Africa and the Middle East who immigrated to Israel in the first two decades of statehood. This gradually changed the composition and character of Israeli society as well as Israeli culture and politics.

Second, the collective memory of the Holocaust became a central, constitutive element in Israeli national identity, influencing not only how Israeli Jews see themselves but also how they see others (including Palestinians, Arabs, and non-Jews in general). This has reinforced a sense of victimhood among Israeli Jews and exacerbated their fears and insecurities, sometimes leading them to exaggerate threats and overreact to perceived dangers. It has also fueled Israeli Jews' feeling of isolation in the world, encouraging them to embrace the notion of self-reliance, especially regarding their own military force. In short, the Holocaust has been a kind of collective trauma for Israeli Jews and it has, in turn, affected Israel's threat perceptions, its foreign and security policies, and even the behavior of the IDF. Hence, though it began well before the Holocaust, Israel's conflict with the Palestinians was and continues to be heavily influenced by it.

What was the United Nations Partition Plan for Palestine?

When the UN inherited the problem of Palestine from the British in 1947, it formed a Special Committee on Palestine (UNSCOP), composed of representatives of eleven states, to investigate the problem and propose a solution. The committee toured Palestine, gathered evidence, held hearings (where they heard presentations from Zionist leaders, but not from Palestinian Arab leaders since they boycotted the committee), and visited Jewish refugee camps in Europe. After months of work, UNSCOP delivered its report, which contained a recommendation by the majority of its members that the British Mandate in Palestine be terminated and the country divided into an Arab state and a Jewish state, with an economic union between them, and with Jerusalem and Bethlehem to be placed under international control. The minority who disagreed recommended a single, federal state with some local autonomy for Arabs and Jews.

In UNSCOP's partition plan (see Map 2), a majority of the territory of Mandatory Palestine (approximately 56 percent) was allocated to the Jewish state, despite the fact that Jews made up only one-third of the country's total population at the time (there were roughly 600,000 Jews and 1.2 million Arabs). The UNSCOP plan made this allocation with the expectation that the approximately 250,000 Jewish refugees and displaced persons in Europe would be resettled in the future Jewish state (there was simply nowhere else for them to go). This was of no relevance, however, to the Palestinian Arabs, who insisted that the fate of Jewish Holocaust survivors was not their problem but someone else's (specifically Europe's since the Holocaust occurred there). They believed that they should not be made to suffer the consequences of the crimes of others. The Palestinian Arab leadership also objected to the fact that the partition plan gave the most fertile regions of the country to the Jewish state (although the barren Negev Desert amounted to more than half of the land allocated to the Jewish state).

Even if the proposed Arab state had been much larger, and included a more fertile area, UNSCOP's partition plan would still have been unacceptable to the Palestinian Arab leadership (dominated by Hajj Amin Al-Husseini and his allies). They rejected any division of Palestine on the grounds that it was fundamentally undemocratic (since the majority of Palestine's population opposed partition), unlawful (since it contradicted the international legal principle of national self-determination), and unjust (since, they maintained, the entire territory was rightfully theirs, and the UN had no right to give any of it away). While Arabs in neighboring countries (Egypt, Syria, Lebanon, and Transjordan) were finally gaining independence from colonial rule and exercising their right to national self-determination, it seemed that Palestinian Arabs were being unfairly denied this same right. Hence, the Palestinian Arab leadership, with the support and encouragement of Arab states, defiantly refused to accept, or honor, the UN partition plan.

The Zionist leadership, on the other hand, officially accepted the UN partition plan since it gave them the state they had long sought, at a time when Jews desperately needed it (the breakaway right-wing Revisionist Zionist movement, however, vociferously opposed partition). But they also had some problems with it. First and foremost, they were concerned that the envisaged Jewish state would contain a large Arab minority, nearly half of the total population, which could, in time, become the majority (the proposed Arab state would also contain a much smaller Jewish minority). Not only would the Jewish state be potentially vulnerable internally due to its large Arab population, it would also be vulnerable to external attack since the proposed borders made it almost indefensible. The Zionist leadership was also disappointed that Jerusalem would be outside the Jewish state and under some kind of international rule (other places of great historic and religious significance to Jews, such as the town of Hebron, were within the proposed borders of the Arab state). Notwithstanding these complaints, the Zionist leadership, headed by David Ben-Gurion, pragmatically embraced, however begrudgingly, UNSCOP's partition plan and actively lobbied UN member states, especially the United States, to vote in favor of it when it came before the UN General Assembly.

On November 29, 1947, after a prolonged and heated debate, a crucial two-thirds majority of the UN General Assembly voted to adopt a slightly modified version of UNSCOP's partition plan, known as UN Resolution 181 (there were 33 votes in favor, 13 against, and 10 abstentions). As some UN delegates applauded, those representing the Arab states walked out in protest. Most Jews in Palestine and around the world, who had been nervously listening to the live radio broadcast of the vote, rejoiced and celebrated. In stark contrast, most Arabs in Palestine, and the Arab world at large, reacted with indignation and outrage. This anger quickly turned violent. In the days following the passage of the partition plan, Arabs in Palestine went on strike, while angry mobs and armed gangs began attacking Jews, and Zionist militias soon retaliated. Civilians on both sides were killed, often deliberately, as the violence escalated. Civil war between the Arab and Jewish communities in Palestine had broken out, while the British, who were still nominally in charge but preparing to leave, largely looked on, refusing to intervene. This civil war, which in May 1948 became an interstate Arab-Israeli war, had enormous and lasting consequences that will be explored in the next chapter.

3

THE ARAB-ISRAELI WARS

How many Arab-Israeli wars have there been, and how many people have been killed?

It is not as easy as you might think to count the number of Arab-Israeli wars or tally the number of casualties in them. Since Israel's founding in 1948 until the present day, its military and security forces have fought constantly against various Arab forces, including non-state militant groups. One could even say that there's been an endless state of war, punctuated by occasional truces and temporary lulls in violence. It is important, however, to distinguish between what military experts call "high-intensity conflicts" and "low-intensity conflicts." The former refers to conventional wars, while the latter refers to guerrilla warfare, terrorism, counterinsurgency, and counterterrorism campaigns. Israel has been continuously engaged in a low-intensity conflict with Palestinians since the early 1950s, when armed Palestinian *fedayeen* (meaning "self-sacrificers" in Arabic) began conducting cross-border attacks against Israel. Over the past three decades or so, Israel has also been fighting a low-intensity conflict with the Shi'ite Lebanese group Hezbollah (which is allied with, and militarily and financially supported by, Iran). During the course of these conflicts, there have been countless guerrilla raids, terrorist attacks, bombings, assassinations, kidnappings, and more, resulting in thousands of casualties, many of them civilians. Along with these low-intensity conflicts, Israel has fought a total of nine wars against various Arab forces (the use of the term "war" here follows the definition commonly used by political scientists who collect quantitative data on them: war is a conflict in which at least a thousand people are directly killed by fighting in a one-year period). These wars, their main protagonists, and estimates of the number of casualties in them (including combatants and civilians) are listed below:

- The 1947–1949 war (Israel's "War of Independence"): Israel vs. Egypt, Jordan, Syria, Lebanon, and Iraq. 6,300 Israelis, 13,000–16,000 Palestinians, and 2,000–2,500 other Arabs were killed.
- The 1956 war ("Sinai War" or "Suez War"): Israel, Britain, and France vs. Egypt. 231 Israelis and an estimated 3,000 Egyptians were killed.
- The 1967 war ("Six-Day War" or "June War"): Israel vs. Egypt, Jordan, Syria, and Iraq. 796 Israelis and an estimated 18,600 Arabs were killed (including approximately 11,500 Egyptian casualties, 1,000 Syrian casualties, and 6,100 Jordanian casualties).
- The 1969–1970 war ("War of Attrition"): Israel vs. Egypt. 1,424 Israelis and an estimated 5,000 Egyptians were killed.
- The 1973 war ("Yom Kippur War," "October War," or "Ramadan War"): Israel vs. Egypt and Syria. 2,688 Israelis and an estimated 15,000 Egyptians and 3,500 Syrians were killed.
- The 1982–1985 First Lebanon War: Israel vs. the Palestine Liberation Organization (PLO) and Syria. 1,216 Israelis and an estimated 21,000 Arabs were killed (including approximately 370 Syrian casualties, 1,000 PLO casualties, and more than 19,000 Lebanese and Palestinian casualties, mostly civilians).
- The 2006 Second Lebanon War: Israel vs. Hezbollah. 165 Israelis (including 44 civilians) and an estimated 1,100 Lebanese were killed, mostly civilians.
- The 2008–2009 First Gaza War ("Operation Cast Lead"): Israel vs. Hamas. 13 Israelis (including 3 civilians) and around 1,400 Palestinians were killed, mostly civilians.
- The 2014 Second Gaza War ("Operation Protective Edge"): Israel vs. Hamas. 72 Israelis (including 5 civilians) and more than 2,100 Palestinians were killed, mostly civilians.

What is immediately apparent from this long list is the sheer number of Arab-Israeli wars, spanning more than seven decades (given this, it is hardly surprising that the conflict has attracted so much international attention). The fact that there have been so many wars between Israelis and Arabs (including Palestinians) is all the more remarkable considering the time period in which these wars have taken place. Since the end of World War II, there has been a general decline in the number of interstate wars, with the vast majority of wars occurring within states (civil wars), not between them. The high number of Arab-Israeli wars has been a notable exception to this global trend.

Not only have there been a great number of Arab-Israeli wars but they have also been fairly frequent, occurring at regular intervals—roughly one a decade—from 1948 until 1982. From the end of the First Lebanon War in 1985 until the outbreak of the Second Lebanon War in 2006, there were no full-scale Arab-Israeli wars, although Israel continued to wage a counterinsurgency war in southern Lebanon until 2000, and two Palestinian uprisings (called *intifadas*) took place from 1987 to 1993 and from 2000 to 2005 (the second of which resulted in over 4,000 deaths—more than the number killed in some Arab-Israeli wars). Since 2006, there has been a resumption of Arab-Israeli warfare, occurring with even greater frequency than in the past as wars have broken out every few years.

These recent Arab-Israeli wars (in 2006, 2008–2009, and 2014) differ from their predecessors in two significant respects. First, they have only been bilateral, not multilateral wars, pitting Israel against a single adversary rather than a coalition of Arab forces. This has given Israel a decisive military advantage, which helps account for the lopsided casualty tolls in these wars with far fewer Israeli than Arab casualties. Second, Israel's adversaries in these wars have been nonstate actors (Hezbollah and Hamas) instead of Arab states. In fact, since 1973, no Arab state has gone to war against Israel. Militarily, the Arab states have effectively dropped out of the conflict, and two of them—Egypt and Jordan—have made peace with Israel. Arab-Israeli wars are no longer interstate wars, but "asymmetric" wars between Israel and nonstate actors that employ guerrilla warfare and terrorism. These wars have led to more civilian casualties but far fewer Israeli fatalities. Hence, wars have become much less costly for Israel, but also less decisive, as it is harder for

Israel to militarily defeat adversaries like Hezbollah and Hamas, who tend to avoid conventional battles and often embed themselves among civilians (to offset their relative military weakness).

Finally, it is worth noting that despite the high number and frequency of Arab-Israeli wars, their lethality is comparatively low. In total, approximately 100,000 people (soldiers and civilians) have been killed in all the Arab-Israeli wars. This figure pales beside the millions who have been killed in many single wars throughout history. Even when compared to other wars in the Middle East, the Arab-Israeli wars have been far less deadly. About ten times as many people were killed in the Iran-Iraq war in the 1980s than in all the Arab-Israeli wars combined, and in recent years, more than four times as many people have been killed in the war in Syria. But while the Arab-Israeli wars have been relatively minor in terms of their casualties, they have had major consequences, not just for the Israeli-Palestinian conflict but also regionally and even globally. The most consequential have been the wars of 1947–1949 and 1967.

Why did Arab states go to war against Israel in 1948?

The 1948 Arab-Israeli war, as it is generally known, was actually two consecutive wars that went on from 1947 to 1949. The first was a civil war in Mandatory Palestine between November 1947 and May 1948, mostly involving guerrilla warfare between irregular Palestinian-Arab forces and Zionist military forces (made up of the Haganah and the more radical Irgun and Lehi militias). The second, immediately following it, was an interstate war between Israel and its Arab neighbors (Egypt, Jordan, Syria, Lebanon, and Iraq), which began the day after the termination of the British Mandate and the declaration of the State of Israel and ended in January 1949. Although they are often described and commemorated as a single event—which Israeli Jews call their "War of Independence" and Palestinians refer to as the *Nakba*—these wars were, in fact, driven by different motives. Contrary to the popular Israeli narrative, the Palestinians and the Arab states were not all intent on preventing the emergence of a Jewish state. While this was true for the Palestinians, who started the civil war to prevent the partition of Palestine and the creation of a Jewish state (as proposed in the 1947 UN partition plan), the Arab states' military intervention was motivated more by inter-Arab rivalries and domestic politics than by a burning desire to destroy the fledgling Jewish state and "drive the Jews into the sea" (as fiery Arab rhetoric at the time declared, and as Israelis like to repeat).

Arab states first became actively involved in the conflict in the 1930s (some were invited by the British government in 1939 to participate in a London conference on the future of Palestine). After gaining independence from Britain and France following World War II, Egypt, Jordan, Syria, Lebanon, and Iraq formed the Arab League, along with Saudi Arabia and Yemen, to strengthen their relations and coordinate their policies. From the outset, the Arab League was divided between the Hashemite-ruled Kingdoms of Jordan and Iraq on one side, and Egypt, Syria, and Saudi Arabia on the other. The latter opposed the regional ambitions of the Hashemites, especially those of King Abdullah of Jordan, who wanted to annex all or part of Palestine (and, possibly afterward, Syria and Lebanon). Although the Arab League rejected the UN partition plan, and its secretary-general publicly threatened a "war of elimination" against the proposed Jewish state, King Abdullah actually supported partition and secretly negotiated an agreement with the Jewish Agency (the de facto government of the Jewish community in Palestine). According to the agreement, Jordan would be allowed to annex territory in Palestine that the UN partition plan had allotted to the Palestinian Arabs in return for not attacking the areas allocated to the Jewish state. The other Arab states were not aware of this secret agreement, but they were rightfully suspicious of King Abdullah and anxious to ensure that Jordan would not take what was left of Palestine for itself. Egypt's King Farouk also competed with Abdullah to be the leader of the Arab world and harbored his own territorial ambitions in Palestine—hoping to annex the southern part of the country (the leaders of Iraq, Syria, and Lebanon also had their own territorial designs on Palestine).

Thus, when the Arab League members (primarily Egypt, Jordan, Syria, Lebanon, and Iraq) went to war against the newly declared State of Israel on May 15, 1948, it was their own national interests—defined by their autocratic rulers—that motivated them first and foremost. While proclaiming to act on behalf of the beleaguered Palestinians, who were on the verge of defeat in the civil war they had been fighting, the intervention of the Arab states was driven more by their own territorial greed and competition for power.

This is not to say that the increasingly desperate plight of the Palestinians, many of whom had become refugees during the course of the fighting, was of no concern to the Arab states. Public opinion across the Arab world was strongly supportive of the Palestinian cause and vehemently anti-Zionist. To ignore such sentiments and idly stand by while the Zionist, and later Israeli, military forces defeated and displaced the Palestinians would have risked incurring significant domestic unrest, which could even threaten the stability of their fragile regimes. Hence, the Arab regimes also militarily intervened to satisfy their domestic publics and safeguard their tenuous hold on power (ironically, their dismal military performance in the war, with the exception of Jordan's British-trained Arab Legion, discredited the Arab regimes and led to a wave of regime change, with the leaders of Egypt, Syria, and Iraq all violently overthrown in the decade following the war).

What appeared to be a concerted Arab attempt to eliminate the Jewish state at its birth was, in fact, a disorganized effort by a fractious coalition of states seeking to advance their own agendas and protect their own interests. This helps explain why the Arab states lost the war, much to their embarrassment. The numerical advantage that they seemingly enjoyed—five Arab armies fighting against the Israeli army with a fifty-to-one advantage in total population—was more apparent than real. Israel was able to field a larger, better-trained force than the five Arab armies combined (approximately 35,000 Israeli troops versus 25,000 Arab troops). There was also very little military coordination on the part of the Arab states, so their armies fought separately, allowing Israel to focus on fighting one adversary at a time. For instance, while the Israelis and Jordanians fought fierce battles around Jerusalem (which was not covered in their agreement), the Jordanians did not fight the Israelis in other areas, and Jordan stayed out of the last round of the war—from November 1948 to January 1949—as the Israel Defense Forces (IDF) drove the Egyptian army out of the southern Negev region. The fact that the Arab military forces arrayed against Israel were smaller and disorganized challenges the traditional Israeli narrative of the war as a miraculous victory of "the few against the many"—a modern-day version of the biblical story of David slaying Goliath. It also demonstrates that Arab unity, and solidarity with the Palestinians, was more rhetorical than real—something that Palestinians bitterly learned in 1948 and many times since.

What were the major consequences of the war of 1947–1949 for Israel and the Palestinians?

The first Arab-Israeli war was, in many respects, the most consequential of them all. Its repercussions continue today, and any attempt to make peace between Israel and the Palestinians cannot avoid addressing them. The most important consequence of the 1948 war is the very existence of the State of Israel. Although the state's establishment had already been officially announced by David Ben-Gurion before a packed hall in Tel Aviv on May 14, 1948, and both superpowers, the United States and USSR, immediately granted the Jewish state diplomatic recognition (a requirement for any new state), it was not until the fledgling state successfully repelled the invasion of Arab armies that its existence was secured. Plainly stated, there would be no Israel if it had lost the war. That's why Israeli Jews celebrate it as their "War of Independence." The consolidation of Israeli statehood as a result of the war was hugely significant not only to Israeli Jews but also to many Jews around the world who regarded the emergence of a Jewish state as an event of profound historical and even theological importance, especially coming so soon after the Holocaust. Israel's survival in the 1948 war is still widely perceived by Jews in Israel and the diaspora as a kind of modern-day miracle, symbolizing both the success of Zionism and the rebirth or "redemption" of the Jewish people after their near-destruction.

Israel not only survived, it expanded. Having been allotted 56 percent of British Mandatory Palestine in the 1947 United Nations (UN) partition resolution, Israel managed to retain this land and conquer some additional territory that had been allocated to the proposed Arab state. As a result, Israel's territory now comprised about 78 percent of Mandatory Palestine, including the western part of Jerusalem (which the UN plan had put under international control). Although Israel's new boundaries were not recognized in any of the armistice agreements it signed in 1949 with Egypt, Lebanon, Jordan, and Syria, they have gradually become accepted over time as its de facto borders by the international community and even by the Palestinians and Arab states (Israelis themselves, on the other hand, are less accepting of these borders). Within these enlarged borders, Israel was a little less vulnerable to external attack, though it was still far from secure.

What was a great triumph for Israel (albeit at a steep cost) was a colossal tragedy for the Palestinians. They refer to it simply as the *Nakba* ("catastrophe"), a term that came from the title of a book written during the 1948 war by Constantine Zureiq, a professor at the American University of Beirut. While the war secured the existence of a Jewish state, it prevented the emergence of a Palestinian one— exactly the opposite outcome of what the Palestinians had hoped. The Arab state envisaged in the UN partition plan never came into being. Instead, the territory was carved up between Israel, Jordan, and Egypt. Jordan occupied and then annexed the eastern half of Jerusalem (including the Old City) and the hilly region of central Palestine (that became known as the "West Bank" because it is west of the Jordan River). Egypt occupied a narrow strip of land along the southern coast around the city of Gaza (the "Gaza Strip"). Jordan and Egypt retained control over these areas until Israel conquered them in the 1967 war.

The Palestinians were effectively dispossessed of their homeland. Their hopes for national self-determination and statehood had been shattered. They were still living under foreign rule, now by Israel, Jordan, and Egypt—none of whom supported Palestinian political independence (Israel and Jordan suppressed and even banned expressions of Palestinian nationalism). Palestinians who became citizens of Israel, initially around 150,000 of them, found themselves living as a minority in a self-declared Jewish state, where they were viewed as a "fifth column" and placed under military rule from 1949 to 1966. Palestinians living in the West Bank under Jordanian rule, and in the Gaza Strip under Egyptian rule, fared no better, as they were also subject to strict surveillance and control.

Not only did Palestinians remain stateless but also about half of them became refugees during the war—600,000–750,000 out of a total of 1.3 million Palestinians (there were widely varying estimates of the number of Palestinian refugees in 1949). Most of the refugees ended up in the West Bank and Gaza Strip, where they were housed in makeshift tent camps (which are now overcrowded shantytowns). Many other Palestinian refugees went to Syria and Lebanon, and others dispersed across the Middle East and beyond. This was the beginning of what became known as the Palestinian refugee problem. The problem has grown enormously in size over the years as these original 700,000 or so Palestinian refugees have had five or six generations of descendants, who are also defined as refugees according to the criteria of the UN Relief and Works Agency (UNRWA), the UN agency that exclusively looks after them (the original refugees and their descendants now number well over five million). Who is to blame for this longstanding and growing problem, and what to do about it—whether Palestinian refugees are entitled to return to Israel or should resettle elsewhere—has been perhaps the most controversial issue in the Israeli-Palestinian conflict, and remains one of the biggest obstacles to ending it.

Israel's survival, and the defeat, dispossession, and displacement of the Palestinians as a result of the war, transformed the nature of the conflict. Before the war, it had been an intercommunal conflict between a Palestinian-Arab majority and a Jewish minority living within the same country—a conflict in which the Palestinians seemed to have the upper hand by sheer virtue of their numbers. After the war, it became a conflict between the State of Israel and a stateless, scattered people, whose very national existence was in question. In this new phase of the conflict, Israel was much more powerful by virtue of its statehood—with centralized leadership, military and economic power, and diplomatic relations and recognition. The Palestinians, by contrast, were left leaderless, largely powerless, and dependent upon the support and largesse of Arab states. With the balance of power so heavily tilted in Israel's favor, there was little chance of reaching a mutual compromise that could peacefully resolve the conflict (just as it had not been possible to resolve the intercommunal conflict during the Mandate period, when the balance of power seemed to favor the Palestinians).

In the two decades following the 1947–1949 war, however, the Israeli-Palestinian conflict was obscured by the bigger and broader interstate conflict between Israel and its Arab neighbors. This conflict, pitting Israel against the Arab world, took center stage and became a focus of regional and often global attention. The Arab states were Israel's primary enemy, especially the surrounding states of Egypt, Jordan, and Syria, whose leaders frequently issued bellicose threats against Israel and whose armies could potentially deliver on those threats. Although Palestinian *fedayeen* regularly staged cross-border raids into Israel, the Palestinians were much less of a concern to Israelis. Indeed, as far as most Israelis were concerned, the Palestinians did not even exist (as a nation).

Across the Arab world, the Palestinians were also largely ignored. Their cause was subsumed in the wider Arab nationalist struggle against Israel—a struggle the Palestinians enthusiastically identified with, but in which they were allowed only a marginal and subservient role. While rejection of the "Zionist entity" (as Israel was called) and a fervent commitment to the "liberation of Palestine" became central and sacrosanct components of Arab nationalism, this was not really for the sake of the Palestinians. Rather, it served the interests of Arab regimes, advanced the ambitions of their authoritarian rulers, and buttressed the ideological worldview of Arab nationalism and pan-Arabism, which saw the creation of Israel as yet another attempt by Western powers to colonize Arab land and weaken and divide the Arab world. Pan-Arabism sought a single Arab state instead of the many that existed, and it was championed most prominently by the charismatic Egyptian leader Gamal Abdul Nasser in the late 1950s and early 1960s and also espoused by the Ba'athist regimes in Syria and Iraq that were established during this time.

Being ostracized in the region and threatened by what appeared to be the combined might of the Arab world (in reality, the Arab world was much less unified than Israelis perceived it to be at the time), fueled a siege mentality among Israeli Jews, sowing a sense of isolation and existential threat that still lingers today. The still-fresh trauma of the Holocaust undoubtedly exacerbated this feeling. Further compounding it was the gradual exodus of around 700,000 Jews from Arab countries between 1948 and 1956, many of them fleeing because of growing persecution and anti-Jewish violence. Although the arrival of these Mizrahi Jews was a huge demographic boon for Israel, it contributed to the popular belief among Israeli Jews that the Arab world was antisemitic, not just anti-Zionist, and that Arabs and Jews were deadly enemies (this led many Mizrahi Jews in Israel to disavow their "Arabness," refrain from speaking Arabic—their native language—in public, and even abandon some of their rich cultural traditions).

Thus, the 1947–1949 war deepened the antagonism on both sides of the conflict, added new issues to it (particularly the issue of Palestinian refugees), and escalated the conflict into a regional and interstate one. In doing so, the war created the Arab-Israeli conflict and made the Israeli-Palestinian conflict much harder to resolve.

Why did many Palestinians become refugees in 1948? Who is to blame?

Of all the fiercely contested issues in the Israeli-Palestinian conflict, none is as fraught with emotion, laden with propaganda, or subject to such prolonged debate as the issue of Palestinian refugees. For many Palestinians, especially those who are refugees (or at least consider themselves to be), it is their paramount issue—the one they are most adamant about and least willing to compromise on. Most Israelis, on the other hand, think that the issue should have been settled long ago and has been artificially kept alive and deliberately inflated. For both sides, the question of who is to blame for creating the refugee problem—and, by extension, who is responsible for resolving it—is not merely a historical dispute. It is central to their clashing national narratives and cuts to the heart of their collective identities. Palestinians, and their supporters, see the plight of Palestinian refugees, which has dragged on for seven decades, as encapsulating their national tragedy. The refugees, in this sense, are the embodiment of Palestinian victimhood, for which, they believe, Israel is to blame. Israeli Jews regard the accusation that Israel is responsible for the Palestinian refugee problem as unfair and inflammatory, aimed at casting them as the villains in the conflict when they are really, in their own eyes, its innocent victims. What is at stake, therefore, in the ongoing argument about the Palestinian refugees are collective memories, narratives, and identities, which is why this issue is so highly charged and resistant to compromise.

There have long been two diametrically opposed explanations for why 700,000 or so Palestinians became refugees during the course of the 1948 war. The Palestinians and their supporters insist that the refugees were violently expelled by Zionist and later Israeli armed forces, who systematically carried out a centrally directed and organized campaign of "ethnic cleansing" to create an ethnically pure Jewish state (i.e., one devoid of Arabs). Israel, according to this account, is solely to blame for the Palestinian refugee problem and must be held accountable for it. In stark contrast, according to the traditional, mainstream Israeli explanation, the Palestinians fled or chose to leave their homes because they were encouraged, and sometimes even ordered, to do so by their own leaders and by outside Arab leaders. They left voluntarily, expecting to return after the Jews had been defeated or driven out by conquering Arab armies. There was no Zionist or Israeli campaign of ethnic cleansing. In fact, Jewish officials even pleaded with Palestinians to stay. Ultimately, the Israeli narrative claims, it was the Palestinians' own fault, or at least their leaders', that they became refugees because they rejected the UN partition plan and started the civil war. The Arab states that attacked Israel are also to blame for escalating the war and, allegedly, encouraging Palestinian civilians to evacuate their homes.

Both of these competing accounts of the origins of the Palestinian refugee problem are one-sided and tendentious. Their purpose is to assign blame, or avoid it, rather than offer a more accurate and complicated explanation for how and why Palestinians became refugees in 1948. Such an explanation has, however, been provided in the work of recent historians, most notably by Benny Morris, a "revisionist" Israeli historian whose archival research (in Israeli archives) has debunked much of the traditional Israeli account. Relying upon extensive documentary evidence, Morris's research showed that Palestinians did not generally leave because they were encouraged or ordered to do so by Palestinian or Arab leaders (except, notably in the case of the Palestinian inhabitants of the city of Haifa), as generations of Israelis had been told. Many Palestinians were, in fact, violently expelled by Zionist and Israeli troops, just as the Palestinian narrative maintains. The largest expulsion (amounting to about a tenth of the total number of Palestinian refugees) occurred in July 1948, when Israeli troops captured the Arab towns of Ramle and Lydda (now called Lod). Under instructions from Ben-Gurion, the local IDF commander (a young Yitzhak Rabin) ordered the 50,000–70,000 Palestinian residents to leave. Some were bused out and others were forced to walk in what became known as the "Lydda Death March."

Was this expulsion part of an orchestrated campaign of ethnic cleansing, as the Palestinians have always contended? Some scholars argue that it was, pointing as evidence to a military plan (Plan D), which was adopted by the Haganah in March 1948 in anticipation of the expected invasion by Arab armies and implemented over the subsequent months. The plan called for the conquest, and destruction if necessary, of Arab-populated towns and villages located close to the borders of the territory that the UN had demarcated for a Jewish state. If the residents resisted, they were to be expelled outside the borders of the Jewish state. Plan D gave Israeli military commanders permission to expel Palestinian civilians, and some acted upon this, but others did not. There was no consistent pattern; it varied from place to place, partly depending upon the behavior of the civilians and the personality and beliefs of the local commander. This leads other scholars, including Benny Morris, to argue that the expulsion of Palestinians was merely a military contingency plan, not a requirement and certainly not a government policy. Morris insists there was no master plan to expel all the Palestinians. Had there been one, he argues, then very few, if any, Palestinians would have remained inside Israel, when, in fact, around 150,000 stayed put. Morris does, however, acknowledge that the Zionist/Israeli leadership not only condoned the expulsion of Palestinians but also looked favorably upon it. They wanted to have a Jewish state without a large Arab minority and had long considered the expulsion or "transfer" of Arabs as a way to accomplish this goal. There was political support for expelling Palestinians, but this does not amount to an official policy of ethnic cleansing.

Whether or not it was premeditated or planned, the expulsion of Palestinian civilians by Zionist and Israeli forces was a war crime according to international law. Palestinian and Arab forces also expelled Jewish civilians from areas that they conquered, and both sides committed various other kinds of war crimes (such as massacring civilians, raping women, and summarily executing prisoners of war). While the Israelis committed more atrocities than the Arabs, this was probably simply because they had more opportunities to do so since they were the superior military force and conquered more territory. It was in response to rumors and reports, sometimes exaggerated, of Jewish atrocities—the most infamous being the slaughter on April 9, 1948, of more than a hundred Palestinian residents of the village of Deir Yassin, including women and children—that many Palestinians fled the fighting.

Most Palestinian refugees were probably not expelled but they fled out of fear and panic, as civilians often do in war. As this fear and panic spread like a contagion, and was also sometimes deliberately induced and encouraged, it contributed to the collapse of Palestinian society, which, in turn, led to a mass exodus (the departure of many middle- and upper-class Palestinians during the early stages of the civil war also contributed to this exodus, as did a lack of centralized leadership). In short, widespread fear gave rise to mass panic and then mass flight. Once this was underway, in the latter half of the war, Israel's leadership, particularly Ben-Gurion, welcomed it as an opportunity to reduce Israel's Arab population. From June 1948, the Israeli government's official policy was to prohibit the return of refugees to the country. From that point onward, Israel barred Palestinian refugees from returning, forcefully prevented them from doing so, razed hundreds of their abandoned villages, and appropriated their homes and lands.

During UN-mediated peace talks in 1949 aimed at resolving the Arab-Israeli conflict, Israel did offer to take in up to 100,000 Palestinian refugees, as long as the Arab states absorbed the rest and agreed to make peace. The sincerity of this offer is questionable since the Israeli government had already decided to bar entry to a mass influx of Palestinian refugees (the offer was made under American pressure and partly because Israel was eager to get accepted into the UN). In any case, the Arab states flatly rejected the proposal, insisting that Israel should admit all the Palestinian refugees before they would even begin to negotiate peace—a demand that Israel interpreted as an attempt to undermine its existence. Subsequently, Israel's position on the Palestinian refugee issue hardened as it refused to allow any Palestinian refugees to return and maintained that the issue could only be resolved within the context of a comprehensive peace agreement. Ultimately, therefore, Israel bears at least partial responsibility for the Palestinian refugee problem. But so too do the Arab states that attacked Israel in 1948 as well as the Palestinian leadership, whose rejection of the UN's partition plan in November 1947 led to the outbreak of the war.

What was the 1956 Sinai War?

The belief that Israel was a tool of Western imperialism was already widespread in the Arab world in 1956, but the war that broke out in October that year—known as the Sinai or Suez War—seemed to confirm this popular suspicion. The war was the result of a secret plot among Israel, Britain, and France to topple Egypt's president Gamal Abdel Nasser. He had taken power in the wake of the "Free Officers" coup in 1952, which overthrew King Farouk and established the Republic of Egypt. A charismatic and popular leader, Nasser advocated pan-Arabism and vociferously opposed Israel's existence and Western influence in the region. Israel, Britain, and France each had their own reasons for trying to get rid of him. Israel wanted to stop the increasingly frequent cross-border raids by Palestinian *fedayeen* coming from the Egyptian-controlled Gaza Strip. It also wanted to restore the ability for Israeli shipping to pass through the Straits of Tiran, a narrow waterway that gave Israel access to the Red Sea and through it to East Africa and Asia, which Egypt had closed off to Israel in September 1955. Above all, Israel was threatened by a potential shift in the military balance of power after Egypt signed a major arms deal in 1955 with Czechoslovakia (a puppet state of the Soviet Union). Rather than sit back and watch Egypt's military buildup, the Israeli government, led by the hawkish Ben-Gurion, opted for a "preventive war" to forestall an anticipated future Egyptian attack. The British and French governments, for their part, were determined to reverse Nasser's nationalization of the Suez Canal, which had been owned by an Anglo-French company. They also saw Nasser as a dangerous demagogue (comparing him to Hitler) who threatened their influence in the Middle East and, in the case of the French, their rule in Algeria (because of Nasser's support for the rebels there).

In accordance with this secret plan, Israel invaded the Sinai Peninsula on October 29, 1956. Shortly afterward, the British and French sent troops to seize control of the Suez Canal Zone on the flimsy pretext of protecting the canal from attack. The collusion fooled no one. It was met with widespread international condemnation, including from the Eisenhower administration in the United States, which worried that the attack on Egypt would drive the Arab world, and possibly the rest of the developing world, into the arms of the Soviet Union. Under intense American pressure, Britain and France quickly withdrew their forces in what was widely seen as a sign that their dominance in the Middle East had come to an ignominious end and that the United States and USSR had taken their place. Threatened with U.S. sanctions, Israel also eventually withdrew its forces from the Sinai and Gaza in March 1957, but only after it secured an American commitment to ensure its right to maritime passage through the Straits of Tiran. A UN peacekeeping force (the first of its kind) was dispatched to monitor the UN-brokered ceasefire, serve as a buffer between Egyptian and Israeli forces, and prevent Palestinian raids into Israel (which significantly declined thereafter). This amounted to a modest achievement for Israel, but it came at the cost of damaging its international reputation and straining its relationship with the United States (though Israel strengthened its relationship with France, which became its main ally and arms supplier, helping Israel to secretly build an embryonic nuclear weapons capability over the next decade).

Nasser, however, was the biggest beneficiary of the Sinai War. Although Egypt's military performed poorly and proved to be no match for the IDF, Nasser's defiant stance throughout the Suez crisis, and his regime's survival despite the Anglo-French-Israeli conspiracy to oust him, catapulted him into the position of leader of the Arab world. Nasser's soaring popularity in the wake of the Sinai War became like a cult of personality and made "Nasserism" the most potent political force in the Arab world. The ideology preached pan-Arabism, Arab socialism, anti-imperialism, anticolonialism, and anti-Zionism, calling for the removal of Western influence from the Middle East, the replacement of "reactionary" Arab regimes, and the "liberation of Palestine." The ideological ascendance of Nasserism generated upheaval across the region, resulting in a military coup in Iraq (1958), civil wars in Lebanon (1958) and Yemen (1962–1970), and a short-lived union between Egypt and Syria (1958–1961). Finally, in boosting Nasser's power and the regional popularity of Nasserism, the 1956 war—the second Arab-Israeli war—sowed the seeds for the third Arab-Israeli war, which broke out in June 1967.

What caused the 1967 war?

There were many factors that contributed to the outbreak of the 1967 Arab-Israeli war—widely known as the "Six-Day War" (Arabs refer to it as the "June War"). Persistent tension between Israel and its Arab neighbors (often heightened by cross-border attacks by Palestinian fighters and harsh Israeli retaliations), Israel's sense of encirclement and vulnerability, an Egyptian–Israeli arms race fueled by the Cold War competition between the United States and the Soviet Union, a water dispute between Israel and Syria that led to frequent border clashes, and inter-Arab rivalries (particularly between Nasser's Egypt and the new Ba'athist regime in Syria) were all indirect or proximate causes of the 1967 war. But the immediate cause of the war was a crisis sparked by a series of provocative actions taken by Nasser in May 1967. It is still unclear what Nasser's actual intentions really were. Most scholars believe that he neither wanted nor expected a war with Israel to break out. Rather, Nasser engaged in a form of brinkmanship that went over the brink. To restore his flagging reputation as the hero of the Arab world and Egypt's status as its unrivaled leader, Nasser drew Israel into a risky game of chicken, confidently expecting it to back down. But under intense public pressure, and at the urging of its military, the Israeli government, led by Prime Minister Levi Eshkol, did not back down. Instead, Israel seized the initiative and attacked Egypt, claiming it was a preemptive strike (some historians have questioned the sincerity of this claim, suggesting that Israel's leadership did not expect Egypt to attack).

While Israel started the 1967 war, and Egypt provoked it, neither side wanted it. It was an accidental war that came about as a result of Soviet misinformation, Nasser's miscalculations, and Israel's fears. It was the Soviets, not the Egyptians or the Israelis, that triggered the three-week crisis that led to the outbreak of the 1967 war. On May 13, 1967, the Soviets falsely reported to Egypt that Israel was massing its troops on Syria's border and planned to invade. Some scholars argue that the Soviets did this because they hoped to solidify the Egyptian–Syrian alliance and bolster the Ba'athist regime in Damascus, while others argue that Moscow wanted to provoke a war in which the Egyptians could destroy Israel's nuclear reactor and thereby prevent it from getting the bomb. Nasser knew that the Soviet intelligence was false, but he took it as an opportunity to demonstrate his willingness to confront Israel and defend Egypt's allies. So he mobilized the Egyptian army and ordered it back into the Sinai (an area it had left as a result of the 1956 war).

Since UN peacekeepers were stationed in the Sinai, Egypt requested that they be redeployed to the Gaza Strip. The UN secretary-general responded that Egypt could not choose where UN peacekeepers were deployed; it could only retract its permission for their deployment on Egyptian territory. Egypt's request had already been made public, giving Nasser little choice but to either back down and risk being perceived as weak or to demand the total withdrawal of the UN Emergency Force (UNEF). Carried away on a wave of popular support, he chose the latter, forcing the evacuation of UNEF (Israel refused to allow the force to be deployed on their side of the border), and moving Egyptian troops right up to Israel's southern border. In response, Israel mobilized its armed forces and called up all its reserve soldiers. This amounted to a large proportion of its male population, making a prolonged mobilization very costly for the Israeli economy. But at this stage of the crisis, war still seemed unlikely (neither the Israeli or U.S. governments expected one).

Nasser's next move, on May 22, made a war almost inevitable. He closed the Straits of Tiran to Israeli shipping, thereby preventing imported goods and vital oil supplies from reaching the Israeli port of Eilat. This crossed a red line for Israel, which had previously clearly stated that such a move would be considered a casus belli (an act of war). Nasser gambled that if Prime Minister Eshkol—who publicly appeared during the crisis as nervous and hesitant—failed to respond, then Israel would be humiliated and he would score a major psychological and political victory. If, on the other hand, Israel struck first and initiated a war, then it would be diplomatically isolated and immediately forced by the United States, USSR, and UN to end its offensive (as had happened in the 1956 war), which Nasser had been led to believe the Egyptian military could cope with.

While Israel nervously waited in vain for the United States and Britain to arrange an international naval flotilla in order to ensure free maritime passage through the Straits of Tiran (which the Americans and British had guaranteed in 1957), Nasser made his final bold move, raising the stakes still further. On May 30, Egypt signed a mutual defense treaty with Jordan, putting the Jordanian army under Egyptian command and establishing a military alliance among Egypt, Syria, and Jordan. As the surrounding Arab armies appeared to be preparing to wage a three-front war against Israel, other Arab states (such as Iraq, Kuwait, and Algeria) sent contingents of troops to join the Arab coalition and Arab leaders, especially Nasser, repeatedly issued threats of destruction, the Israeli public mood went from nervous to near-hysterical. Many Israeli Jews were gripped with fear and panic. The possibility of a second Holocaust, with Nasser now in the role of Hitler, suddenly seemed to them very real and imminent. Although the IDF was quietly confident that it could prevail in a war, its generals, especially Chief of Staff Yitzhak Rabin, thought that Israel had to strike first, and that the longer it waited to do so, the more costly the war would be since the Arab forces would have more time to prepare. As public panic and military pressure mounted, Israel established a national unity government. Then, after receiving what it believed was Washington's acquiescence, if not approval, the Israeli government decided on June 4 to go to war, justifying it as self-defense.

The next morning, on June 5, the Israeli air force carried out a surprise attack on the Egyptian air force, destroying nearly all its aircraft on the ground within minutes. Later that day, Israel also destroyed the Jordanian air force (having failed to convince Jordan to stay out of the war) and most of Syria's air force. This gave Israel complete air supremacy for the rest of the war, helping the IDF to quickly defeat the Egyptian and Jordanian armies, conquer the Sinai Peninsula and Gaza Strip from Egypt, and conquer the West Bank and East Jerusalem (including the Old City) from Jordan. These swift victories enabled Israel to then divert its forces to defeat the Syrian army and conquer the strategically valuable Golan Heights plateau in southwestern Syria. After just six days of combat, a UN-brokered ceasefire was signed on June 11.

Israel had achieved one of the quickest, and most stunning and decisive, victories in modern military history. The Israeli public mood suddenly shifted from despair to euphoria, as Israeli Jews rejoiced in what they regarded as a surprising, if not miraculous, victory (many Jews around the world also celebrated, taking pride in Israel's triumph and subsequently becoming much more committed to the country). In the aftermath of the war, there was a widespread sense of relief and deliverance among Israeli Jews. There was also an air of triumphalism, an intoxicating feeling of power, and, for some Israeli Jews, a new religious fervor. For Arabs, by contrast, the resounding defeat of the Arab coalition (which they refer to as the "Naksa" or "the setback") was a monumental failure and a massive humiliation, which led to years of recriminations and soul-searching in the Arab world. For Nasser personally, the defeat was a severe blow to his status. His gamble in challenging Israel had backfired disastrously. Although he remained in power until his sudden death a few years later (in 1970), his reputation never fully recovered from the failure of the 1967 war, and he lost his ability to dominate Arab politics. It was not only Nasser's own prestige and power that was undermined but also the prestige and power of Nasserism, the ideology he embodied. In the years that followed the war, Nasserism lost much of its popular appeal and political influence in the Arab world (especially in Egypt). This was only one of the war's many important consequences for the region.

What was the impact of the 1967 war?

The 1967 war was brief, but it had a long-lasting and far-reaching impact. Indeed, the consequences of what happened in just six days in June 1967 are still unfolding five decades later, especially in the form of Israel's ongoing occupation and settlement of the West Bank (including East Jerusalem) and Golan Heights, territories it conquered during the war. The war's outcome had a profound impact not only upon its protagonists (Israel, Egypt, Syria, and Jordan) but also on the Palestinians, the entire Arab world, and the Middle East region. In many respects, the 1967 war was a watershed event that transformed Israeli and Palestinian politics and changed the course of both the Arab-Israeli and the Israeli-Palestinian conflicts. Whether it was also, as many believe, a turning point in Arab politics and Middle Eastern history is more debatable, but it undoubtedly contributed to the ideological demise of Nasserism in general, and pan-Arabism in particular, and to the rise of Islamism across the region and even beyond it. Although Islamism predates Nasserism, the discrediting of the latter because of the Arab states' defeat in 1967 enhanced Islamism's popular appeal in the Middle East in recent decades as another militantly anti-imperialist, anti-Western, and anti-Zionist ideology. Islamism also provided a convenient explanation, or excuse, for the humiliating Arab defeat in the 1967 war, blaming it on secularism in the Arab world and a lack of Muslim faith and unity. The 1967 war also contributed to a gradual shift in the balance of power in the Arab world away from Egypt and toward Saudi Arabia (which became more heavily involved in the Arab-Israeli conflict), as well as to much greater American and Soviet involvement in the Middle East. The repercussions of these major developments are still reverberating in the region today. Even the recent wars in Iraq and Syria are, at least in part, long-term consequences of the 1967 war since the war led to the ascendancy of the Assad regime in Syria (Hafez al-Assad, the father of the current Syrian president, Basher al-Assad, seized power in a bloodless coup in 1970), and it eventually led to the attempt by Iraqi strongman Saddam Hussein to become the new Nasser and leader of the Arab world.

Of all its consequences, the 1967 war had the greatest impact on Israel, the Palestinians, and on the Israeli-Palestinian and Arab-Israeli conflicts. In a mere matter of days, Israel was transformed from being a small state surrounded by threatening enemies into a much larger state (in terms of the territory it possessed) that had vanquished its enemies and proven its military prowess. Israel's capture of the West Bank from Jordan, the Golan Heights from Syria, and the Sinai Peninsula and Gaza Strip from Egypt more than tripled the amount of territory under its control (see Map 3). Moreover, the lightning speed with which the IDF conquered these territories and decisively defeated three Arab armies (including Egypt's, then the largest army in the Middle East) demonstrated its tactical ingenuity, technological sophistication, and strategic superiority. Thus, Israel suddenly became the dominant military power in the region. This made it an attractive ally for the United States. Having generally kept Israel at arm's-length before the 1967 war, afterward the United States drew it much closer, gradually developing an informal alliance between the two countries. In 1968, for example, the first big American–Israeli arms deal took place, with the Johnson administration selling fifty Phantom jet fighters to Israel. The strengthening of the U.S.-Israeli relationship in the wake of the 1967 war bolstered Israel's power and regional standing still further.

The dramatic shift in the regional balance of power as a result of the 1967 war had major implications for Israel's conflicts with the Palestinians and the surrounding Arab states. Paradoxically, the war had a contradictory long-term impact—mitigating the Arab-Israeli conflict and escalating the Israeli-Palestinian one. Hence, the war made the Arab-Israeli conflict easier to resolve, but the Israeli-Palestinian conflict harder to resolve.

Arab accommodation with Israel

It might seem odd to claim that the 1967 war led to a lessening of the Arab-Israeli conflict given the fact that Israel and Egypt went to war again, less than two years after the 1967 war ended. Between March 1969 to August 1970, they engaged in what became known as the "War of Attrition," regularly exchanging artillery fire along the Suez Canal and engaging in aerial battles above the Sinai Desert (Soviet pilots occasionally took part in these battles on behalf of Egypt). And just three years after this war ended inconclusively in a cease-fire, another Arab-Israeli war broke out in October 1973 when Egypt and Syria launched a surprise attack against Israel. Although the 1967 war intensified the Arab-Israeli conflict militarily in the years immediately following it, in the long run it had a moderating impact because it convinced Arab leaders, if not the masses, that Israel was too strong to be destroyed militarily, and thus they had to learn to live with it. This realization induced a more pragmatic and moderate approach to Israel, one aimed at both containing its power and accommodating its existence. The change in Arab foreign policy toward Israel already emerged in the aftermath of the war at the Arab League summit in Khartoum in September 1967. While the Arab leaders issued their famous "three no's"—"no peace with Israel, no recognition of Israel, no negotiations with it"—they also stated that they only sought Israel's withdrawal from "the Arab lands which have been occupied since the aggression of June 5" (as opposed to their earlier goal of "liberating Palestine").

As the Khartoum resolution suggested, the 1967 war not only encouraged Arab states to reluctantly come to terms with Israel's existence because it could not be eliminated, it also compelled the defeated Arab states (Egypt, Syria, and Jordan) to do so in order to reclaim the territories that Israel had taken from them in the war. If they wanted these territories back, and they certainly did, then there was only one way to accomplish this, and that was through a peace agreement with Israel. Before the war, the Arab states had little or no incentive to make peace with Israel. After the war, they did, because Israel had a valuable bargaining chip. It had something tangible to trade—land—in exchange for peace. Thus, the war created the possibility of "land for peace," a formula that became the basis for all subsequent Arab-Israeli peacemaking. It led Anwar Sadat, Nasser's successor as president of Egypt, to sign a landmark peace agreement with Israel in 1979, and it also eventually led to a Jordanian–Israeli peace agreement in 1994 (the Oslo Accords between Israel and the PLO in the early 1990s were also based upon the "land for peace" formula).

Although it took a decade, and two wars, until Egypt became the first Arab state to enter peace talks with Israel in 1977, the "land for peace" formula was officially accepted by Egypt, Jordan, and Israel in November 1967 after the UN Security Council unanimously passed Resolution 242 (Syria accepted Resolution 242 after the 1973 war, while the rest of the Arab states, except Libya, formally accepted it in 1982). Resolution 242 was passed after lengthy diplomatic negotiations, and it amounted to a careful balancing act. The resolution emphasized "the inadmissibility of the acquisition of territory by war and the need to work for a just and lasting peace in which every State in the area can live in security" (thereby addressing both Arab and Israeli demands). The text of the resolution went on to affirm that "a just and lasting peace in the Middle East" should involve Israel's withdrawal "from territories occupied in the recent conflict," and the "termination of all claims or states of belligerency and respect for and acknowledgment of the sovereignty, territorial integrity and political independence of every State in the area and their right to live in peace within secure and recognized boundaries free from threats or acts of force." The meaning of this key passage has been the subject of prolonged disagreement—specifically, over whether it requires Israel to withdraw from all of the territory it occupied (as Arab states insist) or just parts of it (as Israel argues, pointing out that the word "all" was deliberately omitted, and that the English version of the resolution referred to "territories," not "*the* territories"). Notwithstanding this ambiguity, Resolution 242 clearly did not call upon Israel to unilaterally and unconditionally withdraw from the areas it had occupied in the 1967 war. Instead, it linked such a withdrawal to peace agreements with Arab states (but not with the Palestinians, whom the resolution only briefly and obliquely made reference to in terms of "a just settlement of the refugee problem").

The reemergence of the Palestinians

The UN Security Council's scant treatment of the Palestinian issue in Resolution 242 was indicative of how far this issue had fallen off the international agenda by 1967. In the eyes of the world, the Palestinians had just become nameless refugees, their demand for statehood ignored and largely forgotten. Even in the Arab world, the Palestinians were often overlooked, as their cause had been subsumed in the broader Arab struggle against Israel. The Palestinians themselves were partially responsible for this, as Palestinian nationalism faded in the wake of the Palestinians' defeat and dispersal in 1948, and many Palestinians embraced pan-Arabism and pinned their hopes and dreams on Nasser. Between 1948 and 1967, therefore, the Palestinians were sidelined, relegated to a supporting role in the wider Arab-Israeli conflict. The 1967 war changed this. The defeat of the Arab states and the failure of their would-be savior, Nasser, shocked Palestinians and convinced them that they could no longer rely upon Arab states for their deliverance, and thus they had to take matters into their own hands. Consequently, in the decades afterward, while the Arab states slowly retreated from their conflict with Israel, the Palestinians returned to take center stage. As they did so, the Israeli-Palestinian conflict gradually eclipsed the Arab-Israeli conflict.

It was not only the bitter disappointment of the 1967 war, the decline of pan-Arabism, and the slow disengagement of Arab states from the conflict with Israel that led Palestinians to reassert themselves and reemerge as an independent actor in the decades after 1967. The resurgence of Palestinian nationalism (including among Arab citizens of Israel) was also, ironically, a result of Israel's conquest of the West Bank and Gaza, Palestinian-populated areas that had been under Jordanian and Egyptian control, respectively. Once both areas came under Israel's control, Palestinians could travel relatively freely between them as well as within Israel proper. Palestinians were reunited, as was "Palestine" itself, albeit under Israeli rule. This rekindled Palestinian nationalism, particularly in opposition to Israel's repressive military-run regime in the West Bank and Gaza, which denied Palestinians many civil liberties, such as freedom of expression, freedom of the press, and freedom of political association (Palestinians in the territories did, at least, benefit economically from employment in Israel and Israeli investment in the territories). While the Israeli authorities tried to suppress Palestinian nationalism, and even criminalized it as a threat to Israeli security (for instance, displaying the Palestinian national colors was a punishable act), this only inflamed Palestinian nationalism and made it more militant.

The resurgence of Palestinian nationalism was reflected in, and reinforced by, a proliferation of Palestinian militant groups (mostly based in Jordan, Lebanon, and Syria because they could not operate in the territories under Israeli control). Groups like Fatah (established in 1959 and led by Yasser Arafat), the Popular Front for the Liberation of Palestine (a Marxist group led by George Habash), and the Democratic Front for the Liberation of Palestine became increasingly active and popular among Palestinians. Inspired by the Algerian War of Independence against France and by other successful anticolonial liberation movements (such as that conducted by the Vietnamese), these groups adopted the strategy of armed struggle, including the use of guerrilla warfare and terrorism. They shot to global attention in the late 1960s and 1970s as they carried out numerous high-profile international terrorist attacks, pioneering the use of airplane hijackings in particular. Most of the Palestinian militant groups were members of the PLO, which was founded by the Arab League in 1964 with the goal of "liberating Palestine" through armed struggle. Initially the PLO was a puppet organization under Egypt's control, but in 1969 Fatah gained control of the PLO and installed Arafat as its new chairman. Under Arafat's leadership, the PLO became much more independent and assertive.

Jordan—where roughly two-thirds of the population was Palestinian (including some 200,000 Palestinians from the West Bank who became refugees during and immediately after the 1967 war)— became the PLO's headquarters and a staging ground for increasing guerrilla attacks against Israel. The heavy Israeli military reprisals that these attacks provoked, and the PLO's growing challenge to Jordan's sovereignty, led to mounting tension between the PLO and Jordan's ruler, King Hussein, whom the PLO tried to assassinate and overthrow. The conflict between the PLO and Jordan culminated in a brief but bloody civil war between September 1970 and July 1971, in which the Jordanian army killed thousands of Palestinians (militants and civilians) and eventually managed to expel the PLO from Jordan to Lebanon. Palestinians refer to this event as "Black September," and an offshoot of the PLO adopted this name and became notorious worldwide when it took eleven Israeli athletes hostage during the 1972 Summer Olympics in Munich and the hostages were killed during a botched rescue attempt at a nearby airport. The terrorist attack was broadcast around the world and became known as the "Munich massacre."

Despite its violent expulsion from Jordan, the PLO steadily emerged during the 1970s as a major player in inter-Arab politics and it became the de facto representative of the Palestinian people on the world stage. In 1974, for instance, the Arab League recognized the PLO as the sole legitimate representative of the Palestinian people, and the UN General Assembly granted it an official status as a "permanent observer." The rise of the PLO brought much more regional and global attention to the Palestinian cause—but whether it garnered more international sympathy for the Palestinians is highly debatable because its methods were often violent and indiscriminate, thereby associating Palestinians with terrorism in many people's minds. The PLO's growing influence and stature made the Israeli-Palestinian conflict harder to resolve because in its early years the PLO officially rejected Israel's existence and opposed the creation of a Palestinian state in just the West Bank and Gaza (though this hardline stance began to soften from the mid-1970s onward when the PLO started to consider the establishment of a Palestinian state alongside Israel, at least as a temporary measure). The PLO's rejectionist stance toward Israel and its frequent use of terrorism made it anathema to Israel and to its ally, the United States (which also opposed the PLO because it received Soviet backing). It would take many years, much bloodshed, and numerous policy shifts on both sides before the Israeli government accepted the PLO as a suitable negotiating partner with whom it could try to resolve its conflict with the Palestinians. Even then, much of the Israeli public fiercely opposed this step and remained deeply suspicious of the PLO.

Israel's new territorial ambition

Palestinian terrorism was one reason why the Israeli-Palestinian conflict worsened as a result of the 1967 war. Israeli expansionism was another. Before the war, Israel accepted the 1949 armistice lines (the

"Green Line") as its de facto borders (it even reluctantly accepted the division of Jerusalem). It harbored no territorial ambitions—all it really wanted was peace with the Arab states. Contrary to Arab claims, Israel did not go to war in 1967 because of territorial greed. In fact, it was not until the war was underway that the Israeli government decided to conquer the West Bank. But as soon as Israel seized this territory, it was reluctant to leave it. It was as if, having tasted the West Bank, Israel's territorial appetite suddenly grew. Although the Israeli government decided immediately after the war ended to return the Sinai to Egypt and the Golan Heights to Syria in return for full peace and the demilitarization of those areas, it made no decision about the future of the West Bank. This area was not only strategically valuable to Israel as a land buffer between it and any army advancing from the east, it was also of great historical and religious significance to Israeli Jews (and Jews elsewhere). It was where the ancient Jewish kingdoms ruled and where the stories of the Bible supposedly occurred (in places like Bethlehem, Hebron, and Nablus). As such, the West Bank—"Judea and Samaria" as Israeli Jews call it—evoked intense nationalist and religious sentiments among many, if not most, Israeli Jews. While some were willing to eventually return the West Bank to Jordan in exchange for a peace agreement, others adamantly opposed this, insisting that the whole "Land of Israel" belonged to the Jewish people and should not be bartered or partitioned. What to do with the West Bank, therefore, became the biggest and most divisive question in Israeli politics in the decades after 1967—and it remains unresolved to this day.

While Israelis argued about the long-term future of the West Bank—and, to a lesser extent, that of the other occupied territories—their government started building civilian settlements there (they were initially intended to bolster Israel's security and were largely restricted to strategic locations in the Jordan Valley). Over time, Israel built settlements in all the territories it occupied after the 1967 war, but its settlement enterprise in the West Bank was the biggest and most consequential because the growing presence of Israeli settlers there not only raised serious questions about Israel's willingness to ever withdraw from this area but also gave birth to an energetic and determined Jewish settler movement led by messianic religious Zionists. They viewed Israel's miraculous "liberation" of Judea and Samaria as divine providence and incontrovertible evidence that the "final redemption" was occurring, which would culminate in the long-awaited arrival of the Jewish messiah (they also believed that this had been prophesied just weeks before the outbreak of the 1967 war by Rabbi Zvi Yehuda Kook, their spiritual mentor and chief theologian). Driven by this religious conviction, after the 1967 war a new generation of religious Zionists burst onto the Israeli scene, much more mobilized and militant than their predecessors (who tended to be politically pragmatic and moderate). They were the vanguard of the Israeli settler movement in the West Bank and Gaza, and they became a highly effective pressure group, often capable of compelling Israeli governments to accept their actions (notably, creating settlements) and acquiesce to their demands (legalizing and protecting such settlements). Although these radical religious Zionist settlers were not solely, or even primarily, responsible for Israel's settlement enterprise in the West Bank, they were, and still are, its most committed participants and advocates. They also be-came the fiercest domestic opponents of any Israeli withdrawal from the West Bank and Gaza. Thus, by giving rise to the Israeli settler movement, the 1967 war made a resolution of the Israeli-Palestinian conflict much harder to achieve.

More broadly, the war made the conflict more intractable by heightening its religious dimension, which had been largely dor-mant. Religious sentiment was most pronounced on both sides in their renewed struggle for control over the Old City of Jerusalem—a place holy to Jews, Muslims, and Christians—and especially over its sacred sites (most notably, the Western Wall and Temple Mount/Haram al-Sharif). Israeli Jews were ecstatic when Israeli paratroopers captured the Old City during the 1967 war, and after-ward they overwhelmingly supported Israel's de facto annexation of East Jerusalem and its reunification with West Jerusalem, which Palestinians strongly opposed. Since the 1967 war, in asserting their rival claims to a capital in Jerusalem, both sides have regularly em-ployed religious rhetoric and appealed to the religious feelings of their coreligionists at home and abroad. In doing so, religion has been increasingly injected into the Israeli-Palestinian conflict.

Israel's occupation of East Jerusalem, the West Bank, and Gaza Strip, along with its expanding settlements in those areas, became a major focus of the Israeli-Palestinian conflict after 1967—so much so, that some people now seem quite unaware that their conflict long predates 1967. Of course, the conflict isn't only about Israel's settlement enterprise or its military occupation of the West Bank and Gaza, but these factors have definitely intensified the conflict (and made it more intimate). They have fueled Palestinian animosity and anger toward Israel, spurred the mass mobilization of Palestinians, and motivated countless protests and acts of violence (including against Israeli civilians). Hence, the 1967 war exacerbated the Israeli-Palestinian conflict and brought much more attention to it—within Israel, regionally, and even globally. Perhaps in the future, however, when the conflict finally ends (as it surely will, somehow), the impact of the 1967 war might ultimately be seen in a different light—planting the seeds for the conflict's resolution, as it has generated an insoluble dilemma for Israelis—how can Israel rule over millions of disenfranchised Palestinians and remain a democracy—and a powerful impetus for Palestinians—to end "the occupation"—that may one day lead them to make peace with each other.

Why was the 1973 war significant?

The 1973 Arab-Israeli war (called the "Yom Kippur War," "October War," or "Ramadan War") was the brainchild of Anwar Sadat, who became president of Egypt after Nasser's death in 1970. He was vice president under Nasser and had also been a senior figure in the Free Officers Movement that overthrew the Egyptian monarchy. Sadat could not emulate Nasser since he lacked his charismatic appeal and popularity across the Arab world, so instead he took a different approach to Egyptian domestic and foreign policy, one that was less ideological and more pragmatic. Abandoning Nasser's pan-Arabism, Sadat focused on Egypt's pressing domestic needs. He prioritized Egypt's ailing economy, not its leadership of the Arab world. To promote economic growth, Sadat had to liberalize Egypt's state-dominated economy and open it up to Western investment. He also needed to reduce Egypt's heavy defense spending, reopen the Suez Canal to international shipping, and regain the Sinai since it contained lucrative oil fields. Sadat recognized that the only way to accomplish these goals was to make peace with Israel, whether he liked it or not. The challenge, for him, was that Israel was not interested in making peace, at least not on terms that were remotely acceptable to Egypt (i.e., one that involved a complete return of the

Sinai). This was evident when the Israeli government, then led by Prime Minister Golda Meir, ignored Sadat's early peace overtures in 1970–1971 (the Nixon administration in the United States supported Israel's intransigence at the time). Israelis, still basking in their stunning victory in the 1967 war, felt confident and complacent and were in no mood to compromise.

Sadat decided that another war was necessary to shake Israelis out of their complacency, prompt the superpowers to launch a peace process, and force the Israeli government to the negotiating table. The war's objective was limited to striking a costly military blow on Israel and restoring Arab pride—not reconquering the Sinai, let alone destroying Israel (which Sadat knew was impossible). Sadat's plan was for Egyptian troops to cross the Suez Canal (where Israeli soldiers were dug in on the heavily fortified eastern bank), rapidly capture some territory in the Sinai, and inflict a large number of Israeli military casualties. The war would be short because the superpowers were expected to quickly end it, but it would break the military and diplomatic stalemate that had set in. To support his war plan, Sadat enlisted Syria, whose leader, Hafez al-Assad, had his own plan to forcefully retake the Israeli-occupied Golan Heights (Sadat didn't tell Assad about the limited nature of Egypt's planned offensive or his ultimate desire to make peace with Israel). By waging a coordinated war against Israel on two fronts, Egypt and Syria hoped to have the strategic advantage, offsetting Israel's military superiority. They also hoped to have a tactical advantage by carrying out a surprise attack at a time when Israeli Jews were least prepared to respond—on the Jewish holy day of Yom Kippur, when most Israeli Jews would be fasting, praying, and resting.

On the afternoon of October 6, 1973, Egypt and Syria launched their attack against Israeli forces in the Sinai and Golan Heights. Although Israeli intelligence received warnings about the planned attack (from Jordan's King Hussein and also from Nasser's son-in-law, who was a close aide to Sadat and a spy for Israel), Israel's military and political leadership had dismissed them, confidently assuming that Egypt and Syria would not dare go to war since the military balance of power was so strongly in Israel's favor (they did not anticipate a limited war—a failure of imagination for which they were later severely criticized). Largely caught off-guard, therefore,

Israel was initially on the defensive as its forces were pushed back and suffered heavy losses. In the early days of the war, Egyptian troops succeeded in crossing the Suez Canal, while Syrian tanks advanced deep into the Golan Heights. At one point the situation seemed so dire for Israel that its defense minister, Moshe Dayan, seriously raised the possibility of using Israel's nuclear weapons (he was rebuffed by Prime Minister Meir).

As the war went on, however, Israel regained the initiative and received a crucial resupply of weapons from the United States (which President Nixon authorized after desperate Israeli appeals). After a successful counterattack against the Syrians on the Golan Heights, which brought Israeli forces to within shelling distance of Damascus, the IDF began a major counteroffensive against the Egyptians. It crossed the Suez Canal, occupied its western bank, and advanced well into mainland Egypt, just a hundred kilometers from Cairo. This dramatic turnaround prompted the Soviets to threaten to intervene militarily to rescue the Egyptian Third Army, which the IDF had surrounded. In response to this Soviet threat, the United States put its nuclear arsenal on high alert in case the war escalated into a superpower conflict, and it pressured Israel to obey a UN ceasefire. After nearly three weeks of intense combat, the war ended on October 26, 1973.

Israel had again managed to defeat Egypt and Syria on the battlefield (it even captured additional Syrian territory), but its victory in the 1973 war felt more like defeat to Israelis. The sudden, unexpected outbreak of the war was a massive shock to them, and they suffered a relatively high number of casualties (2,688 Israeli soldiers were killed—as a proportion of Israel's population this was more than twice the number of Americans killed in the Vietnam war). The Israeli public mood was totally different in the aftermath of the 1973 war than it had been after the 1967 war. There was no jubilation or triumphalism. Instead, there was widespread anger at Israel's political and military leadership for their failure to heed the intelligence warnings and prepare the IDF (Prime Minister Meir and Defense Minister Dayan were later forced to resign in April 1974 following the scathing report by a domestic commission of inquiry into the war). This had major political repercussions in Israel, undermining the longstanding dominance of the Labor Party (which had been in power since the country's founding), and paving the way for the victory of the right-wing Likud Party, led by Menachem Begin, in the 1977 election—a watershed in Israeli politics.

As well as shattering public confidence in Israel's Labor leadership, the 1973 war also forced Israelis to recognize the limits of Israel's military power. Contrary to the conventional wisdom before the war, the Arab states were not deterred from attacking Israel. Moreover, Egypt and Syria had proven that they could really hurt Israel even if they could not defeat it. The IDF lost the aura of invincibility that it had acquired as a result of its triumph in 1967. Thus, unlike the 1967 war, the 1973 war humbled Israelis. It disabused them of their belief that Israel could safely hold onto Arab territories without paying a price and wait for the Arabs to capitulate and sue for peace. Consequently, the war gave Israelis the motivation to make peace that they lacked after 1967 (this helps explain why the Israeli peace movement, led by Peace Now, emerged in the late 1970s).

The 1973 war not only gave Israelis more reason to make peace, it gave Arabs more confidence to do so. For Arabs, especially for Egyptians, the war was a much-needed psychological victory after the humiliating defeat of 1967. The early successes of the Egyptian and Syrian armies restored a collective sense of Arab pride, despite the fact that these armies were later routed. Egyptians, in particular, celebrated the war as a great victory, and to this day the anniversary of the Egyptian army's successful crossing of the Suez Canal on October 6 is one of their biggest national holidays. It is impossible to know how much this restored sense of pride fostered a willingness to make peace with Israel, but it probably emboldened Egypt to enter into negotiations with a feeling that it was at least a more equal partner.

In addition to providing a psychological boost for the Arabs, the 1973 war was a political and strategic success for Sadat. Although his military plan failed, his daring gambit in going to war against Israel worked. It helped convince many Israelis to eventually support Israel's full withdrawal from the Sinai in return for peace, although it took another bold move by Sadat a few years later—his historic visit to Jerusalem in 1977—to get a decisive majority of Israelis to support this concession. Sadat's attempt to violently kickstart negotiations with Israel also succeeded in drawing its government to the negotiating table and getting the Americans and Soviets more actively engaged in attempts to end the conflict (since it now threatened to directly involve them). Intense American and Soviet diplomacy to end the 1973 war produced another major UN Security Council resolution (Resolution 338). This resolution reaffirmed the "land for peace" formula first enunciated in Resolution 242, and it called for "negotiations between the parties concerned under appropriate auspices aimed at establishing a just and durable peace in the Middle East." Resolution 338 was the prelude to a sustained effort by both superpowers to push their respective allies to directly negotiate with each other. It led to the first official face-to-face Arab-Israeli talks since 1949 when Egypt, Jordan, and Israel agreed to participate in a UN-sponsored peace conference, cochaired by the United States and USSR, held in Geneva in December 1973 (Syria refused to participate because the PLO was not invited at Israel's insistence). While the Geneva conference produced no concrete outcomes, the mere fact that it took place at all represented a turning point in the Arab-Israeli conflict away from warfare and toward peacemaking. As then U.S. Secretary of State Henry Kissinger later wrote in his memoirs: "The Geneva conference of 1973 opened the door to peace through which later Egypt and Israel walked."

Kissinger's tireless "shuttle diplomacy" following the Geneva conference played a more direct role in bringing about peace between Egypt and Israel. Kissinger brokered two Israeli-Egyptian disengagement agreements in 1974 and 1975 (the latter was achieved after the United States threatened Israel with a "reassessment" of its relationship). These resulted in a gradual pullback of Israeli forces in the Sinai and the return of some of the territory to Egypt. This paved the way a few years later for the Camp David Accords between Israel and Egypt in 1978 and a full peace treaty in 1979. Kissinger also brokered a disengagement agreement between Israel and Syria in 1974, and although a peace agreement between them has proven to be frustratingly elusive, a decades-long truce has generally prevailed, preventing another full-scale war between Israel and Syria despite their mutual antagonism (and notwithstanding hundreds of Israeli airstrikes in war-torn Syria in recent years).

Peace between Egypt and Israel and a cessation of war between Syria and Israel were arguably the most important and enduring consequences of the 1973 war. But the war also had other significant effects both regionally and globally. In the Middle East, it led to a realignment of Cold War alliances as Sadat took Egypt from the Soviet camp and placed it in the U.S. one, turning Egypt into a U.S. client and a major recipient of American money and arms. Egypt's "defection" from its alliance with the Soviet Union was the beginning of the end of Soviet influence in the Middle East (the Soviets continued to support Syria though). Henceforth, the United States became the only superpower that really mattered in the region. As the United States' diplomatic and military involvement steadily increased, it became the sole external arbiter of Middle Eastern affairs (which, in turn, generated a lot of local resentment).

Finally, the oil embargo that the Arab members of the Organization of the Petroleum Exporting Countries (OPEC) imposed on the United States and the Netherlands during the 1973 war (due to their support for Israel) had global repercussions, causing a spike in oil prices and a worldwide recession that was especially hard-hitting for Western Europe and the United States. It also generated a lingering fear in the West that the Arab Gulf states, particularly Saudi Arabia, would use their "oil weapon" again and cause another costly global oil crisis. This elevated Saudi Arabia's role in the Arab-Israeli conflict (and in Middle East politics more generally) and increased Western interest in seeking a resolution to the conflict.

Why did Israel invade Lebanon in 1982?

There was no territorial dispute between Israel and Lebanon, and unlike Israel's other immediate neighbors, Lebanon hadn't fought any wars with Israel since its limited participation in the first Arab-Israeli war in 1948. Geographically small, militarily weak, and religiously diverse, Lebanon was always more preoccupied with its own, often turbulent, internal affairs than with fighting Israel. Its involvement in the Arab-Israeli conflict was largely involuntary. Lebanon begrudgingly accommodated roughly 100,000 Palestinian refugees from the 1947–1949 war (most of them were confined to squalid refugee camps and denied Lebanese citizenship and equal rights). Lebanon also reluctantly became home to the PLO after its violent expulsion from Jordan in 1970. When the PLO relocated to Lebanon, it set up its headquarters in the capital Beirut, recruited Palestinian refugees in Lebanon to join its ranks, and established military training camps and artillery positions in southern Lebanon adjacent to Israel's northern border. From there, it regularly shelled Israeli towns and villages and launched guerrilla raids into Israel, killing dozens of Israeli civilians. The deadliest terrorist attack in Israeli history (known in Israel as the "Coastal Road Massacre") occurred on March 11, 1978, when eleven PLO commandos took a boat from southern Lebanon, landed on a beach in northern Israel, and then hijacked a taxi and two public buses, resulting in the deaths of thirty-seven Israelis, including thirteen children, and one American tourist.

The PLO's extensive presence in southern Lebanon—strongly resented by the local, largely Shi'ite population—effectively created a "state within a state" (which Israelis dubbed "Fatahland," after the PLO's dominant faction). Inevitably, Lebanon became a target for Israeli military reprisals, just as Jordan had been when it reluctantly hosted the PLO. These deadly reprisals did not stop the PLO's attacks, but they added to growing tensions between the PLO and Lebanese Christians and Druzes. These tensions culminated in the eruption of a devastating civil war in Lebanon in 1975, pitting Christian militias against the PLO and an assortment of other armed groups, and drawing some 35,000 Syrian troops into Lebanon. In March 1978, in the midst of the Lebanese civil war, Israel carried out a major military incursion into southern Lebanon ("Operation Litani," as the IDF called it, came in response to the Coastal Road Massacre). Israel's goal was to drive the PLO away from the area bordering Israel and set up a "security zone" (i.e., a buffer zone) under the control of a Lebanese Christian militia (called the Free Lebanon Army, later renamed the South Lebanon Army) that was supported by Israel. Between 1,000 and 2,000 Palestinians and Lebanese, many of them civilians, were killed during Israel's weeklong offensive, and more than 100,000 people were internally displaced. After three months, IDF troops withdrew from southern Lebanon, following two UN Security Council resolutions (425 and 426) calling for their withdrawal and the deployment of a UN peacekeeping force to the area (the United Nations Interim Force in Lebanon [UNIFIL]).

Israel's invasion of Lebanon on June 6, 1982, was, therefore, the second time that it invaded the country. Like Israel's invasion in 1978, it was ostensibly in response to a Palestinian terrorist attack—this time the attempted assassination of the Israeli ambassador to Britain on June 3, 1982 (he was severely wounded). But this time, the PLO was not actually responsible for the attack (it was carried out by a rival Palestinian splinter group known as the Abu Nidal organization that was based in Iraq and funded by its Ba'athist government, who probably ordered the attack in retaliation for Israel's 1981 bombing of its nuclear reactor). Although Israeli intelligence knew that the PLO was not involved, Israel's right-wing government, headed by Prime Minister Menachem Begin, publicly blamed the PLO and ordered the IDF to immediately retaliate against PLO targets in Lebanon. Predictably, the PLO responded to Israel's air and artillery strikes with its own rocket and artillery barrages into northern Israel, shattering a fragile U.S.-brokered ceasefire that had been in place for almost a year. This was the excuse that Prime Minister Begin, Defense Minister Ariel Sharon, and IDF Chief of Staff Rafael Eitan had been waiting for to implement their preplanned invasion of Lebanon (since they needed to get Israeli cabinet approval and what they believed would be the tacit consent of the Reagan administration in the United States). The next day, on June 4, 1982, the Israeli cabinet authorized what they were told would be a brief and limited IDF ground incursion into southern Lebanon (going no further than 25 miles inside Lebanon and lasting no longer than 48 hours). Officially called "Operation Peace for Galilee," its publicly stated aim was to destroy the PLO's bases in southern Lebanon and push it northward, thereby alleviating the security threat that the PLO posed to northern Israel, which by then had grown into a military threat and not just a terrorist threat (in July the previous year, for instance, a ten-day barrage of PLO rocket and artillery attacks on northern Israel forced tens of thousands of Israelis into bomb shelters and led large numbers to flee).

The real intentions behind Israel's 1982 invasion of Lebanon were far more ambitious than the limited objective approved by the Israeli cabinet and supported by Israeli public opinion. Instead of a quick, geographically restricted, and narrowly defined military operation, what Sharon and Eitan actually had in mind was a much larger and longer military offensive that would penetrate far deeper into Lebanon. The objective was not merely to remove the PLO from southern Lebanon but to completely eradicate its presence in Lebanon as a whole. They hoped that by destroying the PLO's military and political base in Lebanon, they would cripple the organization and cause it to lose its support among Palestinians. This would, in turn, enable the Begin government to overcome the resistance of Palestinians in the West Bank and Gaza to its proposed plan to grant them administrative autonomy under permanent Israeli rule (Begin was ideologically committed to securing Israel's possession of the West Bank and Gaza). Sharon also hoped the PLO's defeat in Lebanon might eventually lead to a mass exodus of Palestinians from Lebanon to Jordan, where they already constituted a majority of the population and could one day, if they wished, establish their own state (Sharon subscribed to the popular right-wing Israeli belief that "Jordan is Palestine"). Sharon's grand plan went even beyond this, as he also wanted to evict Syrian forces from Lebanon and install a pro-Israel, Christian-dominated regime (headed by the leader of a Maronite [Catholic] Christian militia called the Phalange), which would then sign a peace treaty with Israel. In short, for the ultrahawkish Sharon (and possibly for Begin too, though this is less clear), the invasion of Lebanon was the means toward much greater ends—eliminating the Palestinian issue once and for all, ensuring a "Greater Israel," securing its northern border, and establishing its regional hegemony.

After some 80,000 ground troops, accompanied by Israeli tanks, invaded Lebanon on June 6, 1982, it didn't take long for the Israeli cabinet and the Israeli public to realize they had been duped, and that the IDF was conducting a much bigger military operation than what they had been led to expect. Israel was engaged in a full-scale war, and unlike most of its previous wars, this one was entirely voluntary (it was, in Israeli parlance, a "war of choice," whereas the wars of 1948, 1967, and 1973 were regarded by almost all Israelis as "wars of no choice" and hence fundamentally "just wars"). As Israeli forces moved deeper inside Lebanon, reaching the outskirts of Beirut, and as Israeli casualties mounted, the war became increasingly controversial in Israel. For the first time in the country's wartime history, there was widespread public protest against the Lebanon war, and even more unprecedented was the public refusal of some Israelis to fight in it (conscientious objectors even formed their own organization called *Yesh Gvul* ["There is a Limit/ Border"]). Israel's military actions in Lebanon, especially its two-month-long siege and heavy bombardment of West Beirut (June 14–August 21, 1982), where the PLO's leadership was based, also provoked outrage abroad as shocking images of Beirut's destruction and the suffering of its residents were regularly broadcast on television sets around the world. Along with growing criticism in the international media, foreign governments, including Israel's closest ally the United States, also criticized Israel's behavior. Frustrated by its inability to restrain the Begin government, the Reagan administration even considered suspending arms deliveries to Israel and threatening it with sanctions.

Unbowed, and dismissive of all the criticism they faced, Begin and Sharon were determined to force the PLO's surrender and evict it from Beirut. They eventually accomplished this by the end of the summer, with the help of American mediation, when PLO chairman Yasser Arafat reluctantly agreed to leave Beirut along with other senior PLO figures and thousands of PLO fighters. A multinational force made up of American, French, and Italian troops was briefly deployed to oversee the PLO's safe evacuation from Beirut and to protect the Palestinian civilians who remained in the large refugee camps located around the city. Within days of the peacekeeping force's departure, however, the worst atrocity of the Lebanon War occurred after the Israeli army entered West Beirut (violating the U.S.-brokered truce) and allowed their Lebanese Christian ally into Palestinian refugee camps to root out any remaining PLO fighters. Instead, the Phalangist militiamen brutally took revenge for the assassination of their leader Bashir Gemayel, who had been killed in a bombing two days earlier after having just recently been elected president of Lebanon. Systematically moving from house to house, they murdered, mutilated, and raped unarmed Palestinians. The rampage went on for three days (September 17–19, 1982), while Israeli soldiers stood by outside the camps, almost certainly aware of what was happening but not intervening to stop it until they were finally ordered to do so (IDF Chief of Staff Eitan was actually informed of the killings while they were taking place, but did nothing to halt them). Estimates of the number of Palestinians killed range from 800 to as many as 2,750, mostly women, children, and old men.

The "Sabra and Shatila massacre," as it became known (named after the two Palestinian refugee camps where it took place), shocked the world, particularly because of the gruesome pictures of piles of corpses. Although Israeli troops did not perpetrate it, Israel was accused of complicity and bore the brunt of international outrage. Domestically, the Israeli public was also appalled, and a massive demonstration (then the largest in Israel's history) was held in Tel Aviv demanding a judicial inquiry into the massacre as well as the IDF's withdrawal from Lebanon. A commission was appointed and it concluded that Sharon and Eitan were both indirectly responsible for the massacre, calling for their resignations. The Sabra and Shatila massacre was a turning point in the Lebanon war. Faced with intense international criticism, growing American pressure, and declining public support for the war, the Israeli government looked for a way out of Lebanon (Begin himself resigned in August 1983 and was succeeded by Yitzhak Shamir, another hardline Likud leader). It still took two and a half years before Israeli forces withdrew from most of Lebanon in June 1985, marking the end of what had become Israel's longest and most contentious war. Even then, a small contingent of Israeli soldiers remained in a narrow strip of land (about 10 miles wide) stretching along the Lebanese-Israeli border. They patrolled this so-called security zone in concert with a local, mainly Christian militia, the South Lebanon Army (SLA), which Israel funded and armed. It took another fifteen years until the IDF completely withdrew from Lebanon in May 2000. This withdrawal—carried out unilaterally and hastily under orders from Israel's then Prime Minister Ehud Barak (who had promised in his 1999 election campaign to end Israel's unpopular presence in southern Lebanon)—finally took Israel out of what had become a bloody quagmire in Lebanon.

What were the consequences of the First Lebanon War?

The First Lebanon War was in many ways Israel's Vietnam— internationally controversial, domestically divisive, politically and militarily costly, and ultimately unsuccessful. It tarnished Israel's image around the world, harmed its relationship with the Reagan administration, reinforced a "cold peace" in Egyptian–Israeli relations with Egypt's new President Hosni Mubarak (who had taken over after Sadat's assassination in 1981), polarized the Israeli public, and cost the lives of around twelve thousand Israeli soldiers (many more Palestinians and Lebanese, mostly civilians, were killed). The war failed to achieve any of the grandiose objectives of its chief architects (the triumvirate—Begin, Sharon, and Eitan). Although it did succeed in destroying the PLO's military infrastructure in southern Lebanon and ending the threat it posed to northern Israel, the IDF's occupation of the area soon aroused the hostility of its local Shi'ite population (after they had initially welcomed it). This increased their support for the anti-Israel militant Shi'ite Islamist Amal movement, and worse (for Israel), led to the formation of the Iranian-sponsored, radical Shi'ite Islamist group Hezbollah ("Party of God"), which is believed to have been responsible for the October 1983 bombing of the American and French military barracks in Beirut that killed 299 servicemen. With Syrian backing and Iranian funding and arms, Hezbollah became the dominant force in southern Lebanon by 1985.

Ideologically committed to the destruction of the Jewish state, Hezbollah waged a long, highly effective guerrilla war in southern Lebanon throughout the 1980s and 1990s against the IDF and its local ally, the SLA, resulting in a steady stream of Israeli military casualties. Like the PLO before it, Hezbollah also fired rockets into northern Israel (a total of roughly four thousand rockets by May 2000), which, though killing few Israelis, significantly disrupted civilian life. In response, the IDF conducted two large-scale military operations in Lebanon ("Operation Accountability" in 1993 and "Operation Grapes of Wrath" in 1996) in an ultimately unsuccessful effort to prevent Hezbollah's continued rocket attacks on northern Israel. Even after Israel unilaterally withdrew from southern Lebanon in May 2000, ending its eighteen-year-long occupation (since its invasion in 1982), Hezbollah continued to attack Israel, claiming that it still occupied a small strip of Lebanese territory (a claim the UN rejected). After years of periodic rocket attacks by Hezbollah and cross-border raids (the latter aimed at capturing Israeli soldiers and then trading them for Hezbollah prisoners held by Israel), and limited IDF reprisals, in July 2006, following Hezbollah's killing of eight Israeli soldiers and capture of two, Israel's then Prime Minister Ehud Olmert launched a ferocious full-scale military assault on Hezbollah strongholds in Lebanon, including its headquarters in Beirut (Israeli airstrikes also deliberately targeted Lebanese infrastructure).

What Israelis call the "Second Lebanon War" and Lebanese call the "July War" went on for thirty-four days (July 12–August 14, 2006), during which time Hezbollah fired some four thousand missiles into northern Israel, forcing hundreds of thousands of Israeli civilians into bomb shelters and paralyzing life there. Israel could not stop Hezbollah's indiscriminate rocket fire, nor could it overrun the group's heavily fortified positions in southern Lebanon (due to Hezbollah's elaborate network of underground bunkers and its well-equipped and -trained guerrilla army). By the time the war ended inconclusively with a UN-brokered ceasefire, 165 Israelis (including 44 civilians) and at least 1,100 Lebanese had been killed (the majority of whom were civilians), with an estimated one million Lebanese civilians displaced. Having survived the war, Hezbollah claimed victory, and its leader, Hassan Nasrallah, was hailed across the Arab world, briefly becoming the Nasser of his day, a new pan-Arab hero (Prime Minister Olmert, by contrast, suffered a political blow from which he never recovered). Hezbollah's popularity in the wake of the 2006 war increased its domestic political power in Lebanon, eventually enabling the group to wield a growing influence in Lebanon's government (which it first joined in 2005 and at present effectively controls).

Thus, Israel's First Lebanon War led, seemingly inexorably, to its Second Lebanon War. It replaced one capable adversary in southern Lebanon (the PLO) with another one even more capable (i.e., Hezbollah, which is now believed to have 100,000 missiles in its arsenal, ten times as many as it had back in 2006). To make matters worse for Israel, since Hezbollah was, and still is, funded, trained, and armed by Iran, Israel's first war in Lebanon created an opening for Iran to steadily expand its influence in Lebanon over time, posing an even greater potential threat to Israel in recent years. Syria's influence in Lebanon also increased as a result of the First Lebanon War—instead of driving the Syrians out of Lebanon, as the war's planners intended, the chaos and insecurity inside Lebanon caused by the war actually enabled Syria to expand its military presence in the country (and, to some extent, justify it). Nor did the war produce a Lebanese government that was friendlier to Israel (a Lebanese–Israeli peace treaty that was signed during the war in May 1983 was quickly revoked by the Lebanese parliament). It only further undermined the central government and exacerbated the ongoing civil war in the country, which dragged on until 1990.

The impact of the First Lebanon War on the PLO itself was also very different from the war planners' intentions. The PLO's military defeat in the war and eviction from Lebanon weakened the organization but did not destroy it, as Begin and Sharon had hoped. Its leadership regrouped in Tunis, establishing the PLO's new headquarters there, and its fighters dispersed across the Arab world (mainly to Syria, and some later returned to Lebanon). The PLO maintained its dominant political status among Palestinians, including those in the West Bank and Gaza, whose aspirations for national self-determination and opposition to autonomy under Israeli rule remained undiminished. But the war did encourage the PLO to gradually give up its armed struggle against Israel in favor of international diplomacy and eventual peace talks with Israel. The war made it much harder for the PLO to fight Israel by depriving it of a staging-ground bordering Israel from which it could fire rockets and artillery and conduct cross-border raids (although its terrorist attacks continued). This accelerated the PLO's political evolution—from rejecting Israel's existence and a two-state solution to the Israeli-Palestinian conflict to recognizing Israel and embracing the two-state solution (which Yasser Arafat officially did in 1988, creating the possibility for a U.S.-PLO dialogue and, later, for the Oslo peace process with Israel).

In the long term, therefore, the First Lebanon War made the PLO more pragmatic, thereby paving the way for a peace process between Israel and the Palestinians. This was far from the outcome that Begin and Sharon envisioned when they initiated the invasion of Lebanon. Ironically, their plan to crush the PLO as a prelude to Israel's annexation of the West Bank and Gaza ultimately resulted in the PLO taking power in those territories with Israel's support. More broadly, rather than resolving the Palestinian issue, the First Lebanon War only made it more important internationally and within Israel. Together with the First Intifada that erupted a few years later (partly as a consequence of the First Lebanon War), it helped convince many Israelis that there was no military solution to their conflict with the Palestinians, and hence that some kind of territorial compromise was necessary.

4

THE PEACE PROCESS

When was the first attempt to make peace?

Attempts to make peace between Arabs and Jews date back to the beginning of their conflict over Palestine a century ago, before it turned violent. The first attempt involved Chaim Weizmann, the head of the Zionist Organization (who later became Israel's first president), and Emir Faisal bin Hussein, son of the Hashemite leader and king of Hejaz Sharif Hussein bin Ali (Faisal later became king of the short-lived Arab Kingdom of Syria and then king of Iraq). The two men met twice shortly before and after the end of World War I in an effort to promote cooperation between Zionists and Arab nationalists to advance both sides' national aspirations. On January 3, 1919, just before the Paris Peace Conference took place, they signed an agreement in which Faisal accepted the Balfour Declaration and the development of a Jewish homeland in Palestine in return for Zionist support for an independent Arab kingdom in a large part of the Middle East. Faisal, however, stipulated that he would only honor the agreement if the Arabs gained their independence. Arab hopes for statehood were soon dashed by French and British colonialism in the region, so the agreement never went into effect.

The British repeatedly tried to resolve the growing Arab-Jewish conflict in Palestine during their three-decade rule there, first by proposing various power-sharing arrangements, and then (in 1937) by presenting a plan to partition the country into an Arab state and a Jewish one. The United Nations (UN) subsequently adopted this "two-state solution," but its 1947 partition plan failed to settle the conflict and instead provoked a civil war, which then led to the first Arab-Israeli war. Since then, there have been many more attempts to make peace. Indeed, there have probably been more efforts—official and unofficial, public and secret—to resolve the Israeli-Palestinian conflict and the broader Arab-Israeli conflict than attempts to resolve any other international conflict. A succession of UN mediators, American presidents, and U.S. secretaries of state have devoted countless hours trying to launch peace talks or broker peace agreements, often in vain. The history of both the Israeli-Palestinian conflict and the Arab-Israeli conflict is littered with discarded peace plans and unsuccessful peace initiatives, as is clear from just this partial list:

- The Faisal-Weizmann Agreement (1919)
- The Peel Partition Plan (1937)
- The Morrison-Grady Plan (1946)
- The UN Partition Plan (1947)
- The Lausanne Conference (1949)
- The Husni al-Zaim Initiative (1949)
- The Alpha Plan (1954–1955)
- The Rogers Plan (1969)
- The Geneva Conference (1973)
- The Begin Plan (1977)
- The Fez Initiative (1982)
- The Reagan Plan (1982)
- The Brezhnev Plan (1982)
- The London Agreement (1987)
- The Shultz Initiative (1988)
- The Shamir Plan (1989)
- The Madrid Conference (1991)
- The Oslo Accords (1993–1995)
- The Beilin–Abu Mazen Agreement (1995)
- The Camp David Summit (2000)
- The Clinton Parameters (2000)
- The Taba Summit (2001)
- The Arab Peace Initiative (2002)
- The Geneva Initiative (2003)

- The Roadmap for Peace (2003)
- The Annapolis Conference (2007)
- The Kerry Initiative (2013–2014)

The failure of these peacemaking attempts underscores the difficulty of Arab-Israeli peacemaking. It was not because of a lack of diplomatic efforts or international attention that the conflicts between Israel and its Arab neighbors and between Israel and the Palestinians dragged on year after year, constantly claiming more victims. Nor was it simply the fault of any single party in the conflict, as Arab and Israeli propaganda insist. For three decades (1948–1978), Israel, the Arab states, and the Palestinians were all unwilling to compromise to varying degrees, not only regarding how the conflict should ultimately be resolved but also concerning the manner, or procedure, through which peace talks should take place. Israel only wanted direct, bilateral negotiations with each Arab state, whereas the Arab states would only negotiate with Israel collectively, and only after Israel complied with their demands. The Palestinians, for their part, had nobody to negotiate with, since Israel would not recognize them as an independent party in the conflict. For decades, the intransigence of Arab and Israeli leaders, coupled with the mutual mistrust and hostility of their societies, prevented any progress in Arab-Israeli peacemaking. The stalemate was finally broken in 1978 with the signing of the Camp David Accords between Israel and Egypt. Although the negotiations fell short of achieving a comprehensive peace agreement, they produced the first and most important Arab-Israeli peace agreement—the Egypt-Israel Peace Treaty signed in March 1979. After forty years of peace between Israel and Egypt, the Egyptian-Israeli peace treaty remains the most significant diplomatic achievement in the history of the Arab-Israeli conflict.

What were the Camp David Accords, and how did they come about?

The 1973 war fought by Israel, Egypt, and Syria shook the status quo between Israel and the Arabs and reinvigorated international efforts to make peace. It resulted in the UN's Geneva Conference and the U.S.-brokered Israeli–Egyptian and Israeli–Syrian disengagement agreements of 1974–1975. The war created more favorable conditions for Arab-Israeli peacemaking, but there was still a massive "psychological barrier" between the two sides that stood in the way. In the words of Egyptian president Anwar Sadat, this barrier consisted of a "huge wall of suspicion, fear, hate, and misunderstanding that has for so long existed between Israel and the Arabs. It made each side simply unwilling to believe the other." It took a feat of daring diplomacy by Sadat himself to overcome this "psychological barrier" and initiate direct Israeli-Egyptian peace talks, which eventually led to the signing of the landmark Camp David Accords in September 1978.

Determined to regain possession of Egypt's Sinai Peninsula, which Israel had conquered in the 1967 war and retained in the 1973 war, Sadat became increasingly impatient with the slow pace of international diplomacy, which was focused on convening another major UN-sponsored multilateral conference. Just as he had done with his surprise attack against Israel in 1973, Sadat again took the initiative and surprised everyone. In a speech before the Egyptian National Assembly on November 9, 1977, he announced that he was "ready to go to the Israeli parliament itself" to advance peacemaking efforts. Within days, the Israeli government, led by the right-wing Likud party leader Menachem Begin (who had won a shock election victory earlier that year), invited Sadat to visit Israel and address the Knesset.

On November 19, 1977, Sadat went to Israel, becoming the first Arab head of state to visit the country. In doing so, Sadat shocked Israelis, Egyptians, and the entire Arab world. During his three-day trip, he visited Israel's national museum and memorial to the Holocaust, laid a wreath at a monument to Israel's war dead, and, most importantly, gave a speech to the Knesset. He called for a comprehensive Arab-Israeli peace, Israeli withdrawal from all occupied Arab territory, and the creation of a Palestinian state. But it was Sadat's mere presence in Jerusalem that mattered most, not what he said. By visiting Israel and talking directly to Israelis, Sadat broke the prevailing Arab taboo against recognizing Israel, let alone engaging with it. This was a politically courageous act of statesmanship, since it was bound to be highly unpopular in Egypt and across the Arab world and could easily end in failure, especially given Israel's new right-wing government. Sadat's gamble paid off. His actions produced a dramatic shift, literally overnight, in Israeli public opinion. As he intended, his visit convinced Israelis that Egypt wanted peace. Believing that they had, at last, an Arab partner for peacemaking, the Israeli public immediately became much more willing to relinquish the Sinai in exchange for a peace agreement with Egypt. This, in turn, put more domestic pressure on the Begin government to at least engage in serious peace talks with Egypt.

Although Sadat's historic visit to Israel was a game changer, it was not enough to produce a breakthrough in peace talks. This required another politically courageous act of statesmanship—by U.S. President Jimmy Carter. In September 1978, President Carter invited Sadat and Begin to a summit meeting at Camp David, a presidential retreat in the Maryland woods. This was politically risky for Carter because he was putting the prestige of the American presidency, and possibly his own political future, on the line for a summit that could easily have been a fiasco (and almost was). In fact, no American president, before Carter or since, has invested as much time and political capital in trying to broker a resolution of the Arab-Israeli conflict (only President Bill Clinton came close). Carter made Arab-Israeli peace one of his administration's foreign policy priorities. Deeply inspired by his Christian faith, Carter genuinely believed that he was on a mission from God. He also had the naïve expectation that bringing the Egyptian and Israeli leaders together to talk privately in a serene and secluded setting, shielded from the glare of the media and public scrutiny, would break the deadlock and promote mutual compromise. Once the summit got underway, however, this hope quickly evaporated as the personal animosity between Begin and Sadat became apparent and led to heated and angry exchanges between them. Carter himself had to intervene in shouting matches between Begin and Sadat and even physically separate them. Realizing that face-to-face talks between the two leaders were actually counterproductive, Carter and his team kept them apart for the rest of the summit. He had to shuttle back and forth between the two leaders, meeting with them separately in the log cabins where they stayed. After a few days of talks with little progress made and patience running out, Carter and his team decided that they had to take the lead in the negotiations instead of merely facilitating them. Thus, they presented a draft peace plan to each leader, received their comments, and revised the plan accordingly until there was mutual agreement. It was an exhausting, painstaking process—the peace plan went through twenty-three drafts—and it took much longer than anyone had intended (the summit lasted thirteen days, which was a remarkable commitment of time for an American president, especially given the many domestic challenges that Carter was facing at the time, including midterm congressional elections, high inflation, sluggish economic growth, and soaring oil prices). The negotiations broke down on multiple occasions, and both Sadat and Begin threatened to leave. Carter had to personally cajole and pressure them to stay, even threatening U.S. government support for their countries. Without his dogged persistence and indefatigable energy throughout the summit, the talks almost certainly would have collapsed.

It was hard enough to negotiate a peace agreement between Egypt and Israel, largely because Begin did not want to return all of the Sinai to Egypt (as Sadat demanded) and was strongly opposed to abandoning the Jewish settlements that Israel had established there (in the end, Begin reluctantly agreed to allow Israel's parliament to vote on whether to dismantle and evacuate the settlements in the Sinai). But what really complicated and almost derailed the talks was Sadat's insistence on reaching some kind of agreement regarding the Palestinian issue, which Begin preferred to ignore altogether since he was staunchly committed to Israel retaining and ultimately annexing the West Bank. Sadat did not go to Camp David with the intention of making a separate peace with Israel and abandoning the Palestinians. He felt that he had to win at least some Israeli concessions on the Palestinian issue, if only to give him some political cover to make an agreement with Israel (Carter supported him on this). Unfortunately for Sadat, Begin was adamantly opposed to the establishment of a Palestinian state (as most Israelis were at the time), and he was only willing to grant limited autonomy to Palestinians in the West Bank and Gaza. Sadat had little choice but to accept a proposal to install a locally elected Palestinian administration in the West Bank and Gaza for a five-year interim period, after which the final status of the territories would be negotiated (the proposal did not specify what the end result of Palestinian autonomy would be). Begin at least conceded to the inclusion of Palestinians as well as Jordanians in these future final status talks, and he agreed to officially acknowledge "Palestinian national rights," albeit without specifying what these actually were.

But, crucially, the fulfillment of this autonomy plan was not made a condition for peace between Egypt and Israel. Instead, under intense American pressure, Sadat agreed to their proposal to have two separate, weakly linked, agreements, one solely dealing with Israeli-Egyptian relations and the other with the West Bank and Gaza Strip.

After nearly two weeks of contentious negotiations, Begin and Sadat finally accepted two documents: a "Framework for the Conclusion of a Peace Treaty between Egypt and Israel" and a "Framework for Peace in the Middle East." Most notably, the former called for Israel's complete withdrawal from the Sinai in exchange for peace with Egypt, while the latter called for the establishment of a "self-governing [Palestinian] authority" in the West Bank and Gaza, leading to eventual "final status" talks. Together, these two agreements are the "Camp David Accords," and they were signed in the White House on September 17, 1978. The Camp David Accords also included a number of side-letters between the United States and each of the two parties, with the United States promising to provide Egypt with around $2.1 billion in annual aid and Israel with $3 billion annually, making them the biggest benefactors of U.S. foreign aid to this day.

The Camp David Accords were undoubtedly a diplomatic breakthrough in the Arab-Israeli conflict, although they fell short of what Sadat and Carter hoped to achieve. The Accords brought about a peace treaty between Egypt and Israel but did not resolve the Palestinian issue—there was not even a reference to the dispute over Jerusalem or to the fate of Palestinian refugees. The autonomy plan was rejected by the Palestinians and was soon frozen (though it ultimately became the basis of the Oslo Accords between Israel and the Palestine Liberation Organization [PLO] in the early 1990s). The other Arab states didn't follow Egypt's lead and make peace with Israel. It took fifteen more years until another Arab state did so when Jordan finally signed a peace agreement in 1994. Instead of ushering in a new era of Arab-Israeli relations, the Camp David Accords only resulted in a cold peace between Egypt and Israel. Egypt was ostracized in the Arab world (for instance, it was suspended from the Arab League for a decade), and Sadat was widely vilified as a traitor to the Arab cause. For this, he paid with his life. Accused of undermining Arab opposition to Israel and betraying the Palestinians, Sadat was assassinated by Islamist extremists (members of a group called the Egyptian Islamic Jihad) during a military parade in Cairo on October 6, 1981.

Despite being denounced by most Egyptians, Palestinians, and Arabs in general, the Camp David Accords were still a success. By removing Egypt—then the strongest Arab state militarily—from the Arab-Israeli conflict, the Camp David Accords greatly reduced the risk of another major Arab-Israeli war. Without Egypt's army, or the possibility of a two- or three-front war against Israel, the Arab states (primarily Syria and Jordan) no longer really had the option of going to war against Israel, which was far stronger militarily. Thus, while there were four major wars between Israel and its Arab neighbors in the three decades before Camp David (in 1948, 1956, 1967, and 1973), there have been none in the four decades since (although Syria was initially involved in the First Lebanon War). This is the greatest accomplishment of the Camp David Accords. They did not settle the Arab-Israeli conflict, but they did at least stabilize and subdue it, thereby saving countless lives. From then on, the Arab-Israeli conflict gradually died down, and attention increasingly shifted toward the Israeli-Palestinian conflict. Furthermore, by demonstrating the efficacy of diplomacy, and by implementing the formula of "land for peace" (first proposed in 1967 in UN Resolution 242), the Camp David Accords also set an important precedent for later attempts at Arab-Israeli peacemaking (specifically, the Oslo peace process between Israel and the Palestinians, the 1994 peace treaty between Israel and Jordan, and the sporadic peace talks between Israel and Syria in the 1990s). In short, the Camp David Accords didn't produce Arab-Israeli peace, but they made it more possible.

When did Israeli-Palestinian peace talks begin?

Israelis and Palestinians have refused to directly negotiate during most of the duration of their conflict. For decades, this unwillingness to negotiate was rooted in mutual denial—Palestinian leaders regarded any negotiation with Israel as tantamount to recognizing it, which they adamantly refused to do (they even refused to utter Israel's name, instead referring to it as the "Zionist entity"). Israeli leaders, for their part, refused to accept the existence of a distinct Palestinian nation and insisted that Israel's only conflict was with Arab states. Ironically, the first Israeli leader to officially acknowledge the existence of the Palestinians was its most right-wing prime minister (up to that point), Menachem Begin, the head of the Likud Party who came to power in 1977. Even after reluctantly conceding that there were, in fact, Palestinians (and not merely amorphous Arabs), Israeli governments in the 1980s categorically refused to negotiate with the national leadership of the Palestinians, the PLO, on the grounds that it was a terrorist organization—the PLO was, after all, responsible for scores of terrorist attacks against Israeli civilians. Israeli law also forbade Israeli citizens from meeting with, or talking to, members of the PLO (although there were occasionally secret contacts).

It was not until 1991 that this mutual boycott began to end, albeit in a limited manner. In late October that year, an international conference dedicated to Arab-Israeli peacemaking convened with great fanfare in the ornate Royal Palace in the Spanish capital, Madrid. The Madrid Conference was a watershed event in the Israeli-Palestinian conflict and also in the wider Arab-Israeli conflict. The United States and the Soviet Union officially sponsored the conference, but it was the George H. W. Bush administration, especially Secretary of State James Baker, that made it happen. The United States had been occasionally trying to reconvene a Middle East peace conference since Jimmy Carter's presidency (the last one was in Geneva in 1973 under the auspices of the UN), but it took the end of the Cold War and the 1991 Gulf War to finally bring this about. After Saddam Hussein's Iraq invaded and occupied Kuwait in August 1990, the United States assembled an international military coalition to expel Iraqi forces from Kuwait. In order to get neighboring Arab states, particularly Syria, to join the American-led coalition, President Bush promised to make a renewed effort to resolve the Arab-Israeli conflict once the Gulf crisis was over. With the Soviet Union slowly imploding, the United States became the sole superpower. After quickly and decisively defeating Iraq in January–February 1991, the United States was keen to capitalize on its new hegemonic status and also fulfill the promise to its Arab allies. The Bush administration sought to establish a Pax Americana in a post–Cold War Middle East, and it believed that ending the Arab-Israeli conflict was crucial to achieving this goal. More powerful and more determined than ever before, the United States enticed Syria (which had lost its former superpower patron, the Soviet Union) and pressured a reluctant Israel to participate in the Madrid Conference. Israel's reluctance stemmed from its longstanding preference for bilateral negotiations with Arab states, rather than international peace conferences (in which it would be outnumbered by Arab states), and also because Israel's hardline right-wing prime minister at the time, Yitzhak Shamir of the Likud Party, wanted to avoid making any territorial concessions to the Arabs, who he believed were implacably opposed to the Jewish state's existence. Shamir was also committed to maintaining Israel's permanent control over the whole Land of Israel, especially the West Bank (he later said that he intended to drag out negotiations over Palestinian autonomy for ten years, by which time half a million more Jews would have settled in the West Bank, helping to preclude the possibility of a Palestinian state).

The Madrid Conference was historic, but not because of the speeches that were delivered, the substance of the brief negotiations, or even the subsequent intermittent rounds of bilateral and multilateral talks that occurred in the months and years afterward. In fact, nothing new was said at the conference itself, no agreements were reached, and the resulting peace talks ultimately led nowhere. However, the conference was significant simply because it was the first time that formal, face-to-face peace talks took place between Israel and all its immediate Arab neighbors (Syria, Lebanon, and Jordan) and between Israelis and Palestinians. Syria had not previously entered into direct peace talks with Israel. But it was the Palestinian participation in the conference that was most unprecedented and consequential. Unlike the Syrians who were invited to the Geneva Conference in 1973 and refused to attend, Palestinians had never before even been invited to participate in any official peace talks with Israel, primarily because Israeli leaders consistently opposed this step. In Madrid, Palestinians were finally given a seat at the negotiating table, albeit with strings attached.

The Palestinians could only participate in the Madrid Conference as part of a joint delegation with Jordan, because Israel would not agree to a separate Palestinian delegation. Nor would Israel permit any Palestinians linked to the PLO to take part (although the Palestinian delegates only agreed to participate with the PLO's approval and were in constant contact with its leadership in Tunis, and the PLO itself sent an unofficial "advisory delegation" to act as a liaison). And Israel would only talk with Palestinians from the West

Bank and Gaza, not with Palestinians from East Jerusalem or from the Palestinian diaspora. Despite these conditions, the mere fact that Palestinians were represented at all was historic. Henceforth, it would be impossible to exclude Palestinians from peace talks or to pretend that they were not independent actors in the conflict with Israel who were entitled to represent themselves. Moreover, once it became known that the Palestinian delegates at the Madrid Conference, and in the subsequent rounds of negotiations held at the U.S. State Department between December 1991 and July 1993, were taking instructions from the PLO, the case for initiating direct talks with the PLO became much stronger. After all, if Israel was already indirectly negotiating with the PLO, then why not stop the charade and just directly negotiate with it, especially since the PLO could, and in practice did, prevent any progress in Israeli-Palestinian peace talks it was excluded from? It was this line of thinking that eventually led the next Israeli government, headed by Yitzhak Rabin of the center-left Labor Party, to engage in secret talks with the PLO in Oslo, Norway, which resulted in the Oslo Accords.

What are the Oslo Accords?

There have been tragically few occasions during the long, blood-soaked, and bitter conflict between Israelis and Palestinians when it seemed that they could overcome their enmity, compromise, and make peace. Among these rare moments, by far the most significant and memorable was the handshake between Israeli Prime Minister Yitzhak Rabin and PLO chairman Yasser Arafat on the White House lawn on September 13, 1993. The now-iconic image of these two longtime enemies shaking hands, as a beaming President Bill Clinton stood between them with his arms outstretched, was viewed around the world with astonishment and joy as many people thought that peace had finally been achieved or was, at least, imminent. This optimism was soon shattered by subsequent events, but even at the time it was based upon wishful thinking and a misunderstanding of the agreement that was signed on that sunny, hopeful September day.

The agreement was called the "Declaration of Principles on Interim Self-Government Arrangements" (DOP). It was the first of a series of interim agreements between Israel and the PLO collectively known as the "Oslo Accords," because they resulted from secret, back-channel talks held in Oslo, Norway, from January to August 1993 (the Norwegian foreign ministry hosted the talks). Contrary to popular belief, the DOP agreement (referred to as "Oslo I") was not a peace agreement. It only called for Israel to withdraw from the Gaza Strip (but not from its settlements there) and from the West Bank city of Jericho. Further withdrawals from other unspecified parts of the West Bank were supposed to take place during a five-year transitional period. During this period, a quasi-governmental Palestinian entity (the Palestinian Authority [PA]) would be created and given responsibility for much of the day-to-day management of the areas from which Israeli troops had withdrawn (i.e., it would handle internal security, policing, direct taxation, healthcare, social welfare, education, culture, and tourism). The DOP agreement also identified the main issues that needed to be resolved in a future peace agreement: the nature of the Palestinian entity and its borders, the future of Israeli settlements and settlers, security arrangements, the Palestinian refugee problem, and the status of Jerusalem. The Israeli and Palestinian negotiators who drew up the agreement chose to defer tackling these highly contentious issues to a later date, when they hoped it would be easier to make concessions as trust grew between Israel and the PLO and their respective publics became more conciliatory. The agreement set a timetable for resolving these "permanent status issues"—negotiations between Israel and the PLO were to begin within two years, and a comprehensive peace agreement had to be reached within five years. Nothing was written about what this "final status agreement" would actually entail—and, in particular, whether it would involve the establishment of a Palestinian state.

The DOP agreement between Israel and the PLO, therefore, was merely a commitment to negotiate and to give Palestinians in some areas a degree of autonomy. It fell far short of Palestinian demands for self-determination (i.e., statehood) and for Israel to completely withdraw its soldiers and settlers from the West Bank and Gaza. The agreement only required Israel to redeploy its troops, not withdraw them, and it did not require Israel to stop building or expanding its settlements—a glaring omission that Israel insisted on and the PLO reluctantly acquiesced to. Nevertheless, for all its limitations, the DOP agreement represented a historic break-through in Israeli-Palestinian relations, setting in motion a peace process between Israel and the PLO to gradually end the conflict. Equally important was the exchange of letters between Arafat and Rabin that preceded the signing of the DOP agreement in September 1993. In these letters, the PLO renounced the use of terrorism and explicitly recognized "the right of the State of Israel to exist in peace and security," while Israel recognized the PLO as the "representative of the Palestinian people" and its official negotiating partner (Israel did not, however, recognize a Palestinian right to statehood). This mutual recognition ended decades of mutual boycotts—when Israeli governments refused to talk with the PLO because it was a terrorist organization, and the PLO refused to accept Israel's existence—but it did not end their mutual suspicion.

The Oslo Accords also consist of another major agreement between Israel and the PLO: the "Interim Agreement on the West Bank and the Gaza Strip" (referred to as "Oslo II"), which was signed in Washington, DC, on September 28, 1995. This was a more detailed agreement that divided the West Bank into three noncontiguous areas of jurisdiction (see Map 4): Area A—containing all the Palestinian cities, except Hebron—would be under full Palestinian control; Area B—containing smaller Palestinian towns and villages (then making up 24 percent of the West Bank)—would be under joint Palestinian-Israeli control with the PA handling civil affairs and Israel in charge of security; and Area C—containing smaller Palestinian villages and all Israeli settlements and military bases, as well as agricultural land, main roads, and natural water reserves (initially amounting to 73 percent of the territory)—would remain under Israeli control, pending final peace talks that were scheduled to be completed by the summer of 1999. This administrative division of the West Bank into Areas A, B, and C, was meant to be temporary—lasting no more than five years—but more than two decades on, it remains in effect, much to the frustration of Palestinians. The only thing that has changed is the relative size of these different areas as Israel has transferred full or partial jurisdiction over more parts of the West Bank to the PA.

By adopting an incremental, step-by-step approach to resolving the Israeli-Palestinian conflict, the Oslo Accords were premised upon the recognition that peace could not be achieved quickly or easily. Peace talks were doomed to fail if they were not preceded by confidence-building measures undertaken by both sides. In particular, the PLO had to demonstrate its ability to govern and its willingness to prevent violence against Israelis, while Israel had to gradually cede control over more of the West Bank to the PA and move its soldiers away from Palestinian population centers. The architects of the Oslo Accords hoped that as both sides carried out their commitments and worked together, public attitudes would soften, extremists would be marginalized, and peace would move within reach. But things turned out very differently. Neither side lived up to its commitments. Deadlines were missed, promises were broken, and trust never developed. As hardliners on both sides vociferously and, at times, violently opposed the Oslo peace process, Israeli and Palestinian public support for it declined. Consequently, peace became harder, not easier, to achieve. Yet, notwithstanding these failures, the Oslo Accords were still a momentous achievement. They were a victory for diplomacy over violence and marked a politically daring initiative by the Israeli government (chiefly, Prime Minister Rabin and Foreign Minister Shimon Peres) and the leadership of the PLO (particularly, Arafat and his longtime deputy, Mahmoud Abbas). Acknowledging this, the Nobel Prize committee awarded the 1994 Nobel Peace Prize jointly to Rabin, Peres, and Arafat "for their efforts to create peace in the Middle East."

The Oslo Accords did not, of course, succeed in creating "peace in the Middle East." Nor did they bring Israelis the security they sought or Palestinians the freedom they yearned for. The high hopes that the Oslo Accords raised on both sides were dashed, leaving Israelis and Palestinians bitterly disappointed. But although they are widely regarded as a failure, the Oslo Accords did at least deliver some benefits to both sides. For Israelis, they paved the way for a peace agreement with Jordan and a wider rapprochement between Israel and its Arab neighbors, especially the Arab Gulf states (with whom trade relations commenced). For Palestinians, the Accords led to the withdrawal of Israeli troops from their major cities and an easing of Israeli control over their daily lives (at least for the majority of Palestinians who lived in urban areas). And by creating the PA, the Oslo Accords gave Palestinians in the West Bank and Gaza a degree of self-rule and some of the trappings of statehood (such as Palestinian passports).

Why did Israel and the PLO sign the Oslo Accords?

The Oslo Accords represented a radical break from the longstanding positions of Israel and the PLO. Both sides radically changed their policies and accepted things that had once been unthinkable, and remained highly controversial, to their respective publics. The PLO's policy shift was most pronounced. It had previously rejected proposals for Palestinian autonomy in the West Bank and Gaza (such as that put forward in the 1978 Camp David Accords), and it had always opposed any kind of interim agreement that did not guarantee eventual Palestinian statehood. By signing the Oslo Accords, the PLO accepted both an autonomy plan and an interim agreement (with a lengthy transitional period before any permanent settlement of the conflict would even be discussed, let alone implemented). In other words, the PLO reversed course and adopted essentially the same piecemeal approach to resolving the conflict that Israeli governments had long been promoting. This was a major concession by the PLO's leadership that was extremely controversial among Palestinians, including among PLO members themselves. Critics, such as the well-known Palestinian writers Edward Said and Mahmoud Darwish, accused Arafat of capitulating to the Israelis and betraying the Palestinian cause to satisfy his own desires and political ambitions (since the Oslo Accords enabled Arafat to return from exile and become president of the newly created PA.

The PLO's perilous predicament

Whatever Arafat's personal motives may have been, his decision to sign the Oslo Accords (and it was really *his* decision) was largely driven by perceived necessity. It was, above all else, a means of ensuring the PLO's survival in what had become desperate circumstances for the organization. Since its defeat in the First Lebanon War, and the forced departure of its leadership from their headquarters in Beirut to the more distant Tunisian capital, Tunis, the PLO had been struggling to maintain its leadership of the Palestinian people, especially over those living in the Israeli-occupied West Bank and Gaza Strip. The PLO's heroic image among Palestinians had been tarnished, and it no longer had fighters and armaments deployed in areas bordering Israel, making it much harder for the PLO to continue its armed struggle.

An even greater challenge to the PLO came when Palestinians in the occupied territories spontaneously started protesting in huge numbers against Israeli rule. The protests began on December 8, 1987, in a Gaza refugee camp as a reaction to the killing of four Palestinians by an Israeli army vehicle (Israel insisted it was a traffic accident, but Palestinians believed it was deliberate). Protests quickly spread across the Gaza Strip and the West Bank, and they escalated into a popular uprising, which was called the *Intifada* in Arabic (meaning "shaking off"). Along with large-scale demonstrations and rioting (particularly stone-throwing), the First Intifada also involved nonviolent, mass protests against the Israeli occupation such as general strikes, boycotts of Israeli products, and refusal to pay taxes. Local Palestinian activists, mostly from a younger generation who had grown up under Israeli rule, initially organized these protests. Desperately wanting to end the military occupation they lived under, and the restrictions, humiliations, and daily frustrations that went with it, they had lost patience with the PLO's ineffectual armed struggle against Israel, and they felt abandoned by the wider Arab world (which was more concerned in the 1980s with the Iran-Iraq war than with the Palestinian issue).

Surprised by the sudden eruption of the First Intifada, and in danger of losing popular support and being sidelined by the so-called insiders leading it, the PLO responded by making what it described as a "historic compromise" (it was also a response to Jordan's renunciation of its claim to the West Bank, which was itself a response to the Intifada). At a meeting in Algeria in November 1988, the Palestinian National Council, the PLO's parliament, issued a Declaration of Independence—known as the "Algiers Declaration"—for a Palestinian state located only in the West Bank and Gaza (an area that amounted to just 22 percent of Mandate Palestine). In doing so, the PLO for the first time formally accepted UN Resolutions 181 (the Partition Plan), 242, and 338 (the latter two proposed the formula of "land for peace"). A month later, Arafat himself publicly endorsed a two-state solution to the conflict, renounced the use of terrorism, and recognized Israel's right to exist. This gave the PLO more international legitimacy and enabled the U.S. government to begin an official "dialogue" with the organization (that lasted until June 1990).

Although the PLO gradually gained more control over the First Intifada, its dominance over Palestinian politics was also challenged by the rise of Hamas (which means "zeal" in Arabic and is also an acronym for the words "Islamic Resistance Movement"). Founded in Gaza in December 1987 soon after the Intifada began, Hamas was a militant offshoot of the Muslim Brotherhood, a Sunni Islamist group based in Egypt with branches in many Arab countries. Blending Palestinian nationalism with radical Islamism, Hamas called for the creation of a Sharia-ruled Islamic state in all of historic Palestine. It categorically rejected a two-state solution to the conflict with Israel, instead advocating a violent *jihad* (holy war) to destroy the Jewish state and "liberate" Palestine (in recent years, Hamas's opposition to a two-state solution has softened, as its leaders have suggested that the group could live with one under certain circumstances). Just as the PLO moderated its tactics and limited its territorial ambitions, Hamas emerged as a more uncompromising and violent competitor (a smaller, even more radical, Palestinian Islamist group called Palestinian Islamic Jihad was also increasingly active during the First Intifada). Growing popular support for Hamas, particularly among poorer and more devout Palestinians in the Gaza Strip, put the PLO under increasing pressure to reassert its leadership over the Palestinians and achieve some concrete gains for those living under Israeli occupation.

In addition to the political challenges it faced, the PLO also had to contend with mounting financial challenges, which eventually brought it to the brink of bankruptcy. The PLO's finances were strained by the economic cost of sustaining the Intifada (for example, by providing payments to striking Palestinians or to those imprisoned in Israel), and by the decline and then loss of financial support from the Soviet Union. But Arafat's decision to support Iraq after it invaded and occupied Kuwait in August 1990 proved to be particularly costly. The oil-rich Arab Gulf states that were financial patrons of the PLO, most notably Saudi Arabia, retaliated by cutting off their funding (the large Palestinian population in Kuwait was also forced to flee the country during and after the 1991 Gulf War). Without financial support from the Gulf states or the Soviet Union, the PLO's survival was in jeopardy.

The Oslo Accords, therefore, were a lifeline for the PLO at a time when it was politically challenged and financially imperiled. The

PLO gained Israel's official recognition that it was the sole, legitimate representative of the Palestinian people and henceforth its only negotiating partner. Perhaps even more importantly, the PLO gained entry to the West Bank and Gaza, enabling its leaders, officials, and fighters to return from their long exile and assume positions of power and patronage within the PA. This helped ensure the PLO's primacy in Palestinian politics for at least another decade.

To be sure, the PLO's decision to sign the Oslo Accords and begin a peace process with Israel was not only self-serving. Arafat and Abbas also expected, or at least genuinely hoped, that the Oslo peace process would eventually result in the establishment of a Palestinian state. But their willingness to sign agreements with Israel that did not explicitly promise statehood and to temporarily accept a limited degree of Palestinian self-rule over a limited amount of Palestinian territory, and their acquiescence to postpone negotiating, let alone resolving, crucial issues (such as the refugee issue) that Palestinians cared deeply about, can only be adequately explained by the PLO's weakness, if not outright desperation, at the time.

Israel's opportunity

The weakness of the PLO was also partly why Israel signed the Oslo Accords. For decades, successive Israeli governments had adamantly refused to negotiate with the PLO because of what it did (terrorism), and because of what it wanted (a Palestinian state). When Rabin became Israel's prime minister for the second time following the Labor Party's victory in the 1992 election, he continued to oppose negotiating with the PLO (Rabin was also initially more interested in a peace agreement with Syria than with the Palestinians, who posed no military threat to Israel). But Rabin changed his mind a year later in May 1993, after Shimon Peres informed him of the surprising progress being made in unofficial, clandestine talks in Oslo between senior members of the PLO and two Israeli academics (which Rabin had been unaware of). Despite his distrust of Arafat, Rabin sent two Israeli officials to join these talks, thereby upgrading them to an official status. By then frustrated with the continued stalemate in the U.S.-sponsored Israeli-Palestinian peace talks that had been intermittently taking place in Washington, DC, Rabin sought to exploit the PLO's weakness and test its readiness to make unprecedented concessions by directly negotiating with it.

The PLO's weakness presented the Rabin government with an opportunity to make a deal on terms that were favorable to Israel, but it also posed a serious risk. If the PLO collapsed, the more extremist Hamas movement might replace it as the preeminent Palestinian organization. In such a scenario, there would be no possibility for peace talks (since Hamas stridently opposed them), let alone a peace agreement. The Israeli-Palestinian conflict could be transformed from a nationalist struggle to an unending religious war. Compared with Hamas, the PLO was the lesser of two evils from Israel's point of view. By signing the Oslo Accords with the PLO, therefore, the Rabin government effectively rescued it and ensured that it had a suitable Palestinian interlocutor for future peace talks.

The Rabin government had other compelling reasons for signing the Oslo Accords. It was a "dovish" coalition government, led by Rabin's center-left Labor Party, whose resounding victory in the 1992 election broke the domestic political deadlock between the left and the right that had largely paralyzed Israeli politics for much of the previous decade (the last Labor victory was nineteen years earlier in 1973). There were many reasons for Labor's victory, so it would be simplistic to attribute it solely to a popular yearning for peace. Labor's election campaign emphasized Rabin's reputation as "Mr. Security," and it highlighted the social and economic concerns of Israelis, which it claimed the previous Likud-led government had neglected. Labor's proclaimed willingness to make peace with the Palestinians—whom most Israelis still deeply distrusted—was not its biggest draw. Nevertheless, the Israeli public, as a whole, had become more amenable to compromise on the Palestinian issue, largely because the Intifada convinced many Israelis that Palestinians would not quietly acquiesce to Israel's continued control over the West Bank and Gaza and that the price of trying to maintain it was prohibitive. Public opinion polls showed that growing numbers of Israelis favored a withdrawal from the territories, supported the idea of "land for peace" with the Palestinians, and were even willing to negotiate with their archenemy, the PLO.

The Labor Party appealed to this new public sentiment in the 1992 election. When it subsequently came to power, its leadership—chiefly Rabin and Peres (who were longtime rivals)—felt that they not only had a political incentive to at least try to make peace but also had a popular mandate to do so. Both men also believed that the time was right for peacemaking with the Palestinians and the wider Arab world. They viewed the momentous regional and global developments that had been taking place—notably, the end of the Cold War (1989), the Gulf War (1991), the Madrid Conference (1991), and the dissolution of the Soviet Union (1991)—as creating a window of opportunity for Israel to make peace from a position of strength. Israel was stronger than ever (and backed by a hegemonic United States), while its adversaries were weak and divided. With the regional balance of power so heavily in Israel's favor (if only temporarily), Rabin and Peres hoped that the Palestinians, Jordanians, Syrians, and the rest of the Arab world might finally be ready to end the Arab-Israeli conflict once and for all.

Alongside this lofty goal, Rabin also had a more pressing concern that helped persuade him to reluctantly make a deal with the PLO. He wanted to end the Intifada, which had become increasingly costly to Israel—diplomatically, militarily, economically, and morally. Although the Intifada was running out of steam by the time the Rabin government was formed in July 1992, it was also becoming more militarized and more violent (against Israelis and Palestinians). Having been Israel's defense minister during the first two years of the uprising (when he notoriously instructed Israeli soldiers to "break the bones" of Palestinian protesters), Rabin was acutely aware of the damage the Intifada inflicted on the Israel Defense Forces' (IDF) morale and military readiness as well as on Israel's reputation abroad. He also knew better than anyone that there was no military solution to it. Making a deal with the PLO and allowing its leadership to return from exile and take charge of a semiautonomous Palestinian entity that would help Israel govern and police parts of the West Bank and Gaza was, in his mind, probably the least worst option.

To this day, it is unclear whether Rabin himself regarded the Oslo Accords as a prelude to ending Israel's control over the West Bank and Gaza or as a more convenient and cheaper means of maintaining it. Rabin remained publicly opposed to Palestinian statehood and to a complete Israeli withdrawal from the West Bank (he also opposed a division of Jerusalem). But to many observers that was, in fact, the endgame of the Oslo peace process. Sadly, we will never know how far Rabin was prepared to go to make peace with the Palestinians. On the evening of November 4, 1995, after addressing a huge rally in Tel Aviv in support of the peace process, Rabin was gunned down by a right-wing Israeli extremist who believed that Rabin was betraying and endangering the Jewish people by giving away parts of their sacred homeland to the Palestinians. Convinced he was carrying out religious decrees and acting under divine guidance, Rabin's assassin wanted to stop the Oslo peace process by killing Rabin. Many people believe he succeeded. When Arafat, for instance, was informed of Rabin's assassination, he is reported to have responded: "Today the peace process has died." This grim announcement turned out to be premature. The assassination of Rabin was a severe, but not fatal, blow to the peace process. It limped along for five more years before collapsing in the wake of the failure of the Camp David summit and the outbreak of the Second Intifada.

How did the assassination of Yitzhak Rabin impact the Oslo peace process?

Rabin's murder profoundly shocked Israelis, not only because it was the first time that an Israeli prime minister was assassinated but also because the assassin was Jewish, not Palestinian. Despite the incitement and deaths threats against Rabin by Jewish extremists prior to his assassination, most Israelis had assumed that a Jew would never murder an Israeli leader. In the aftermath of the assassination, there was an outpouring of public grief, accompanied by angry recriminations and anguished national soul-searching. Religious Zionists, especially settlers, were accused of fomenting a political subculture that scorned democracy, disregarded the rule of law, and legitimized political violence (Rabin's assassin, Yigal Amir, was not actually a settler, but he was a frequent visitor to Jewish settlements in the West Bank and a fervent believer in messianic religious Zionism). Many left-wing Israelis went further, blaming the right in general, including the leader of the opposition Likud Party, Benjamin Netanyahu, for condoning, and even encouraging, the vilification of Rabin by opponents of the Oslo peace process. (Netanyahu, for example, gave a fiery speech at a demonstration in which Rabin was denounced as a traitor and depicted on placards wearing a Nazi uniform). What Rabin's assassination, and the Israeli public's reaction to it, made abundantly clear was that Israelis were deeply and dangerously divided over the peace process, so much so that there were even fears of a civil war breaking out. In response, there were frequent pleas for "national unity" and numerous efforts to promote intra-Jewish dialogue and understanding. Peace among Israeli Jews, rather than with the Palestinians, became the national priority. This diminished the importance of the Oslo peace process in the minds of many Israeli Jews and shifted public energy and attention elsewhere, ultimately to the detriment of the peace process.

A bigger blow to the peace process was Netanyahu's surprise narrow victory (by only 29,000 votes) over Shimon Peres, who had been serving as acting prime minister, in the election for prime minister held seven months after Rabin's assassination (it was the first time that Israelis voted directly for prime minister as well as for a party). Although many left-wing Israelis and international observers believe that Netanyahu would not have been elected prime minister in 1996 were it not for Rabin's assassination, it is by no means clear that Rabin would have won the election. After all, before his death, Rabin's government had lost its majority in the Knesset along with support from a majority of Israeli Jews (prompting its right-wing opponents to claim that the Rabin government, and its peace policy, lacked legitimacy). Moreover, Netanyahu won the election despite Rabin's assassination, not because of it. There was a surge of Israeli public support for the peace process and for the Labor Party in the wake of the assassination, but Peres failed to take advantage of this and squandered a huge lead in the polls. This was, however, more due to Hamas's suicide bombers than to Peres's political shortcomings. In February and March 1996, suicide bombers boarded four packed public buses and detonated explosive vests, killing fifty-nine Israelis (Hamas ordered these bus bombings in retaliation for Israel's assassination of its chief bomb maker, Yahya Ayyash, in December 1995). This wave of terrorism shortly before the election made Peres's vision of a "New Middle East," without armies and borders, seem completely out of touch and dangerously unrealistic to most Israelis, whereas Netanyahu's campaign promise to achieve "peace with security" resonated widely.

Netanyahu was a fierce critic of the Oslo Accords—he insisted that the PLO was still a terrorist organization committed to Israel's destruction and that it could not be trusted. But once he came to power, he did not stop the peace process, largely because of American pressure and continued domestic support for it. Instead, Netanyahu slowed the peace process down and undermined it. He put off talks with Arafat and delayed implementing steps that Israel had already agreed to. For example, his government repeatedly delayed the construction of an airport and maritime port in Gaza, and for long periods of time the government refused to transfer money belonging to the PA. It was not only what Netanyahu didn't do that undermined the peace process—it was also what he did do. In particular, his government lifted a partial freeze on settlement building in the West Bank that had been in place under the previous Labor-led government, enabling a rapid increase in the number of Jewish settlers there. Netanyahu's government also authorized the controversial opening of an ancient underground tunnel that led to the Western Wall in Jerusalem in September 1996. This sparked Palestinian riots and armed clashes between Israeli soldiers and PA security forces in which seventeen soldiers and seventy Palestinians were killed.

Despite a severe deterioration in Israeli-Palestinian relations, the peace process survived due to the Clinton administration's intensive mediation efforts. In January 1997, Netanyahu and Arafat signed the Hebron Protocol, in which Israel agreed to transfer control of the West Bank town of Hebron to the PA, while keeping 20 percent of the town—the central area where more than 400 Jewish settlers lived among 130,000 Palestinians—under Israeli control. In October 1998, they signed the Wye River Memorandum, which expanded the areas of the West Bank under the PA's full or partial jurisdiction (Areas A and B). By signing these agreements, albeit reluctantly, Netanyahu lost the support of his right-wing base and coalition partners and was forced into early elections in May 1999. He was resoundingly defeated by Labor Party leader Ehud Barak in the election for prime minister. Barak, a former general who was the most decorated soldier in Israel's history, boldly pledged to withdraw Israeli troops from Lebanon and make peace with Syria and the Palestinians. To many, he appeared to be Rabin's true heir, lifting Israeli and Palestinian hopes that he would rescue the faltering peace process and at last bring peace. Instead, it was during Barak's brief term in office (1999–2001) that the peace process finally collapsed (Barak did unilaterally withdraw the IDF from Lebanon in May 2000).

Why did the Oslo peace process collapse?

The Oslo peace process collapsed in January 2001 when Israeli and Palestinian negotiators meeting at the Egyptian Red Sea resort of Taba failed in a desperate, last-ditch effort to reach a peace agreement. Although they declared in a joint statement at the end of the Taba talks that "they have never been closer to reaching an agreement and it is thus our shared belief that the remaining gaps could be bridged with the resumption of negotiations following the Israeli elections," peace talks did not resume after the election in February 2001 because it was won by the hawkish Likud leader Ariel Sharon, who opposed the Oslo peace process. Sharon's landslide victory over Barak in the election for prime minister expressed the Israeli public's response to the outbreak of the Second Intifada a few months earlier. Sharon himself provided the spark that ignited the Second Intifada (also known as the Al-Aqsa Intifada) when he paid a brief, but highly controversial, visit on September 28, 2000, to the Temple Mount/Noble Sanctuary in Jerusalem (where the Al-Aqsa Mosque and Dome of the Rock are located). The site is sacred to Jews and Muslims and claimed by both Israel and the Palestinians (it had been under Israeli control since the 1967 war, but Israel allowed an Islamic religious trust to continue to administer the area). Palestinians were outraged by Sharon's visit, which was accompanied by more than one thousand Israeli police. The Palestinians perceived the visit as a deliberate provocation to them, while most Israelis viewed it as merely a domestic political stunt. In responding to Palestinian protests and rioting the next day, Israeli police killed four Palestinian demonstrators and wounded two hundred. This was the beginning of a bloody cycle of escalating Israeli-Palestinian violence that continued for four years (until 2005), in which about 1,000 Israelis and 3,200 Palestinians were killed.

Unsurprisingly, both sides blame each other for the outbreak of the Second Intifada and the collapse of the Oslo peace process. Israelis, along with their supporters overseas, tend to pin the blame on Palestinian leader Yasser Arafat. They accuse him of failing to prevent Palestinian terrorism during the peace process (particularly in the mid-1990s, when there was a surge of terrorist attacks, including suicide bombings, by Hamas and Islamic Jihad), and then encouraging, and even funding, Palestinian violence against Israel during the Second Intifada. This violated the PLO's commitment in the Oslo Accords to countering anti-Israel violence and suggested to most Israelis that the PLO, and especially its leader, had not genuinely given up the use of violence (some speculated that Arafat was psychologically incapable of transforming himself from a guerrilla fighter to a statesman). Israelis also hold Arafat solely responsible for the failure to reach a peace agreement at the Camp David summit in July 2000, convened by President Clinton at the urging of Barak. At Camp David, Barak proposed a Palestinian state in approximately 91 percent of the West Bank, all of Gaza, and parts of East Jerusalem, which Israelis regarded as extremely generous—it was by far the most that any Israeli leader had ever offered the Palestinians until then. Arafat's unwillingness to accept this unprecedented offer is widely seen as proof that he was not a genuine partner for peace, at least not on terms that Israelis could ever accept. According to this popular Israeli narrative, then, Arafat's intransigence and his predilection for violence destroyed the peace process.

Palestinians and their supporters have a different explanation for why the Oslo peace process collapsed and the Second Intifada erupted. They emphasize relentless Israeli settlement building, particularly by the Netanyahu and Barak governments, which they regard as a violation of the spirit, if not the letter, of the Oslo Accords (the agreements did not explicitly prohibit Israel from building new settlements or expanding existing ones). The number of Israeli settlers increased by around 70 percent, from 115,000 to 200,000, during the years of the Oslo peace process. Palestinians saw the continued growth of Israeli settlements and the settler population as incontrovertible evidence that Israel had no intention of ever withdrawing from Palestinian territory. The Palestinians also highlight Israel's failure to fulfill commitments that it made (such as opening a safe passage between the West Bank and Gaza) and its reluctance to redeploy its soldiers and hand over territory in the West Bank to PA control. Moreover, the Palestinians point out that instead of bringing them greater freedom and prosperity, as they hoped it would, the peace process was actually accompanied by a steep decline in Palestinian living standards and increasing restrictions on their freedom of movement (for instance, they were no longer able to easily enter Israel for work). And they regard the supposedly generous offer that Barak made at the Camp David summit as woefully inadequate, adding insult to injury, and falling far short of what they demanded and felt minimally entitled to—a Palestinian state encompassing Gaza and the entirety of the West Bank and East Jerusalem. Thus, according to the Palestinian narrative, the Second Intifada broke out because the accumulation of these grievances, and the continuation of the Israeli occupation, eventually led to an explosion of popular frustration and anger. The uprising became increasingly violent in response to Israel's aggressive use of force (for example, the IDF fired more than a million bullets in just the first month of the Second Intifada) and was, in any case, entirely justified as "armed resistance."

Both Israelis and Palestinians had good reason to feel let down by the Oslo peace process. Neither side's hopes or expectations were satisfied. The peace process did not bring Israelis the security they longed for. On the contrary, it brought more Palestinian terrorism, not only against Israeli settlers but also against Israeli civilians inside Israel. Nor did the peace process liberate Palestinians from Israeli control or improve their living conditions (except for a small minority who grew rich as a result of rampant corruption and nepotism within the PA). In fact, most Palestinians became poorer—Palestinian per capita GNP plummeted by almost 40 percent after 1993—and in some significant respects, they became less free. Both Israelis and Palestinians are also justified to some extent in their criticisms of each other's actions and inactions during the Oslo peace process. Neither side carried out all its commitments, met deadlines, or really tried to convince the other side of their willingness to compromise and make peace. Instead of building mutual trust and cooperation, the peace process was marred by frequent delays and setbacks, prompting accusations and recriminations, which only deepened distrust and undermined cooperation. The "permanent status negotiations" to reach a comprehensive peace agreement, for example, were supposed to begin no later than 1997 and be completed by 1999, but they did not even get underway until the Camp David summit in July 2000, by which time public opinion on both sides had soured on the peace process and was unwilling to make major concessions.

Both Israeli and Palestinian leaders bear some of the responsibility for the breakdown of the Oslo peace process. Rabin repeatedly sealed off the West Bank and Gaza in response to Palestinian violence, thereby preventing Palestinians from going to work in Israel and depriving them of a vital source of income. Netanyahu fanned Israeli suspicions of Arafat and the PLO, slowed the peace process, and escalated Israeli settlement building (including a new settlement in East Jerusalem). Barak continued expanding Israeli settlements, refused to redeploy Israeli troops in the West Bank in accordance with agreements that Israel had signed, and pushed for final peace talks despite American reservations and Palestinian reluctance. He then publicly blamed Arafat for the failure of the talks, convincing Israelis that they had, in Barak's words, "no partner for peace." On the Palestinian side, Arafat initially tolerated Hamas and Islamic Jihad's campaign of terrorism against Israelis (possibly because he hoped to benefit from it), encouraged incitement against Israel, and presided over a Palestinian administration that was authoritarian and corrupt—suppressing Palestinian dissent—while allowing his cronies to enrich themselves at the expense of ordinary Palestinians. Arafat made little effort at state-building and no serious attempt to convince Israelis of his desire to make peace (unlike what the late Egyptian President Anwar Sadat had famously done when he visited Jerusalem in 1977). On top of all this, Afafat rejected Barak's proposals at the Camp David summit without even making a counteroffer.

It is easy to blame these political leaders for the collapse of the peace process. Indeed, it is often argued that they lacked the requisite political will, diplomatic skill, and empathy and understanding to make peace. No doubt, there is some truth to these charges. These leaders, however, were not operating in a vacuum. They had to constantly contend with domestic opposition and maneuver within, and sometimes around, the political constraints imposed on them by public opinion. The failure of the Oslo peace process, therefore, was also due to the entrenched suspicion and hostility of the Israeli and Palestinian publics toward each other. Although there was at first a great deal of public support and enthusiasm on both sides for the peace process, this support declined as the process dragged on and its promised benefits failed to materialize. But it was not just flagging public support that undermined the peace process. More fundamentally, it failed because popular beliefs, attitudes, and perceptions on both sides hardly changed, or at least they did not change nearly enough.

Most Israelis and Palestinians continued to perceive each other as enemies, to suspect each other's intentions, to think of themselves as the sole victims in the conflict, and to view their relationship in zero-sum terms. This was hardly surprising given the long, bitter conflict between them. It was difficult to overcome decades of fear, antagonism, and mistrust and to fashion new collective identities that were not based on victimhood and memories of past traumas. While numerous grassroots initiatives tried to promote dialogue, understanding, and reconciliation between Israelis and Palestinians, especially among children and youth, these were only small-scale, generally poorly funded efforts that reached a limited audience. For the most part, the Oslo peace process was a top-down, elite-driven undertaking. The vast majority of Israelis and Palestinians were not participants in the process but spectators watching from the sidelines. Hence, the psychological barrier between them remained in place, and little to no reconciliation occurred. This meant that when peace talks took place at the Camp David summit, neither side's public was prepared to support the kinds of concessions that a peace agreement required. It also meant that when the Second Intifada started, most Israelis and Palestinians were all too ready to endorse their own sides' increasingly violent actions and blame the other side.

The architects of the Oslo peace process were well aware of the suspicion and hostility that Israelis and Palestinians felt toward each other. This was one reason why they deferred tackling the hardest and most contentious issues until the end of the peace process, by which time they hoped that trust would have developed and hostility would have diminished. The fact that this did not happen was not only due to how deeply ingrained suspicion and hostility were (and how limited efforts were to overcome them) but also because of the violent actions taken by some extremist groups and individuals who fiercely opposed the peace process and tried to sabotage it. These "spoilers," as political scientists call them, strategically used violence to stall the peace process and undermine public support for it. The long time-frame and incremental nature of the peace process offered ample opportunities for this to happen.

The most notorious example of "spoiling" during the peace process was the assassination of Rabin by an Israeli Jewish religious extremist who wanted to prevent Israel's withdrawal from the West

Bank. For the same reason, the year before, on February 25, 1994, another Israeli extremist killed twenty-nine Palestinians while they prayed at a mosque in Hebron (in retaliation for this act of terrorism, Hamas carried out two terrorist attacks in Israel in the months afterward). Hamas and Islamic Jihad (who both received support from Iran) regularly perpetrated attacks against Israeli soldiers and civilians, killing hundreds, in order to derail the peace process. They played the role of spoilers most successfully in the spring of 1996, when their intense campaign of suicide terrorism helped defeat Peres, Rabin's successor and Oslo's leading Israeli champion, and bring Netanyahu, Oslo's chief critic, to power.

It is tempting to believe that the peace process would have succeeded were it not for all this violence but, as I have argued, the violence was not the only cause for the collapse of the peace process. Extremist violence, public mistrust, and political mismanagement and misdeeds all undermined the Oslo peace process. There were many reasons for the failure to achieve peace, so it would be wrong to single out only one or to place all the blame on just one side, however politically and intellectually convenient that might be. Moreover, even if the Oslo peace process had gone as smoothly as its planners hoped, without any delays, backtracking, or broken promises, it is still doubtful whether Israel and the PLO could have reached a comprehensive peace agreement back then. As the failure of the Camp David summit demonstrated, neither side was willing, or able, to accept a peace agreement based on anything close to the other side's terms.

What are the main issues that need to be resolved in an Israeli-Palestinian peace agreement?

There are four main issues that have bedeviled peace talks and are the chief obstacles to reaching a comprehensive peace agreement: (1) the future of the contested city of Jerusalem, (2) the fate of Palestinian refugees, (3) the borders of a future Palestinian state, and (4) the security arrangements between Israel and a Palestinian state. These so-called final-status issues are by no means the only important issues that need to be resolved in a peace agreement. There are many crucial economic and resource issues (for example, regarding water-sharing) that must also be tackled. But Israel and the PLO (which officially represents the Palestinians in peace talks) both agree that the issues of Jerusalem, refugees, borders, and security are the most important (Israel's recent demand that the Palestinians officially recognize it as a Jewish state is not mutually accepted as a final-status issue since the Palestinians insist that such recognition is unnecessary). In order to explain why these four issues have been so contentious and difficult to resolve, I will summarize the conflicting positions of both sides, based upon what is publicly known about the official negotiations that have taken place over them during the past two decades (including the Camp David summit in July 2000, the Taba talks in January 2001, the "Annapolis process" in 2007–2008, and the last round of indirect peace talks in 2013–2014 mediated by then U.S. Secretary of State John Kerry).

Jerusalem

The future of Jerusalem has been the most contentious and challenging of all the issues in the peace talks between Israel and the Palestinians. The city's historical and religious significance to Jews, Muslims, and Christians worldwide makes it a particularly highly charged issue at the negotiating table. The struggle for sovereignty over Jerusalem has long been a central feature of the Israeli-Palestinian conflict, which is why the 1947 UN partition plan proposed an international administration for the city. This administration never came into being. Instead, Israel gained control over the western half of the city in the war of 1947–1949, while Jordan seized the eastern half, including the Old City and its holy sites. Jerusalem remained a divided city (much as Berlin was during the Cold War), until Israel conquered—or "liberated" as many Israelis would put it—East Jerusalem from the Jordanians in the 1967 war. Israel subsequently effectively annexed the area and gave its Palestinian inhabitants residency rights, but not citizenship (though they can apply for Israeli citizenship, few do, and thousands of Palestinians have had their residency stripped over the years). Israel also greatly expanded the municipal boundaries of Jerusalem to incorporate a large amount of West Bank land, including many Palestinian villages. To strengthen its hold over East Jerusalem, Israel has built a dozen large Jewish "neighborhoods" there (or "settlements," as most of the world calls them), where roughly 280,000 Israelis now reside (many of them ultra-Orthodox Jews). The Israeli authorities have also used a variety of bureaucratic methods, such as zoning regulations and building permit laws, which restrict the growth and development of Palestinian neighborhoods, forcing some Palestinians from East Jerusalem to live elsewhere. Palestinian residents of East Jerusalem also lack many municipal services. Yet despite suffering from years of discrimination and neglect, the Palestinian population of East Jerusalem has grown more than fivefold since 1967 and now numbers around 370,000, amounting to roughly 40 percent of Jerusalem's total population.

Israelis and Palestinians both want Jerusalem as their national capital. It has been Israel's self-declared capital since 1949, although only the United States and a few other countries officially recognize this (U.S. President Donald Trump controversially announced this recognition in December 2017). The PLO no longer claims all of Jerusalem for a Palestinian capital. It now limits its territorial claim to East Jerusalem, which it regards as occupied Palestinian territory (as does the UN). For decades, Israeli leaders categorically rejected this claim, insisting that "Jerusalem is the eternal, undivided capital of Israel," and vowing never to divide it. Although Israeli politicians still frequently repeat this phrase, in negotiations with the Palestinians Israeli leaders have actually been willing to accept Palestinian sovereignty over parts of East Jerusalem. Ehud Barak broke the Israeli taboo against dividing Jerusalem at the Camp David Summit when he offered Arafat a Palestinian capital in outlying areas of East Jerusalem (Arafat rejected the offer because he wanted more of East Jerusalem, including at least parts of the Old City). When Ehud Olmert was Israel's prime minister (from 2006 to 2009), he went further than this in his negotiations with Arafat's successor, Mahmoud Abbas, proposing Palestinian sovereignty over Palestinian-populated neighborhoods in East Jerusalem and Israeli sovereignty over its Jewish "neighborhoods" (this idea was first suggested by President Clinton shortly before he left office). Abbas accepted this general formula, but he and Olmert disagreed about the future of Har Homa, a Jewish neighborhood/settlement in East Jerusalem that cuts Bethlehem (in the West Bank) off from Jerusalem.

It is quite conceivable that an agreement could eventually be reached to allow the Palestinian neighborhoods of East Jerusalem to become the capital of a Palestinian state, while West Jerusalem and the Jewish neighborhoods of East Jerusalem would be Israel's capital. The fact that the Jewish neighborhoods in East Jerusalem are largely contiguous with West Jerusalem facilitates this. It is, however, much easier to divide Jerusalem on a map than on the ground. For one thing, a growing number of Israeli Jews have deliberately moved into Palestinian neighborhoods in East Jerusalem so as to make any partition more difficult to implement. For another, many Palestinians now work in West Jerusalem (about half the East Jerusalem Palestinian labor force), so they might lose their jobs and livelihoods if the city were divided. Palestinians in East Jerusalem could also lose valuable access to Israeli hospitals, universities, and welfare benefits.

An even more difficult challenge arises when it comes to the Old City of Jerusalem, an area less than one square kilometer in size that is packed with historical and religious sites, including Judaism's holiest site (the Temple Mount) and, sitting on top of it, Islam's third-holiest site (the Haram al-Sharif). The Old City is also home to a few thousand Jews and more than thirty thousand Palestinians, and it attracts hordes of foreign tourists, making it a lucrative asset for Israel or for a future Palestinian state. Both sides want sovereignty over the Old City, and especially over the Temple Mount/Haram al-Sharif. The Camp David summit collapsed primarily because neither side was willing, or even able, to give up its claim to this sacred space (Arafat allegedly feared that he would be assassinated if he accepted Israeli sovereignty over the Haram al-Sharif). Since then, some creative proposals have been made to divide the Old City and give both sides, or neither side, sovereignty over the fiercely contested Temple Mount/Haram al-Sharif, but none of these proposals have been accepted by Israeli or Palestinian leaders.

An alternative approach, put forward by Olmert in his talks with Abbas, is for both sides to forgo sovereignty over the Old City and the area around it (known as the "Holy Basin" because it also contains many religious sites) and instead place it all under the control of an international consortium, consisting of Israel, Palestine, the United States, Saudi Arabia, Egypt, and Jordan (the latter already has a role in managing the Haram al-Sharif). Abbas reportedly accepted this approach, but he and Olmert could not agree on the size of the area to be internationalized. Olmert was then forced to resign due to multiple corruption charges against him (he was subsequently imprisoned), and his more hardline successor as Israeli prime minister, Likud leader Benjamin Netanyahu, has publicly rejected any kind of division of Jerusalem. Behind closed doors, however, Netanyahu might be more willing to compromise over Jerusalem, but for now at least his political survival largely depends on his intransigence on issues concerning the Palestinians.

A future Israeli leader might well be prepared to divide, or even share, sovereignty over Jerusalem with the Palestinians. This would undoubtedly be highly controversial among Israeli Jews (and among Jews around the world). But now that proposals to divide or share Jerusalem have been circulating and gaining currency for some time, they are no longer completely unacceptable to the Israeli public (as numerous opinion polls show). Just as most Palestinians have reluctantly come to terms with Israeli rule over West Jerusalem, most Israelis may have to concede, sooner or later, to Palestinian rule over parts of East Jerusalem and possibly even over some of the Old City (specifically, over the Palestinian-populated Muslim and Christian quarters).

Refugees

If giving up sovereignty over some of Jerusalem will be the hardest concession that Israelis will have to make, then giving up an unqualified "right of return" for Palestinian refugees will probably be the hardest concession for Palestinians. For them, the issue of Palestinian refugees is the most emotional of all the final-status issues because it concerns what Palestinians call the *Nakba*, the national tragedy that happened to them when Israel was founded in 1948, which is still central in the collective memory and national identity of Palestinians. Ever since approximately 700,000 Palestinians fled or were expelled during the course of the civil war and then the Arab-Israeli war between 1947 and 1949, Palestinians have insisted that these refugees, and their immediate descendants, have a right to return to their homeland and reclaim their property (they also demand this for the 300,000 or so Palestinians who became refugees as a result of the 1967 war). Many Palestinian refugees, in fact, still have the keys to their former homes, which have become treasured family heirlooms. Palestinians believe that the right of return for Palestinian refugees is not only morally justified—since they blame Israel for deliberately and systematically expelling Palestinian civilians during the war, and then forcibly preventing them from returning to their homes and villages after the war—but also legally mandated by international law. In particular, they insist that the right of return was established in UN Resolution 194, passed in December 1948, which, among other things, stipulated that "the refugees wishing to return to their homes and live at peace with their neighbors should be permitted to do so at the earliest practicable date" (this has been reaffirmed in multiple UN resolutions since then).

Israel's decades-long refusal to admit Palestinian refugees, and denial of responsibility for displacing them in the first place, is one of its chief crimes in the minds of Palestinians—its "original sin," according to them. Hence, they have always conditioned their willingness to make peace with Israel on its willingness to accept responsibility for the historical injustice inflicted on Palestinian refugees, to compensate them for their suffering and their material losses, and to allow any refugee (and their descendants) wishing to return home to do so. For many Palestinians, these demands are nonnegotiable. No peace, let alone reconciliation, is possible for them without this accountability and restitution. Many Palestinian refugees are still stateless seventy years after the *Nakba*, and many still live in squalid, overcrowded refugee camps in the West Bank, Gaza Strip, Syria, and Lebanon (in the latter, they also suffer from official discrimination). These circumstances add to the salience of the refugee issue for Palestinians, making it an ongoing humanitarian issue in addition to a moral, legal, and historical one.

Israel's longstanding official position on the issue of Palestinian refugees is diametrically at odds with Palestinian demands. Israeli governments, left and right alike, have always adamantly rejected a right of return for Palestinian refugees on the grounds that Israel is neither morally responsible for their original displacement nor legally required to admit them, let alone their descendants (who should not be considered refugees, according to Israel and the current U.S. administration, since this status should not be inherited). Israel has insisted that most of the refugees from the 1947–1949 war left voluntarily, and that the responsibility for this exodus lies with the Arab states and the Palestinian leadership at the time since they rejected the UN's partition plan and went to war to stop Israel's creation. In addition to absolving itself of responsibility for the creation of the Palestinian refugee problem, Israel blames the Arab states for the perpetuation of the problem because (with the exception of Jordan) they have been unwilling to integrate Palestinian refugees into their own populations (as Israel has done with Jewish refugees, including those from Arab countries), preferring to keep them as pawns to be used in their conflict with Israel. Finally, regardless of who is at fault for the Palestinian refugee problem, Israel argues that it is not required by international law to admit Palestinian refugees, pointing out that UN Resolution 194 does not stipulate an unconditional "right of return" and, in any case, is not legally binding since it was passed by the UN General Assembly rather than the Security Council (only Security Council resolutions are mandatory).

Along with these arguments, Israel has another major objection to a right of return for Palestinian refugees—it fears that this could lead to the demise of the Jewish state. There are now 5.4 million Palestinians registered as refugees by the UN agency that still looks after them (the United Nations Relief and Works Agency for Palestine Refugees, or UNRWA). At least two million more Palestinians, scattered around the world, claim to be refugees, putting the total number somewhere between seven and eight million people. Israel's Jewish population is around 6.5 million, so if Palestinian refugees were entitled to live there, the country's demographics could be completely upended. Palestinians could quickly outnumber Jews (there are already roughly 1.5 million Palestinian citizens of Israel), and then simply vote the Jewish state out of existence. Even if this nightmare scenario for Israeli Jews is unlikely to happen, a large influx of Palestinians could severely strain the already fragile relationship between Jews and Arabs in Israel and pose a potential security risk. Hence, Israel argues that because of these demographic and security concerns it would be very dangerous, if not suicidal, to allow potentially hostile refugees to return en masse.

For all these reasons, therefore, a Palestinian right of return is absolutely unacceptable to Israel, just as it is essential for the Palestinians. On the face of it, the dispute over this issue seems irresolvable, dooming any attempt to negotiate a peace agreement. However, in the actual negotiations that have taken place, both sides have displayed more flexibility than their public postures, and propaganda, would suggest. In the same way that Israeli leaders have been willing to compromise in negotiations behind closed doors on the hot-button issue of Jerusalem, Palestinian leaders have been willing to compromise on the refugee issue. While insisting upon a Palestinian right of return in principle, they have conceded that this will be restricted in practice.

Acknowledging Israel's demographic concerns, and grudgingly accepting that Israel will never agree to jeopardize its identity as a Jewish state by allowing a mass return of Palestinian refugees, Palestinian negotiators have proposed that only a limited number, agreed upon by Israel, will be permitted to gradually return to Israel, while the rest will voluntarily be resettled in a future Palestinian state, in their current host countries in the Arab world, or in other countries willing to take them in. As for the number of Palestinian refugees to be admitted to Israel, Palestinian negotiators have gone from suggesting at least hundreds of thousands to asking for 150,000 over a ten-year period (i.e., fifteen thousand per year)—a tiny fraction of over five million who claim to be refugees. In fact, in confidential internal documents that were leaked (called the "Palestine Papers"), the chief PLO negotiator, Saeb Erekat, is recorded as being prepared to accept just ten thousand refugees in total being admitted into Israel. Abbas, himself a refugee from the 1947–1949 war, is quoted as saying in a 2009 meeting: "On numbers of refugees, it is illogical to ask Israel to take 5 million, or indeed 1 million. That would mean the end of Israel."

For their part, Israeli leaders—specifically, Barak and Olmert—have expressed a willingness to admit a token number of Palestinian refugees, as long as they were admitted as a humanitarian gesture under the rubric of a family-reunification program rather than in accordance with a right of return. In his negotiations with Abbas in 2008, Olmert offered to accept a total of five thousand refugees over five years, but he was reportedly willing to accept as many as thirty thousand. Israeli leaders have also offered to contribute to an international fund that would compensate Palestinian refugees for their losses and help pay for their resettlement and rehabilitation (although it has been estimated that the total cost of this would be between $55 to $85 billion, so Israel's financial contribution would probably be a drop in the bucket).

Both sides, therefore, are not far from agreeing on practical measures to resolve the ongoing plight of Palestinian refugees. But while an agreement over numbers—of refugees and dollars—is within reach, there is little likelihood that both sides can agree about who is responsible for what happened to Palestinians in the 1947–1949 war. Although, by and large, Israeli Jews have slowly and painfully come to accept that their side did carry out some mass killings and expulsions during the war, they furiously deny accusations of "ethnic cleansing" and strongly object to being blamed for the suffering of Palestinian refugees. Israeli Jews might be willing to acknowledge the Palestinians' suffering, but they will not accept any responsibility for it, and certainly not sole responsibility. For Palestinians, on the other hand, though they now recognize that their own leaders and Arab leaders at the time were guilty of various failures before, during, and after the 1947–1949 war, they continue to place the bulk of responsibility for their collective dispossession and displacement upon Israel. Their demand that Israel officially accept this responsibility, and make amends for it in some significant way, is one that they are unlikely to give up any time soon. Ultimately, an agreement on the Palestinian refugee issue will depend upon whether Israeli and Palestinian negotiators can somehow finesse this highly sensitive subject, and come up with a joint statement that their respective publics can live with. For example, in the "parameters" for resolving the conflict that President Clinton presented to both sides in December 2000, he suggested that Israel "acknowledge the moral and material suffering caused to the Palestinian people as a result of the 1948 war and the need to assist the international community in addressing the problem."

Borders

Unlike the refugee issue, on which Israeli and Palestinian negotiators are much closer to agreement regarding practical measures than the guiding principle (i.e., the right of return), on the issue of borders they have agreed on the general principle but cannot agree on the details. It took many years, and much bloodshed, but both sides have officially accepted the principle of territorial partition, involving the establishment of a Palestinian state alongside the State of Israel. The PLO accepted this in 1988, after a long-running and fractious internal debate, when it first announced its support for a two-state solution to the Israeli-Palestinian conflict and declared the establishment of a Palestinian state in the West Bank (including

East Jerusalem) and Gaza Strip. Twelve years later, Barak became the first Israeli prime minister to accept the Palestinian demand for statehood (at the Camp David summit). Israel's current leader, Netanyahu, verbally endorsed a two-state solution in a major speech in June 2009—delivered under pressure from President Obama, who had recently entered office—but he has since backed away from this without renouncing it altogether (which most of the members of his current cabinet, and his party, would like him to do).

The borders of a future Palestinian state, however, have been the focus of fierce disagreement. Having abandoned their claim to the vast majority of the land they believe is rightfully theirs (amounting to 78 percent of Mandate Palestine)—which Palestinians regard as a massive concession—the PLO, and most Palestinians, have been strongly opposed to making any more territorial concessions. Both Arafat and Abbas have insisted that the future border between Israel and a new Palestinian state runs along the "Green Line"—the 1949 armistice line that was drawn on a map with a green marker at the end of the first Arab-Israeli war (which then served as the de-facto border between Jordan and Israel until the 1967 war). Since Israel captured the West Bank from Jordan in the 1967 war, Israeli governments, and a majority of Israelis, have consistently opposed withdrawing back to the Green Line for a variety of reasons. The most commonly cited objection has been that Israel needs "defensible borders" because of the security threats it faces. The Green Line, it is argued, is not a defensible border since it would put Israeli population centers within easy reach of Arab armies and, more recently, rockets and missiles. Israeli governments have also argued that the existence of numerous Jewish settlements in the West Bank— where as many as 400,000 Israelis now live—makes it almost impossible for Israel to completely withdraw from the territory. The political, social, and economic cost of dismantling these settlements and evacuating all their residents would be prohibitive for any Israeli government. Hence, Israeli leaders have insisted that the future border between Israel and a Palestinian state must be drawn in a way that allows most of the settlers to stay where they are. Since the vast majority of settlers live in sprawling, densely populated blocs of settlements located near the Green Line—in areas adjacent to urban areas within Israel (these settlements are like suburbs of Israeli cities)—Israel wants to annex these large "settlement blocs."

If the Palestinians want a border between Israel and a Palestinian state to be based on the Green Line, and the Israelis want a border that allows them to annex Israeli settlement blocs beyond the Green Line, then agreement on this issue seems unattainable. Indeed, this was a major source of disagreement between Barak and Arafat at the Camp David summit. Barak made what he, and most Israelis, considered to be a magnanimous offer to the Palestinian leader: a state in 91 percent of the West Bank (by Israeli calculations) plus the Gaza Strip. For Arafat, however, a Palestinian state encompassing less than 100 percent of the West Bank was insufficient. When Arafat spurned Barak's offer, most Israelis concluded he was not genuinely committed to making peace with them, while most Palestinians felt he had done the right thing.

Despite the failure of the Camp David summit, one idea that American officials suggested during the talks as a way of reconciling the seemingly incompatible territorial demands of both sides has gained traction—land swaps. Israel could give some of its own land to the Palestinians in exchange for annexing some West Bank land. Both sides have accepted this idea, but they disagree about whether an equivalent amount of land has to be exchanged. At the Taba talks in January 2001, for example, Israeli negotiators proposed a Palestinian state on 94 percent of the West Bank (upping the previous offer that was made at Camp David), with a 3 percent land swap from Israel, for a total of 97 percent. The Palestinians rejected this proposal, insisting upon an equal land swap, in terms of both the quantity and the quality of the land exchanged. In negotiations since then, Israel has moved closer to meeting this demand. In exchange for Israel annexing around 6 percent of the West Bank (thereby allowing about 80 percent of Jewish settlers to stay in place), Olmert offered to give the Palestinians around 5 percent of Israeli land— not a 1:1 ratio, but close (to make up the difference, he also offered a "safe-passage corridor" consisting of tunnels or roads connecting the West Bank to the Gaza Strip). Abbas proposed that Israel annex about 2 percent of the West Bank (including East Jerusalem), with the Palestinians receiving the same amount of land from Israel.

Now that the principle of land swaps has been accepted by both sides, all that remains to be decided are the details: How much land should be traded, and where? Israel favors a larger land swap so that it can keep as many settlements as possible, thereby minimizing the number of settlers it would have to evacuate. In exchange for annexing the large settlement blocs, some right-wing Israeli politicians (most notably, former defense minister Avigdor Lieberman) have advocated that Israel give the Palestinians territory within Israel that is adjacent to the West Bank and largely inhabited by Palestinian citizens of Israel (who strongly object to such a proposal). The Palestinians, on the other hand, prefer a much smaller land swap, so that they can get almost all of the West Bank and ensure that it is contiguous, thereby minimizing any disruption to Palestinian life. And they will not accept Israeli land that is already populated, whether by Jews or Arabs.

It remains to be seen whether Israel has enough empty land, of comparable value, that it can trade for West Bank land. The more Israeli settlements expand and multiply in the West Bank, the more land Israel will probably have to give the Palestinians to compensate them. For a small, densely populated country, much of it desert, this will be difficult to say the least. Even if such uninhabited land is available within Israel, and adjacent to the West Bank, the Palestinians are still likely to oppose Israel's annexation of settlements located deep inside the West Bank in order to preserve the territorial contiguity of a Palestinian state. For example, the large Israeli settlement of Ariel, a university town with a population of 20,000, lies approximately 11 miles inside the West Bank, nearly halfway between the Green Line and the Jordan River. If Israel annexed this settlement, as it hopes to do, it would keep a long sliver of land stretching across much of the northern West Bank, effectively bisecting it. The Palestinians are adamant that they will never agree to this, so the prospects for an agreement on the borders of a Palestinian state may ultimately depend on Israel's willingness to relinquish Ariel and other outlying settlements. Although not completely inconceivable, it is doubtful whether any Israeli prime minister (certainly not the current one) will voluntarily agree to this since it would most likely entail the eviction of their residents—as many as 80,000–100,000 Israeli settlers (some of whom, numbering in the thousands, are religious extremists)—and incur stiff domestic resistance, probably including violence. Allowing these settlers to stay put, if they wish, and become citizens of a Palestinian state, as some have suggested, is also an unpalatable option for an Israeli leader given the high risk that these settlers would become an easy target for violent attacks by Palestinians or carry out attacks themselves against neighboring Palestinians. It is also absolutely unacceptable for most Palestinians.

Security

For decades, Israel's powerful security establishment opposed the creation of a Palestinian state in the West Bank and Gaza on the grounds that it could pose an existential threat to Israel. They were particularly concerned about the risk of a hostile foreign army (such as the Iraqi army) entering a future Palestinian state, whether by invitation or invasion, and using it as a staging ground from which to attack or invade Israel. The country's small size and "narrow waistline"—the short distance between the Mediterranean Sea and the West Bank (only 9 miles, or 15 kilometers, at its narrowest point)—means it lacks strategic depth, making it especially vulnerable to such a conventional military attack. Although this concern has not entirely abated, the Israeli security establishment no longer views the prospect of a Palestinian state with the same alarm. On the contrary, Israeli generals and security chiefs now tend to regard a Palestinian state as a strategic necessity for Israel, rather than a strategic threat, and retired security officials have become some of the most outspoken advocates for Palestinian statehood.

Nonetheless, the West Bank remains strategically important to Israel because of its proximity to the Israeli heartland (where most of its population and economic infrastructure is located), and its topography (the West Bank's hilly terrain overlooks Israel's coastal plain). For this reason alone, Israelis are wary about withdrawing from the West Bank and giving up Israel's control over this strategic territory. Even if an Israeli government were otherwise willing to withdraw from the vast majority of the West Bank and evacuate (forcibly if necessary) tens of thousands of Israeli settlers, it would only do so if Israel's security were not seriously jeopardized. Indeed, the Israeli government's official rationale for the IDF's presence in the West Bank is that it keeps Israelis safe, and a majority of Israelis continue to believe this (whether it is true or not is another question entirely).

Most Israelis would probably support an Israeli withdrawal from the West Bank if they were not so worried, quite understandably, about the security threats that could follow it. Foremost in their minds is the threat of Hamas taking over the West Bank—as it has already done in Gaza following Israel's withdrawal in 2005—and using it as another launching pad for indiscriminate rocket attacks on nearby Israeli cities and towns (and its international airport). The frequent shelling of Israeli communities in the south since Israel's "disengagement" from Gaza, and Hezbollah's missile attacks on Israeli communities in the north after Israeli forces unilaterally withdrew from southern Lebanon in 2000, has convinced many Israelis that territorial withdrawals only lead to more violence against them, not less. Israelis are also concerned about the risk of a Hamas-run Palestinian state entering into a dangerous military alliance with Israel's chief enemy, Iran (which has long been a patron of Hamas). The risk that a future Palestinian state could collapse into disorder and civil strife, which would surely spill over into Israel, also worries Israelis, as they have recently witnessed the collapse of Arab states (Syria, Libya, and Yemen) and the horrific violence that resulted. Along with this potential threat, there is the risk that jihadist terrorist groups (specifically, the Islamic State and Al Qaeda) could infiltrate, find sanctuary in, or even overrun a weak or failed Palestinian state, as has happened in recent years in Iraq, Yemen, and neighboring Syria and Egypt (in its Sinai region). Indeed, nowadays Israelis are more worried about whether Palestinian security forces could maintain order and stability in the West Bank in the aftermath of an Israeli withdrawal than whether they will attack Israel.

For all these reasons, security has been Israel's top priority in peace talks with the Palestinians (especially for Netanyahu, who has conditioned his acceptance of a Palestinian state on his security requirements being met). Barak, Olmert, and Netanyahu have all made similar security demands: that a Palestinian state be demilitarized (i.e., it would only be permitted to have a police force and not an army, air force, or any heavy weaponry); that the Palestinian state would be prohibited from making military agreements or alliances with states hostile to Israel; that no foreign armies would be allowed to enter a Palestinian state without Israel's permission; that imports into a Palestinian state would be monitored by Israel to prevent weapons smuggling by terrorist groups; and that Israel would have guaranteed access to the air space of a Palestinian state and to its electromagnetic spectrum (i.e., its broadcast frequencies).

Despite the fact that these Israeli security demands infringe on the sovereignty of a future Palestinian state—especially the demand that it be demilitarized—the Palestinians have been surprisingly accommodating. In his negotiations with Olmert, for instance, Abbas largely agreed to all these demands, and both sides believed the issue of security was more or less resolved. The major sticking point in the negotiations over security has been Israel's desire to maintain a long-term military presence in the Jordan Valley (such as early-warning stations manned by Israeli soldiers), located inside the West Bank along the border with Jordan. Since conquering the West Bank in 1967, the Israeli army has stationed soldiers in the Jordan Valley to stop foreign troops, terrorists, or arms from entering. Although the threats have changed to some extent—Israel now has a peace treaty with Jordan and is more concerned with jihadists crossing the border than Arab troops—the belief that it is critical for Israel's security to keep its forces in the Jordan Valley has persisted (not without challenges, of course). Israel's purported need to maintain a military presence in the Jordan Valley conflicts with the Palestinians' desire to completely rid the West Bank of Israeli soldiers. Abbas has reluctantly agreed to accept a small Israeli military presence in a future Palestinian state for a limited and fixed amount of time (he proposed a five-year time frame to Olmert), but he has refused to allow a long-term presence, let alone an indefinite one (as Netanyahu has demanded). Having endured five decades of Israeli military occupation, it is hardly surprising that the Palestinians insist that Israel commit to fully withdrawing its forces from the West Bank by a specified time. For them, this is a deal breaker, since the Palestinian public perceives Israeli soldiers as a threat (with good reason, it should be noted) and as the literal embodiment of Israel's occupation of their land.

American mediators in the peace talks have proposed a compromise, whereby Israel could keep a military presence in the Jordan Valley for a limited period of time, after which a U.S.-led international force (possibly NATO) would be deployed in the area. Arafat and then Abbas have both accepted this proposal, but different Israeli leaders have given different responses. Barak accepted it during the Camp David summit, as did Olmert in his negotiations with Abbas, but Netanyahu has insisted (at least publicly) that only the IDF can ensure Israel's security, not a temporary, unreliable, international peacekeeping force, even one under American command. The poor performance of UN peacekeepers in southern Lebanon (from Israel's perspective), and the failure of UN peacekeepers in the Sinai to prevent the 1967 war, has meant that many, if not most, Israelis endorse Netanyahu's position and share his disdain for foreign peacekeepers.

Before concluding this discussion of the four main issues at the center of the negotiations over the past two decades, it is worth emphasizing the fact that neither side's positions are set in stone. They have shifted when different leaders came to power, and in response to changing domestic, regional, and international circumstances. It would be mistaken, therefore, to simply assume that their positions are irreconcilable. Neither side is as rigid as their public rhetoric often conveys, and both sides have displayed some willingness to compromise, albeit obviously not enough. Nevertheless, their stances have changed over time, often in subtle but significant ways. To a certain extent, they have converged on some extremely important and contentious questions (such as whether Jerusalem can be divided, whether Palestinian refugees can all "return" to Israel, or whether all Israeli settlements have to be dismantled). But there are still some wide gaps between the positions of the two sides, and in some cases they have only grown wider in recent years.

Unfortunately, the prospects for achieving a breakthrough appear bleaker now than they have for some time. There is currently widespread pessimism about the possibility of negotiating a peaceful resolution of the conflict. Indeed, if there is one thing that Israelis and Palestinians agree upon it is that a comprehensive peace agreement is impossible, at least for the foreseeable future. This pessimism is entirely understandable given the record of failed peace talks and the situation in the West Bank and Gaza (discussed in the next chapter), but it fails to appreciate the progress that has been made in previous rounds of negotiations. Now that both sides have expressed their views on the final-status issues and clarified their "red lines," the outlines of a peace agreement are much clearer than they ever have been. And since they have even come agonizingly close to reaching an agreement (at the Taba talks in January 2001 and in the negotiations between Olmert and Abbas in 2007–2008), there is no reason to believe that such an agreement is beyond reach. But it is by no means easy to achieve, and it may well require some outside help, probably from the United States.

What role has the United States played in the peace process?

No other country in the world has been as intensely and intimately involved in the peace process between Israel and the Palestinians as the United States. As the world's most powerful state and Israel's closest ally, the United States has enjoyed a near monopoly over international efforts to resolve the Israeli-Palestinian conflict, at least since taking the lead role in convening the Madrid Conference in 1991, which was when formal, face-to-face peace talks between Israelis and Palestinians first began. American engagement in the Israeli-Palestinian peace process is an extension of its broader, and much longer, attempt to broker an end to the Arab-Israeli conflict. Since the outbreak of the first Arab-Israeli war in 1948, many American presidents and secretaries of state have tried, with varying degrees of success, to impose ceasefires in Arab-Israeli wars, initiate peace talks, mediate negotiations, settle disputes, and put forward principles and plans for peacemaking. This seven-decades-long diplomatic effort to resolve the Arab-Israeli conflict is unparalleled in the history of U.S. foreign policy. It is probably safe to say that more American government attention, time, money, and manpower have been devoted to brokering a resolution of this conflict than toward any other international conflict.

American policymakers have been exceptionally committed to Arab-Israeli peacemaking primarily because they have always believed that it serves American national interests (no doubt, they have also believed that it advances Israel's interests, but this is secondary). They have had a variety of strategic motivations. Since the end of World War II, the Middle East has been a focus of U.S. foreign policy, largely because of the plentiful oil reserves in the Gulf. United States foreign policy toward the region has consistently been driven by its desire to ensure a reliable supply of reasonably priced Gulf oil to itself and its allies (containing the influence of the Soviet Union was also an overriding interest during the Cold War). This goal has required the United States to cultivate relationships with oil-rich Gulf states, especially Saudi Arabia, and, more broadly, to maintain or restore stability in the Middle East. Since the Arab-Israeli conflict is seen as a major source of regional instability, U.S. efforts to broker peace are partly motivated by the belief that this will bring more stability to the region, and particularly bolster the stability of pro-American regimes there.

Another strategic motive behind American peacemaking efforts has been a desire to mitigate a longstanding irritant in its relations with Arab states, who have strongly objected to U.S. support for Israel (less so today). Keeping America's staunch commitment to the survival of the Jewish state while at the same time cultivating ties with Israel's Arab adversaries has been a difficult balancing act for American policymakers, particularly when the Arab-Israeli conflict was at its height in the 1950s, 1960s, and 1970s. Hence, making peace between Israel and the Arabs was seen as a way of removing the tension between the United States' support for Israel and its need for good relationships with certain Arab states. Even if the United States could not actually resolve the Arab-Israeli conflict, just trying to do so could help alleviate some of this tension. Moreover, in the wake of the 1973 Arab-Israeli war, then U.S. Secretary of State Henry Kissinger developed an ingenious new strategy, using American leverage over Israel as a way of enticing hostile Arab states aligned with the Soviet Union, primarily Egypt, into the American orbit. By brokering the disengagement agreements between Israel and Egypt in 1974 and 1975, Kissinger not only managed to lay the groundwork for the subsequent Camp David Accords (1978) and Egyptian-Israeli peace treaty (1979) but also converted Egypt—the most important Arab state at the time—from a Soviet ally into an American one, helping the United States establish its hegemony in the region. In a similar manner, but less successfully, American policymakers in the 1990s tried to strengthen U.S.-Syrian relations first by offering, and then by overseeing, peace talks with Israel.

The United States' involvement in the Arab-Israeli peace process, therefore, has been a way for it to manage, and even develop, its alliances in the Middle East. For the past two decades or so, American efforts to broker Israeli-Palestinian peace (particularly during the Obama administration) have also been driven by the belief that this will improve its standing in the Muslim world—since the Palestinian cause resonates among Muslims worldwide—as well as by the hope that resolving the Israeli-Palestinian conflict peace might help diminish the popular appeal of jihadism and ultimately reduce terrorism against the United States and its allies. Most recently, during the Trump administration, American policymakers have expressed the belief that peace between Israel and the Palestinians will facilitate an emerging de facto alliance between Israel and the Sunni Arab states, especially Saudi Arabia, against their common enemy, the Islamic Republic of Iran.

Although the pursuit of Arab-Israeli peace, or at least a peace process, has long been a goal of American foreign policy, it has not always been a priority. Some U.S. administrations have prioritized it. Others have put it on the back burner because they have had more pressing international issues, conflicts, and crises to deal with, or because they have been reluctant to devote significant political capital to Arab-Israeli peacemaking, particularly when the prospects for peace, or even just progress toward it, appeared slim. Likewise, some administrations have put more effort into peacemaking and been more deeply engaged in the peace process than others. Several U.S. presidents have taken the lead by hosting summits, proposing peace plans, mediating peace talks, and personally pressuring and/ or cajoling Arab and Israeli leaders. And others have taken a back seat and empowered their secretaries of state or official emissaries to convene talks, conduct negotiations, and broker disputes (and some presidents have done both at different points in their presidency). Jimmy Carter's tireless personal diplomacy with Begin and Sadat, for example, was instrumental in bringing about the Camp David Accords between Israel and Egypt. Bill Clinton acted in a similar manner with Barak and Arafat during the second Camp David summit in 2000, but without success. By contrast, neither George W. Bush nor Barack Obama were as willing to really immerse themselves in the Israeli-Palestinian peace process, spend political capital, and risk failure. Not only has the extent and manner of American involvement in Arab-Israeli peacemaking varied considerably over time, so too have the methods and tools used (such as presidential summits, backchannel talks, shuttle diplomacy, public outreach, and rewards and threats).

So how successful has the United States been over the years? Entire books have been written addressing this question, but the short answer is: not very successful. By far its greatest achievement has been the peace treaty between Egypt and Israel, which has withstood the test of time and many challenges. The United

States (specifically, President George H. W. Bush and his Secretary of State James Baker) can also claim credit for the historic Madrid Conference of 1991, which brought Israel and numerous Arab states to the negotiating table for the first time and launched official Israeli-Syrian, Israeli-Jordanian, and Israeli-Palestinian peace talks. But only Israel and Jordan went on to sign a peace agreement (in 1994), which the United States had little to do with because they did not really need American assistance to make peace. As archenemies, Israel and Syria did need the United States to broker a peace agreement between them—which both wanted—but the Clinton administration's repeated efforts to do so in the 1990s ended in failure and recriminations.

The United States has also, obviously, failed to make peace between Israel and the Palestinians, despite many years of trying. It has not even been able to engineer any major breakthrough in Israeli-Palestinian peacemaking. The Oslo Accords, the only breakthrough to have occurred, came about without any initial American involvement (Norway hosted and mediated the backchannel talks that led to the Oslo Accords). For all the effort and money the United States subsequently devoted to the Oslo peace process, its biggest achievement—if it can be considered an achievement at all—has been keeping the peace process going and restarting it when it has stalled. For better or worse, the peace process between Israel and the Palestinians would probably have died long ago were it not for the United States' determination to keep it alive, albeit occasionally on life support. The United States has also kept the PA—a product of the Oslo Accords—afloat by providing it with billions of dollars of aid (since the PA was established in 1994, it has received about $5.2 billion from the U.S. government). In recent years, the United States has also helped the PA restore order in the West Bank and crack down on violence against Israel by funding, training, and equipping its security forces.

The United States sustained the Oslo peace process but also contributed to its collapse by failing to enforce the commitments that Israel and the PLO had made or to punish them when they behaved in ways that undermined the peace process. If the Clinton administration had done more to hold Israel and the PLO accountable for their actions and inactions, the Oslo peace process would at least have had a greater chance of success. Similarly, if the Clinton administration had prepared better for the pivotal Camp David summit in July 2000, and if President Clinton had mediated the talks more effectively—for instance, by pressuring Barak as well as Arafat, and by getting the leaders of Egypt, Jordan, and Saudi Arabia to encourage Arafat to make certain concessions—the summit may well have had a different outcome. The negative repercussions of the summit's failure, which contributed to the outbreak of the Second Intifada, could also have been lessened had Clinton emphasized the progress that was made and not publicly blamed Arafat for its failure (thereby helping to convince Israelis they had "no partner" for peace).

Nevertheless, President Clinton should not be held responsible for Barak and Arafat's inability to negotiate a peace agreement (Clinton also deserves credit for presenting his "parameters" for a peace agreement during his last month in office, which have since helped to advance negotiations). Nor should the United States in general be blamed for the continuation of the Israeli-Palestinian conflict. This exaggerates American influence over the course of events and minimizes the responsibility of Israelis and Palestinians. But as the custodian of the peace process and the patron of both Israel and the PA, the United States could do more to bring about a peaceful settlement of the conflict. For example, some suggest that the United States should be more "even-handed" in mediating between Israel and the Palestinians. According to this view, the United States has not been the "honest broker" it claims to be. Rather, it has acted as "Israel's lawyer," in the words of Aaron David Miller, a former senior State Department official who participated in the peace process and helped formulate U.S. policy. Palestinians and their supporters frequently complain about what they see as U.S. bias toward Israel (for instance, by shielding it from international criticism and pressure, particularly at the UN). They want the United States to not simply be neutral when trying to broker a peace agreement but to actually favor the Palestinians by applying pressure on Israel to offset the massive power imbalance between the two sides. Others have advocated that, instead of acting as a mediator by trying to get Israel and the Palestinians to voluntarily negotiate the terms of a peace agreement, the United States should be more of an arbitrator by putting forward its own peace plan and pressuring both sides to accept it.

Whatever the merits of these suggestions, the Trump administration is unlikely to follow them. In fact, so far it has taken the opposite approach, unequivocally and uncritically backing Israel, especially Prime Minister Netanyahu, and vociferously criticizing the Palestinians, particularly President Abbas. The Trump administration has also relocated the U.S. embassy from Tel Aviv to Jerusalem, closed the PLO's office in Washington, slashed U.S. aid to the PA, stopped funding Israeli-Palestinian coexistence programs involving Palestinians in the West Bank and Gaza, and canceled the sizable U.S. financial contribution to UNRWA (the UN agency that takes care of Palestinian refugees). It is too soon to tell whether this hardline approach toward the Palestinians—which President Trump summed up as, "If we don't make a deal, we're not paying [the Palestinians]"—will succeed in forcing them to accept the "deal of the century" that Trump hopes to achieve to resolve the Israeli-Palestinian conflict, but as yet it has only resulted in Palestinian defiance and Arab disapproval. Given this negative reaction, it is unlikely to work (if the Trump administration's long-awaited and still secret peace plan is even released).

5

THE OCCUPIED TERRITORIES

Why are the West Bank and Gaza Strip considered "occupied territories"?

The Israeli-Palestinian conflict has always been fought with words as well as weapons. The public rhetoric of both sides, and their respective supporters, has been deliberately formulated to discredit the other side's claims, delegitimize their actions, and even to deny their very existence. In this long-running war of words, language has become highly politicized. Specific words, phrases, or terminology are politically loaded, carrying certain connotations or associations that can subtly influence people's opinions about the conflict and their perceptions of the actors involved. A clear example of this is the use of the term "occupation" in characterizing Israel's control over the West Bank, East Jerusalem, and, to a lesser extent, the Gaza Strip. It is common to hear Palestinians, left-wing Israelis, and pro-Palestinian activists refer to the "Israeli occupation" or simply to "the occupation," whereas Israeli governments and most Israeli Jews object to the term "occupation" because of its negative connotations (it implies, for instance, that the West Bank belongs to someone else—the Palestinians—and that Israel has no right to be there). Indeed, in May 2003, Israel's then prime minister, Ariel Sharon, shocked many Israelis, and outraged those on the right, when he told a group of Likud Party supporters "I think the idea that it is possible to continue keeping 3.5 million Palestinians under occupation—yes, it is occupation, you might not like the word, but what is happening is occupation—is bad for Israel, and bad for the Palestinians." Israel's current prime minister, Benjamin Netanyahu, by contrast, publicly declared in November 2018 that "the 'occupation' is nonsense."

Referring to the West Bank and Gaza Strip as "occupied territories" is also controversial in Israel and in some circles elsewhere, particularly in the United States. While the term "occupied territories" has taken on a political meaning for many people—casting Israel as the overlord and oppressor of Palestinians—international organizations like the United Nations (UN) and the European Union (EU), along with the international community in general, use this term because of its widely accepted legal meaning. In international law, a territory is defined as occupied when it is under the effective control of a state that is not recognized as having sovereignty over that territory (the legal definition of what is officially termed "belligerent occupation" is codified in the Hague Convention of 1907 and the Fourth Geneva Convention of 1949). A territory becomes occupied when it falls under the control of a foreign army, typically when that army invades the territory and conquers it during a war. Whenever a state forcibly takes control of territory beyond its existing (de jure or de facto) borders, the international law of armed conflict defines that territory as occupied. The territory's history and prior status are irrelevant. Nor does it matter who the territory was taken from or the circumstances in which it was taken (e.g., whether the war was defensive or not). In other words, a "belligerent occupation" is simply a legal fact, not a political or moral judgment. There are numerous examples of such occupations: Indonesia's occupation of East Timor (1975–1999), Vietnam's occupation of Cambodia (1977–1989), Turkey's occupation of Northern Cyprus (1974–present), Morocco's occupation of Western Sahara (1975–present), and, most recently, Russia's occupation of Crimea (2014–present), to name just a few.

The West Bank and Gaza Strip, therefore, are regarded as occupied territories under international law because they were not part of Israel before the June 1967 war, when the Israeli army conquered them. Israel took the West Bank from Jordan and the Gaza Strip from Egypt; it also captured the Golan Heights from Syria, which it still occupies, and Egypt's Sinai Peninsula, which it later returned after making peace with Egypt. While it is true that Israel did not go to war in 1967 to conquer these territories, that Israelis believe the war was forced upon them, and that the West Bank (Judea and Samaria) is of great historical and religious importance to Jews, these factors are irrelevant in terms of international law. Nor does it matter whether or not Israel's military occupation is "benevolent," as many Israelis once believed it to be (until the First Intifada disabused them of this reassuring belief). All that matters legally is that Israel conquered the West Bank and Gaza Strip and that territorial conquest is forbidden by international law (this was not the case before the twentieth century).

The Israeli government has consistently opposed the designation of the West Bank and Gaza Strip as "occupied territories." Instead it prefers to officially call them "disputed territories" or "administered territories." Israeli officials and legal experts have argued that Israel's control over those territories is not an occupation in the legal sense because that only applies when a state conquers and occupies another state's territory. The Gaza Strip was not Egyptian territory when Israel conquered it (Egypt captured it in the Arab-Israeli war of 1948 but never annexed it), nor was the West Bank legally Jordanian territory (Jordan annexed the West Bank after taking it in the 1948 war, but the international community did not ratify this annexation). Hence, Israel argues that since no state had recognized sovereignty over the West Bank and Gaza prior to Israel's conquest of them in 1967, these territories cannot legally be defined as occupied, and international conventions relating to belligerent occupations do not apply to them. However, the International Court of Justice (the principal judicial organ of the UN) and most experts on international law have rejected this legal argument on the grounds that nonsovereign territory can still be occupied. Moreover, Israel's own High Court of Justice has effectively treated the West Bank and Gaza Strip as occupied territories, and the Israeli government itself has even argued in cases before the High Court of Justice that its authority in those territories is based on the international law of belligerent occupation.

Since Israel withdrew from the Gaza Strip in 2005, Israeli governments have also argued that, even if Israel occupied Gaza before then, it no longer does because it completely removed all its soldiers and settlers. Israel claims that the Gaza Strip is not under its control anymore—it has been ruled by Hamas since 2007—so it insists that it is not occupied territory. This argument has also been rejected by the UN and by many, if not most, international legal experts because Israel is still seen as exercising "effective control" over Gaza since it controls Gaza's airspace, territorial waters, five of six land crossings, and population registry.

It might seem that this is all merely a debate over semantics and technicalities. What does it matter, you may wonder, what wording one uses to characterize the West Bank and Gaza Strip? In fact, it matters a lot, because if these territories are designated as occupied, then Israel, as the occupier, must abide by the international laws of war that govern military occupations (these are largely aimed at protecting the population of the territory under occupation). In particular, Israel has to comply with the terms of the Fourth Geneva Convention that were adopted in 1949 in the aftermath of World War II (when civilians, especially Jews, living in territories under German occupation suffered enormously). The Fourth Geneva Convention includes regulations that prohibit forcible deportations, detention without trial, and destruction of civilian property. While Israel rejects the legal applicability of the Fourth Geneva Convention to the West Bank and Gaza, it has always claimed that it complies with it in practice in its treatment of Palestinians. Such a claim is easy to challenge given the Israel Defense Forces' (IDF) well-documented history of using deportations, administrative detention, and home demolitions. Israeli settlement-building is the most glaring violation of the Fourth Geneva Convention since it clearly prohibits an occupying state from moving its own civilians into the territory it occupies. The Israeli Foreign Ministry's own legal adviser, Theodor Meron, acknowledged this in a secret memo written shortly after the 1967 war for then Israeli prime minister Levi Eshkol, which stated: "Civilian settlement in the administered territories contravenes explicit provisions of the Fourth Geneva Convention." By officially sanctioning and subsidizing the growth of Israeli settlements, the Israeli government is, indisputably, breaking international law, regardless of its denials.

More debatable is the question of whether Israel's continued occupation of those territories is itself illegal under international law. Military occupations are not, in and of themselves, illegal, as long as they are temporary and dictated by "military necessity." Although Israel has legitimate security concerns about withdrawing from the West Bank, its military occupation there has lasted for more than half a century, the longest of any modern occupation. Understandably, Palestinians and many international observers have come to view the Israeli occupation as permanent. Indeed, with no peace process underway, and hopes for a two-state solution fading, the belief that Israel's occupation of the West Bank is only temporary—and hence technically legal—is becoming increasingly untenable.

What restrictions does Israeli military rule place upon Palestinians in the West Bank?

While the West Bank, East Jerusalem, and Gaza Strip are all under Israeli occupation according to international law (so is Syria's Golan Heights), the Israeli government treats these areas, and their Palestinian inhabitants, differently (the Israeli public also views them differently). East Jerusalem is, or at least was, part of the West Bank, but soon after the 1967 war it was effectively annexed by Israel (it was formally annexed in 1980). Since then the Israeli government and Supreme Court have treated East Jerusalem as part of Israel's sovereign territory. The international community has not recognized Israel's annexation of East Jerusalem and for the most part continues to regard it as occupied territory—which is one reason why President Donald Trump's recognition in December 2017 of Jerusalem as Israel's capital, without any mention of East Jerusalem, was met with widespread criticism around the world. The roughly 370,000 Palestinians who currently reside in East Jerusalem—more than a third of the city's total population—are legally defined in Israel as "permanent residents" (not citizens, but they can become eligible to apply for citizenship). This means that Palestinian residents of East Jerusalem live under Israeli laws. They can vote in municipal, but not national, elections—though in practice very few do because of a longstanding boycott—and they are entitled to receive Israeli welfare benefits, to get treated in Israeli hospitals, to attend Israeli universities, and to work and travel inside Israel. In all these respects, their situation is better than that of Palestinians living in the rest of the West Bank and in Gaza (albeit worse than that of Jews living in Jerusalem).

Unlike East Jerusalem, Israel has not annexed the rest of the West Bank or the Gaza Strip (although the Likud Party, and many right-wing Israeli Jews, want Israel to annex more of the West Bank). For many years, their Palestinian inhabitants lived under strict Israeli military rule. Both territories were completely under the Israeli military's direct control, and the Civil Administration, a branch of the Israeli military, managed the day-to-day affairs of Palestinian residents. After Israel unilaterally withdrew from the Gaza Strip in 2005 (at the end of the Second Intifada), the circumstances of West Bank Palestinians and Gazans significantly diverged, especially after Hamas violently seized control of Gaza in 2007. Since then, the Israeli government has treated Gaza as an "enemy entity." It has imposed a land, sea, and air blockade that severely restricts imports and exports and prevents almost all Palestinians from leaving and entering the territory except in extremely rare cases. Rather than controlling the territory from the inside, the Israeli military now tries to control it from the outside (although it has twice invaded Gaza during its wars with Hamas in 2009 and 2014, and it regularly carries out incursions and airstrikes). Inside the Gaza Strip, Hamas is fully in control on the ground, and the territory is exclusively governed by Hamas rather than the Israeli military—which is why Israel insists that Gaza is no longer occupied territory, and most Israelis share this view.

Since 2005, it is only Palestinians in the West Bank who remain under Israeli military rule. For the three million or so who live there, Israeli military occupation is a fact of everyday life, affecting nearly every aspect of their lives, and coping with the myriad restrictions imposed by the occupation is a constant struggle. But while all Palestinian inhabitants of the West Bank live under Israel's overarching military occupation, as they have done for more than half a century now, their circumstances also differ depending on where they reside. For the first quarter of a century of military rule, the IDF, through the Civil Administration, governed all of the West Bank and its Palestinian residents, which meant that the Israeli military managed and monitored every aspect of Palestinian civilian life. This changed after Israel and the Palestine Liberation Organization (PLO) signed the Oslo Accords, which, as part of the Oslo peace process, created a Palestinian Authority (PA) to manage and control certain areas of the West Bank (and Gaza) after the Israeli military withdrew from them. The PA was granted limited powers and autonomy—it is not a Palestinian government, let alone a state—but it allowed Palestinians to exercise partial self-rule until a comprehensive peace agreement could be reached. The creation of the PA also allowed Israel to subcontract some of the burdensome tasks that the IDF was hitherto solely responsible for, such as providing social services to Palestinians and, in some areas, policing and security. The PA was put in charge of civil affairs and security in all the Palestinian cities and large towns of the West Bank, where most Palestinians live (this was designated Area A, now covering approximately 18 percent of the West Bank). In some other places (Area B, now encompassing 22 percent of the territory), the PA was given responsibility for civil affairs, while Israel retained control over security. The rest of the West Bank (Area C, currently 60 percent) stayed under full Israeli military control.

Since the vast majority of Palestinians live in the cities and towns where the PA has full or partial jurisdiction (Areas A and B), as far as the Israeli government is concerned (and most Israelis), the PA is solely responsible for the lives of most Palestinians in the West Bank. In reality, however, whatever the PA does depends to a large extent on the consent, even if tacit, of the Israeli military and, by extension, the Israeli government. More to the point, wherever they live in the West Bank, Palestinians still face numerous restrictions because of Israel's ongoing military occupation. They are also frequently subjected to humiliating treatment and human rights abuses by Israeli soldiers, which have been painstakingly documented by Israeli human rights groups like B'Tselem and Breaking the Silence, the latter run by former Israeli soldiers who served in the West Bank and witnessed Palestinians, including children, being beaten and humiliated by their fellow soldiers. Rather than try to catalogue all the Israeli military practices, regulations, and laws that restrict Palestinians in the West Bank, for the sake of brevity, I will focus on three interlocking systems used by the Israeli military to maintain control in the West Bank and protect Israelis, especially settlers. Though they are certainly not the only means the IDF uses, these three "systems of control" affect the lives of Palestinians across the territory, seriously restricting where they can go and what they can do. They are: (1) the checkpoint system, (2) the permit system, and (3) the legal system.

The checkpoint system

The first thing that any visitor to the West Bank immediately notices is an Israeli military checkpoint, manned by heavily armed

Israeli guards. It is mandatory to pass through these checkpoints to enter or exit the West Bank, but Israelis and foreigners are generally waved through and rarely stopped or searched, whereas Palestinian residents of the West Bank are almost always stopped, often searched, frequently kept waiting, and sometimes detained. Entering and leaving the West Bank is difficult for the Palestinians who live there, as Israel controls all the crossing points between the West Bank and Israel and between the West Bank and Jordan. For Palestinians in the West Bank, to enter Israel for whatever reason—to travel abroad, to visit friends and relatives in East Jerusalem, to pray at the Al-Aqsa Mosque, to receive treatment at an Israeli hospital, or to commute to work in Israel—they must cross these checkpoints and come into contact with Israeli soldiers. For the roughly 70,000 or so Palestinians who legally work in Israel (most in the construction industry), this often turns what would otherwise be a quick commute into a lengthy, laborious, and frustrating journey, as they can be stuck waiting in long lines for hours, sometimes standing under a hot sun or in the pouring rain, until they can go through the narrow concrete corridors, metal turnstiles, and electric gates of the major checkpoints standing between Israel and the West Bank.

Palestinians in the West Bank have to cross Israeli military checkpoints not only to enter Israel or East Jerusalem but also when traveling within the West Bank. Going from one Palestinian city or town to another necessitates traveling along roads that are under Israeli military control (Israel controls all the roads leading to Areas A and B). As of January 2017, there were approximately a hundred permanent military checkpoints and hundreds more temporary ones dotted along these roads throughout the West Bank. In addition to all this, the IDF has placed hundreds of physical obstacles along West Bank roads, including dirt mounds, concrete blocks, and gates installed at the entrances to some Palestinian villages.

Many of the checkpoints and roadblocks inside the West Bank were put there by the IDF during the Second Intifada (2000–2005), when it was engaged in "low-intensity warfare" with various Palestinian militant groups who frequently carried out terrorist attacks against Israeli civilians, including dozens of suicide bombings. To this day, the Israeli government claims that all the military checkpoints and roadblocks in the West Bank are there solely because they help keep Israelis safe from potential Palestinian violence. Whether one accepts this claim or not, the restrictions they place on Palestinian freedom of movement inside the West Bank are undeniable. Whatever security benefits Israelis derive from the IDF's elaborate system of checkpoints in the West Bank, Palestinians who live there suffer the consequences. Military checkpoints not only disrupt the daily lives of Palestinians, making travel within the West Bank and between it and anywhere else much more time-consuming and costlier (according to several studies by the World Bank, the Israeli military's restrictions on Palestinian movement within the West Bank significantly impede economic growth there). They also undermine the predictability of daily life for Palestinians since they never know how long it will take to get anywhere or, for that matter, whether they will even be able to get there. This uncertainty complicates their everyday lives, making it harder to carry out mundane tasks, since there is always the possibility of being delayed at a checkpoint, denied passage, or even detained. The fact that any of this can happen for no apparent reason makes it all the more difficult. It is not uncommon for Israeli soldiers at checkpoints to refuse to allow Palestinian civilians to pass through or to delay them without any explanation.

The permit system

If checkpoints are the most visible markers of Israeli military rule in the West Bank, then permits are the most pervasive. The checkpoint system and the permit system reinforce each other, since Palestinians need specific permits to cross certain checkpoints. If they want to enter Israel for any purpose, for instance, Palestinians in the West Bank (and in Gaza) must obtain a permit, even if they are just passing through on their way to the airport. This never used to be the case. For the first twenty-five years of the Israeli occupation, Palestinians in the West Bank and Gaza Strip could freely enter Israel, travel around, and easily move between both territories. Beginning in the early 1990s, however, in response to Palestinian attacks against Israelis, Israel began closing its borders to Palestinians from the West Bank and Gaza, sometimes sealing them off. Nowadays, only Palestinian residents of the West Bank with travel or work permits are generally allowed to enter Israel (those living in Gaza are almost completely banned from entering). Palestinians also need permits to drive on certain roads in the West Bank, as they are restricted or pro-hibited from traveling on some major roads or sections of roads to keep them far away from Israeli settlements (Israelis can travel freely on these roads). Some Palestinian farmers must even have permits to access their own land if it lies on the other side of the barrier that Israel has built in the West Bank. All told, there are more than a hundred different kinds of permits issued to West Bank Palestinians by the Israeli military's Civil Administration. Obtaining these permits can be a bureaucratic nightmare for Palestinians. It can take time, money, and a lot of patience. Applications are often denied with no explanation given and no recourse to appeal. In fact, the difficulty of receiving permits and keeping them—since they can always be rescinded—has enabled Israel's internal security service (the Shin Bet) to recruit Palestinian informers and collaborators because it has the power to approve or deny permits.

Palestinians who live in Area C, the majority of the West Bank under exclusive Israeli control, must apply to the Civil Administration for a permit to carry out any kind of construction, no matter how minor, even on privately owned land. These applications are almost always rejected. Since it is so difficult, if not impossible, for Palestinians in Area C to obtain building permits, many do not bother applying for one and build without a permit. This can result in Palestinian homes and other buildings being demolished, sometimes repeatedly, by the IDF because they lacked building permits. With construction in Area C subject to Israeli military approval, Palestinians in the West Bank are effectively restricted from building anything—whether for private or public use—on most of the West Bank's land.

The legal system

Perhaps the most obvious way in which Israeli military rule restricts Palestinians in the West Bank is through the military court system that Israel has operated there since 1967. Over the years, hundreds of thousands of Palestinians in the West Bank, including many children, have been brought before Israeli military courts. To this day, thousands of them are tried in Israeli military courts every year by Israeli military officers in uniform serving as judges and prosecutors, enforcing laws or regulations that were all written by Israeli military officers for the express purpose of controlling the Palestinian population. All Palestinians in the West Bank, wherever they live, are subject to Israeli military law and can be brought before a military court, whether their alleged offenses were committed in the West Bank or not. They can be tried on a wide range of charges, ranging from the most serious (security-related offenses such as planning or carrying out terrorist attacks against Israelis), to regular criminal offenses, to the most trivial (such as traffic violations). Most of those tried in military courts, in fact, are not charged with "security offenses." Palestinians in the West Bank can even be prosecuted in military courts for organizing, or just attending, a peaceful political protest if it is not authorized in advance by the IDF.

A Palestinian brought before an Israeli military court faces almost certain conviction. The threshold for convictions in military courts is lower than it is in Israeli civilian courts, and the sentences are harsher. The vast majority of cases never even go to trial because the military courts keep most defendants in detention—long after they have been interrogated and charged—until their legal proceedings are finished. Rather than sit in prison waiting for a trial that will probably end in their conviction, most Palestinian defendants prefer to take plea bargains, whether they are guilty or not. This practice effectively undermines their right to a fair trial, since it means that what really matters is what happens in the interrogation room rather than in the courtroom. Another common practice within the military legal system, particularly in cases of alleged security offenses, is denying Palestinian detainees access to a defense lawyer for at least thirty days, and up to ninety days, from the day of their arrest, unless they make a confession. This helps interrogators gain information and extract confessions, but it also infringes upon the "due process rights" of Palestinian detainees. The most severe violation of Palestinian detainees' right to due process is the frequent use of what is known as "administrative detention," which means that Palestinians can be imprisoned without charge or trial for a period of up to six months, and this can be renewed indefinitely. Hundreds of Palestinians are held in administrative detention every year, and not only those accused of security offenses.

Finally, it is worth noting that, unlike Palestinians, Israelis living in the West Bank ("settlers") are under Israeli law, not military law, and they are tried in civilian courts in Israel rather than military courts in the West Bank (although the military court system officially has jurisdiction over them). The fact that Israelis and Palestinians in the West Bank live under two different legal systems, with the former having more legal rights than the latter, creates a situation in which they are not equal before the law. Simply put, a Palestinian resident of the West Bank is more likely than an Israeli settler to be convicted and receive a harsher sentence for exactly the same crime. However one might try to explain or justify it, this is legal discrimination.

Why has Israel built a long barrier in the West Bank?

The barrier between Israel and the West Bank that the Israeli government has been building since 2003 has many different names. Israelis call it the "security fence" or the "separation barrier." Palestinians, by contrast, call it the "annexation wall" or the "apartheid wall." These different names underscore the contrasting perspectives that Israelis and Palestinians have toward it, as each believes that it serves fundamentally different purposes. For most Israelis, it is a necessary means of protection, aimed at saving the lives of Israeli civilians by stopping Palestinian terrorists from infiltrating into Israel. For Palestinians, it is a symbol of the Israeli occupation and another tool for Israel's territorial expansion, designed to take their land and displace Palestinians.

Before giving the reasons for these conflicting perceptions of the West Bank barrier, it is first essential to explain what the barrier really is. Is it a fence or a wall? In fact, it is both, and more. The most common images of the barrier that appear in the media are pictures of a towering, grey concrete wall (sometimes covered with murals and graffiti), but most of it is not actually a wall. A concrete wall 8 meters high (26 feet), punctuated by watchtowers, constitutes no more than 10 percent of the existing barrier, primarily in urban areas and along major highways used by Israeli drivers. The rest of the barrier, running through rural areas, consists of a chainlink fence 2 meters high (6.5 feet), equipped with electronic sensors that alert the Israeli army to any intrusion or movement along the fence. This high-tech fence is flanked on one side by a trench and stacks of barbed wire, and on the other side by a smooth dirt road (to track the footprints of intruders), a military patrol road, and another barbed-wire fence. Projected to run a total length of roughly 700 kilometers (435 miles) upon completion—about two-thirds of the barrier has been completed to date—each kilometer of the barrier has cost around $2 million to build, and the total cost of its construction so far exceeds $2.6 billion, making it the biggest infrastructure project in Israel's history.

Why, then, did the Israeli government undertake such an expensive and controversial project? Although Israel built an electrified fence around the Gaza Strip in 1994, and official consideration had been given to building one between Israel and the West Bank as well, it was not until the Second Intifada that the idea of a West Bank barrier became popular with the Israeli public, and it was politically impossible for the Israeli government at the time to resist. Whereas the First Intifada was a largely nonviolent mass uprising, in which Palestinian women and children were heavily involved, the Second Intifada began in September 2000 with mass demonstrations, but it quickly escalated into a low-intensity war of attrition between Israeli security forces and an assortment of armed Palestinian groups. The weapon of choice for these groups was the suicide bomber—an individual strapped with explosives, or carrying them, who operated as a kind of "smart bomb" targeting crowds of people and detonating the explosives when they could inflict maximum casualties. Palestinian suicide bombings had taken place in Israel in the 1990s, but they dramatically increased during the Second Intifada with devastating effects. Buses, shopping malls, supermarkets, outdoor markets, cafes, restaurants, bars, and nightclubs in Israeli cities were all targeted, making it seem to Israelis as if no urban public space was safe. More Israelis were killed by suicide bombings during the Second Intifada than by any other violent tactic (such as rocket attacks and sniper fire) used by Palestinian militant groups, and most of these suicide bombings were launched from the West Bank. From September 2000 to August 2005, there were 151 Palestinian suicide bombings, killing 515 people and injuring almost 3,500 (the total death toll during the five years of the Second Intifada was about 1,000 Israelis and 3,300 Palestinians—the majority of those killed on both sides were civilians). The bloodiest year of the Second Intifada was 2002. There were fifty-three Palestinian suicide bombings that year, most during the first half of the year. In March 2002, they were happening on a weekly and almost daily basis. The worst of these attacks occurred in a hotel dining room on the evening of March 27, when Abdel-Basset Odeh, a young Palestinian man from a nearby West Bank town, blew himself up during a Passover meal, killing thirty people (mostly elderly Israelis). It became known as the "Passover massacre," and it was the deadliest terrorist attack against Israelis during the Second Intifada (Hamas claimed responsibility for it).

This was the context in which the Israeli government, then led by the Likud Party and headed by Prime Minister Ariel Sharon, decided in April 2002 to build the West Bank barrier (it also launched "Operation Defensive Shield," in which the IDF, using tanks and heavy weaponry, reoccupied the West Bank's major cities, from which it had withdrawn during the Oslo peace process). Prime Minister Sharon and his right-wing cabinet were initially reluctant to build the barrier because they were concerned that it could be construed as a future Israeli-Palestinian border, cutting off many Jewish settlements in the West Bank from Israel (the center-left Labor Party, then in opposition, championed the idea of a barrier, and its leader, Ehud Barak, was the first to publicly propose it). But as suicide terror attacks escalated and Israeli public support for a barrier grew, Sharon, who had previously dismissed the idea of a barrier as "populist," reluctantly bowed to mounting domestic pressure. His cabinet officially authorized the barrier in June 2002, and construction started the following year.

Since then, as the barrier went up, suicide bombings in Israel went down (from fifty-three in 2002 to zero in 2009). According to Israeli authorities, this is clear evidence that the barrier has been extremely effective. The Israeli government claims that it has prevented hundreds of terrorist attacks. Many analysts, however, argue that the steep decline in suicide bombings was due not only to the construction of the barrier but also to a combination of factors, including the IDF's military offensive in the West Bank in 2002 and closer security cooperation with the PA after the Second Intifada ended. But even if the barrier was not the only reason why suicide terror attacks declined, it undoubtedly played a part. Regardless, the simple fact that far fewer Israelis have been killed in Palestinian terrorist attacks since construction of the barrier began (the number dropped from more than 130 fatalities in 2003 to less than 25 two years later) has convinced the majority of Israelis that the barrier has saved the lives of many of their fellow citizens and is therefore necessary for their security. This consensus among Israelis has endured until the present day (with the notable exception of Israeli settlers in the West Bank, who have generally opposed the barrier's construction).

While most Israelis, understandably, perceive the West Bank barrier in terms of the added security it purportedly brings them, Palestinians, equally understandably, perceive the barrier in terms of what it takes from them—their land and, in some cases, their livelihoods. Israelis focus on their security-driven rationale for building the barrier, and they tend to pay little attention to its actual route—many are not even aware that the barrier remains unfinished—or to its impact upon Palestinians. The latter, on the other hand, even those Palestinians willing to acknowledge Israeli security concerns, emphasize the route the barrier has taken and the harm it has caused them. They point out that the barrier could have been built within Israel or along the Green Line, but instead Israeli governments chose to build it mostly inside the West Bank—the vast majority of the barrier's route, about 85 percent, runs inside the West Bank. Hence, Palestinians argue that even if Israelis' fear of terrorism was the original motivation for the barrier, its actual route was determined by Israel's territorial ambitions.

One only has to look at a map showing the barrier's long and winding route to understand why Palestinians see it as a land grab. The route is clearly drawn with Israeli settlements in mind, since some sections loop deep into the West Bank to incorporate dozens of settlements on the Israeli side of the barrier. By routing the proposed barrier around the large blocs of settlements near the Green Line, the Israeli government has laid the groundwork for their future annexation. When/if construction is completed along the entire planned route of the barrier, nearly 200 square miles of land—amounting to almost 10 percent of the West Bank—will be enclosed behind the Israeli side of the barrier and cut off from the rest of the West Bank. This large enclosed area sandwiched between the barrier and the Green Line (Israel officially refers to it as the "seam zone") contains seventy-one Israeli settlements and thirty-two Palestinian villages. Palestinians believe that Israel wants to annex at least this area— which Israeli policymakers have openly acknowledged—so they see the construction of the barrier as yet another Israeli attempt to take land that Palestinians want for their future state. Whether or not one accepts the Palestinian claim that the barrier's route has been driven by Israel's desire for territorial expansion, the Israeli government's claim that security considerations alone have dictated its route is untenable—indeed, Israel's own High Court of Justice has rejected this claim on more than one occasion. Most likely, the route of the barrier has been determined by a mix of Israel's security needs, territorial ambitions, and demographic concerns—namely, to include the largest number of Jews and the smallest number of Palestinians behind its side of the barrier.

Whatever the reasons for the barrier's existence and its circuitous route, the negative impact it has upon Palestinians is incontrovertible. Israel insists that it has tried to minimize any harm to Palestinians affected by the barrier, and the barrier's route has been modified in response to rulings by the Israeli High Court of Justice that called for it to be rerouted in order to make it less harmful to some nearby Palestinian communities (one village was bisected by the barrier, with neighbors finding themselves on opposite sides of a wall). Nevertheless, in practice the barrier has made life much more difficult for many Palestinians, particularly those who live on either side of it. Farmers, for example, need special permits from the Israeli authorities to work in their fields, with permission often limited (if it is granted at all) to certain hours of the day or certain times of year (such as the olive harvest season), making it harder, if not impossible, for them to cultivate their land or grow certain crops. Some eleven thousand Palestinians living in the villages located in the so-called seam zone are stranded on the Israeli side of the barrier, cut off from their family and friends on the other side (who need a permit just to visit them). It is not only villagers and farmers who are severely affected by the barrier. The fifty thousand or so Palestinian residents of the city of Qalqilya in the northern West Bank are surrounded on three sides by the barrier, and they can only enter and leave their city through a single IDF military checkpoint. The inhabitants of many Palestinian towns near Jerusalem have been hard-hit economically because the barrier wraps around Jerusalem (incorporating most, but not all, of East Jerusalem), cutting them off from their former customers and clients there. Palestinians in East Jerusalem who live on the Israeli side of the barrier have been effectively cut off from the West Bank. And those living in the areas of East Jerusalem located on the other side of the barrier have basically been left to fend for themselves as municipal services have largely stopped and Israeli police no longer enter these areas, turning them into squalid, crime-ridden slums. In the long run, by severing most of East Jerusalem from the West Bank, the barrier undermines the possibility that East Jerusalem could one day become the capital of a Palestinian state, frustrating the nationalist aspirations of most Palestinians.

In July 2004, following a request from the UN General Assembly, the International Court of Justice (ICJ) issued an advisory opinion (a nonbinding ruling) on the West Bank barrier's legality according to international law. Although it recognized Israel's security concerns, the ICJ declared that building the barrier within the West Bank was contrary to international law (the Israeli High Court of Justice, by contrast, has ruled that the barrier is legal even though it runs in the West Bank). The ICJ also stated that the proposed route of the barrier illegitimately confiscated land from Palestinians, and its construction imposed unnecessary hardships upon them. Finally, it called upon Israel to stop building the barrier, dismantle the sections that were already built inside the West Bank, and pay compensation to Palestinians who had been adversely affected by its construction. This was a legal and diplomatic victory for the Palestinians and a serious rebuke to Israel, but fifteen years later the barrier still stands (despite the growth of a generally nonviolent, Palestinian-led, grassroots protest movement against it). Thus, while Israel continues to insist that the West Bank barrier is only temporary, it looks increasingly permanent.

Why are there Israeli settlements in the West Bank, and why do Israelis choose to live in them?

In May 1967, not a single Israeli citizen lived in the West Bank, which was then under Jordanian control. Fifty years later, approximately 400,000 Israelis lived in more than 100 civilian communities, known as "settlements," spread all across the West Bank (and another 200,000 or so lived in a dozen Jewish "neighborhoods" in East Jerusalem). These settlements range from small clusters of trailers, which house a few families, to sprawling cities with tens of thousands of residents living in rows of prefabricated red-roofed houses with green manicured lawns or in multistory apartment blocks (for this reason, the generic term "settlement" is misleading insofar as it conveys an image of outposts consisting of a few ramshackle homes).

The skyrocketing population of Israeli settlers in the West Bank and the proliferation of Israeli settlements throughout the territory since Israel conquered it in the 1967 war—in short, Israel's colonization of the West Bank—has undoubtedly been one of the most consequential, and controversial, developments in the Israeli-Palestinian conflict over the past five decades. It has provoked Palestinian resistance, international condemnation, bitter arguments between Israelis (and even violence), and much agonizing among Jews elsewhere. Indeed, the Israeli settlement enterprise in the West Bank has probably received more attention, most of it critical, than any other aspect of Israel's behavior in its conflict with the Palestinians (which is why some people mistakenly think that the settlements themselves are the cause of the conflict).

The growth of Israeli settlements in the West Bank—numerically and geographically—has been gradual, incremental, and seemingly inexorable. They have grown under every Israeli government over the past half-century despite Palestinian opposition and consistent international criticism. In 1968, a year after Israel took control of the territory, there were only five sparsely populated settlements in the West Bank, with just 250 Israeli settlers. In 1977, a decade after the 1967 war, there were 38 Israeli settlements with 1,900 settlers. Ten years later, in 1987, the number of settlements had increased to 118 and the number of settlers reached 49,000. By 1997, the settler population had tripled to about 150,000, and by 2007, it had grown to around 280,000. In 2017, it reached a total of about 400,000 settlers and 130 official settlements (as well as nearly 100 so-called outposts, much smaller, fledgling settlements that were not unauthorized by the Israeli government, but were retroactively approved despite the fact that many of them were built on land privately owned by Palestinians).

The most common explanation for how this happened largely attributes it to the activism and willpower of a small minority of religious fundamentalists within the Israeli Jewish population. In the wake of what they saw as Israel's miraculous victory in the "Six-Day War" of 1967, they fervently embraced a hitherto marginal, messianic version of religious Zionism (chiefly expounded by Rabbi Zvi Yehuda Kook). This messianic religious Zionism sanctified the whole Land of Israel as the inalienable God-given possession of the Jewish people for all eternity, and commanded its followers to settle in Judea and Samaria (the West Bank's biblical names), not just as a means of ensuring Jewish control over them but as part of a divinely guided process of bringing about messianic redemption. Driven by ideological conviction and religious devotion, and inspired by the example of the early Zionist settlers, messianic religious Zionists did whatever they could (including civil disobedience, intimidation, and violence) to establish settlements in the West Bank, irrespective of the wishes of Israeli governments, who frequently capitulated to their single-minded resolve. In 1968, led by Rabbi Moshe Levinger, they settled in Hebron (which had a Jewish community before 1948 and is a holy city for religious Jews), and a few years later the settlement of Kiryat Arba was established just outside the city. In 1974, in response to the shock of the "Yom Kippur War" the year before, and their resulting worry that the Israeli government might try to trade the "liberated territories" for peace treaties, religious-nationalist activists formed *Gush Emunim* ("Bloc of the Faithful"), which pressured the government to promote settlement-building in the heartland of the West Bank. According to this account, there-fore, the relentless expansion of Israeli settlements in the West Bank is primarily due to the messianic zeal and political cunning of a Jewish settler movement, which has successfully lobbied, bullied, and manipulated the Israeli state to do its bidding.

There is certainly some truth to this. Messianic religious Zionists have been, and still are, the vanguard of Israel's settlement enter-prise, and the settler lobby has been a powerful political force within Israel, which Israeli leaders have both courted and been wary of challenging. But for all its guile and determination, the settler move-ment is no match for the Israeli state. This movement has never been strong enough to single-handedly force its will upon Israeli governments. Rather, it has generally worked in tandem with Israeli governments, regardless of the latter's political makeup. To be sure, the settler movement has sometimes been in conflict with Israeli governments (especially those led by center-left parties), but more often it cooperates with Israeli governments (especially with Likud-led governments) and carries out their wishes. On the few occasions when there has been a major clash between settlers and an Israeli government over the dismantling and evacuation of settlements, the latter has prevailed—most notably, in 1982 when Israeli settlements in the Sinai Desert were demolished following Israel's peace agreement with Egypt, and in 2005 when its settlements in the Gaza Strip were razed as part of Israel's unilateral "disengagement."

Israel was not simply forced to build settlements in the West Bank by a domestic social movement/political lobby. It did so because successive Israeli governments since 1967 onward chose to do so for a variety of reasons. Both of the country's major political parties, Labor and Likud, have supported settlement building in the West Bank, albeit for different purposes. It was under the Labor Party (then known as Mapai) that the first Israeli settlement, Kfar Etzion in an area south of Jerusalem, was established shortly after the end of the 1967 war (the name and site of the settlement were chosen because a Jewish community of that name had been there in the prestate era until it was overrun and destroyed during the 1947–1949 war). In the decade of Labor rule from 1967 to 1977, more than two dozen settlements were created, most of them situated along the length of the Jordan Valley in the West Bank as a first line of defense against an invading army (these became small agricultural communities with IDF soldiers working as farmers and guards). Labor's settlement policy in the West Bank was unofficially guided by a plan devised in July 1967 by Yigal Allon, a cabinet member and the head of the Ministerial Committee on Settlements. The "Allon Plan" essentially regarded settlement building as a defensive measure, calling for small settlements to be placed in strategic locations to protect against an Arab attack and only in areas sparsely inhabited by Palestinians. The plan was predicated upon the hope that most, but not all, of the West Bank would eventually be returned to Jordanian control in exchange for a peace agreement.

While Labor started building settlements in the West Bank (and in the Gaza Strip, the Sinai, and the Golan Heights), it was only when the Likud Party came to power in 1977 that settlement construction significantly accelerated, settlements expanded (becoming towns in some places), and the number of settlers rapidly increased. In contrast to the limited settlement activity under the Labor government, which was designed with a future territorial compromise with Jordan in mind, under the Likud Party the Israeli government's settlement policy in the late 1970s and early 1980s was designed to prevent any territorial compromise. To remove "any shred of doubt regarding our intention to hold Judea and Samaria [the West Bank] forever," as an official government settlement plan openly stated in 1981, the goal was to increase the number of Jewish settlers and spread them all over the West Bank. Hence, under Prime Minister Menachem Begin (1977–1983), Israel built dozens of settlements in the heart of the West Bank, some deliberately positioned between Palestinian cities. The Begin government's intention was to ensure that the West Bank would forever remain in Israel's possession and that a Palestinian state could never be created there. The next Likud-led government, under Prime Minister Yitzhak Shamir, followed a similar settlement policy in the late 1980s and early 1990s.

The Labor Party's return to power after the 1992 election, and the beginning of the Oslo peace process in 1993, resulted in a long freeze on new settlement building (but not settlement expansion, which continued throughout the peace process and afterward). For more than twenty years (until 2017), no new Israeli settlements were established in the West Bank, in large part due to American pressure. Nevertheless, the number of Israeli settlers there has not stopped growing. In fact, according to Israel's Central Bureau of Statistics, over the past two decades the population of Israeli settlers in the West Bank has grown at a much faster rate per year than the Israeli population in general (although the annual growth rate of settlers has significantly slowed down, with much of the growth now coming from births—"natural growth"—rather than migration from Israel proper). The relentless increase in the number of Israeli settlers raises the question of why Israelis choose to live in West Bank settlements.

There are, no doubt, as many individual reasons for making this decision as there are settlers (excluding those who were born and raised in the settlements). In 2018, an estimated total of 430,000 Israeli Jews lived in the West Bank, nearly 7 percent of Israel's 6.5 million Jewish citizens (and about 15 percent of the West Bank's total population). This sizable population is more diverse than most people think. The popular stereotype of a settler is that of a Jewish zealot, driven by his or her religious and/or nationalist convictions to reclaim all of the ancient homeland that they believe was given to Jews by God, or at least to live in a place saturated with thousands of years of Jewish history and filled with holy sites (such as the Cave of the Patriarchs in Hebron, Joseph's Tomb in Nablus, and Rachel's Tomb in Bethlehem). There are certainly many settlers who have chosen to live in the West Bank because of their ideological beliefs, which typically consists of some kind of religious Zionism. Such ideological settlers—who are often referred to as "national-religious settlers"—generally live in smaller settlements that are located deep inside the West Bank. They make up a large majority of the 100,000 or so settlers living beyond Israel's West Bank barrier. But they represent only a minority, about a quarter, of settlers in general, albeit a highly visible and vocal minority.

Most Jewish settlers in the West Bank do not fit the popular stereotype, at least not any longer. They live there primarily for economic rather than ideological reasons. Some are staunchly secular (particularly those Jews from the former Soviet Union who immigrated to Israel and moved to the West Bank), while others are extremely religious (such as ultra-Orthodox Jews). But they all moved to settlements because the housing there is generally cheaper and/ or the quality of life better than inside Israel. The need for affordable housing is especially acute for ultra-Orthodox families (with an average 6.9 children per family), and there is a severe shortage of it in Israel proper. This has led a large number of them in recent years to move into exclusively ultra-Orthodox Jewish settlements in the West Bank. In fact, the fastest-growing and most densely populated settlements today are two ultra-Orthodox cities located near the Green Line, Modi'in Illit and Beitar Illit. With a combined population of about 125,000, they now account for almost 30 percent of the total settler population in the West Bank. Those economic or "quality-of-life" settlers (as they are sometimes called) who are not ultra-Orthodox generally live in large suburban-style settlements clustered in blocs close to the Green Line. This location allows the residents to quickly and easily commute to work inside Israel on roads built specifically for them (the majority of Israeli adults living in the West Bank work in Israel). For example, the settlement city of Ma'ale Adumim, home to some forty thousand people, is just a few miles east of Jerusalem, where many of its residents work.

Housing tends to be cheaper and the quality of life higher in Israeli settlements in the West Bank than in Israel itself because Israeli governments have provided settlements and settlers with a huge amount of financial support (foreign donors, Jewish charities, and Christian evangelical groups, mostly based in the United States, also provide financial support to Jewish settlements in the West Bank, but much less than that given by the Israeli government).

Proportionally, Israeli governments have spent much more per capita on West Bank settlers and settlements than they have spent on other Israelis and communities, including cities and towns, inside Israel (for example, it is estimated that settlement municipalities received nearly $900 million in additional funding from the Israeli government in the 1990s compared to funding for municipalities within the Green Line). West Bank settlers receive numerous government benefits that other Israelis do not, such as subsidized mortgages, tax breaks, special transportation, and education benefits. On average, schools in settlements receive more state funding than schools in Israel, and teachers there are generally better paid.

The Israeli government's massive investment in the settlements, and the generous benefits that government ministries provide for settlers, are aimed at encouraging Israeli Jews to move to the settlements and stay there (funding for the settlements and settlers has also been a convenient way for Israeli politicians, including cabinet ministers, to essentially buy the political support of the settler lobby, and a means for fragile Israeli coalition governments to survive when they have depended upon the support of small settler-backed political parties, such as the Jewish Home Party and its predecessors). Since the Begin government in the late 1970s and early 1980s, Israeli policymakers have understood that the West Bank settlement enterprise could not succeed if it was only populated by ideological settlers. National-religious settlers were the vanguard of the settler movement, but they were too few in number to populate all the settlements that Likud-led governments, in particular, wanted to establish (in order to preclude a Palestinian state). Hence, it became necessary to offer financial incentives to ordinary Israelis to entice them to live in the West Bank. This is why so many of them live there today. Thus, just as Israeli settlements in the West Bank would not exist were it not for the will of Israeli governments (of both the left and the right), the phenomenal growth of the Jewish settler population would not have occurred without the government's active support (not to mention the Israeli army's protection).

Why are Israeli settlements so controversial?

Israel's settlements in the West Bank (and those in East Jerusalem) have always been controversial, but in recent years they have become the focus of intense controversy, attracting more critical attention than almost any other contemporary issue in the Israeli-Palestinian conflict. There has been a noisy and well-publicized grassroots campaign in Europe and the United States calling for a consumer boycott of goods produced in West Bank settlements (including products made in factories located in large Israeli industrial zones within the West Bank). This campaign is related to, but distinct from, the transnational BDS movement (an acronym for Boycott, Divestment and Sanctions), which calls for a total boycott of all Israeli products and institutions. But it is not only grassroots activists who have targeted Israeli settlement products. In 2015, the European Union (EU), Israel's biggest trading partner, instructed its member states to ensure that imports from Israeli settlements were clearly labeled as such, thereby enabling European consumers to distinguish between goods produced inside Israel and those made in its settlements. In 2017, the EU went even further, imposing customs duties specifically on Israeli settlement products (a 1992 free trade agreement between Israel and the EU means that products made in Israel are exported tariff-free to Europe). In the United States, by contrast, there has recently been a raft of bills introduced in statehouses across the country that seek to ban and penalize any kind of boycott of Israel, including settlement products. These bills have stirred up the controversy over Israeli settlements and elicited strong opposition, including from civil liberties groups who see them as violating Americans' First Amendment rights (i.e., freedom of speech). And on many American college campuses, Israeli settlements have been the subject of heated arguments between pro-Palestinian and pro-Israel students when their student governments vote on resolutions demanding that their universities divest from multinational corporations like Caterpillar, Hewlett-Packard, and Motorola who are accused of profiting from Israel's occupation of the West Bank.

Israeli settlements are a contentious issue even among Israelis. Some left-wing Israelis refuse to visit West Bank settlements or buy goods produced in them, and a few risk being sued (due to a law passed by the Knesset in 2017) by publicly advocating for such boycotts. The Israeli public in general has long been divided between supporters and opponents of Israel's settlement enterprise in the West Bank. In opinion polls conducted in 2017, for instance, Israelis were equally split between those who thought the Israeli government's policy of building settlements in the West Bank was "wise in terms of Israel's national interest" and those who thought it was unwise (46 percent on each side). They were also quite divided over whether Israel should expand settlement construction in the West Bank (40 percent favored this, but 55 percent were opposed). Similarly, when asked in surveys whether most West Bank settlements should be dismantled as part of a peace agreement with the Palestinians, roughly half of Israelis support this and the other half oppose it (the numbers fluctuate slightly in response to changing developments).

There are numerous reasons why Israeli settlements are so controversial, and some of them probably have little to do with the settlements themselves. Moreover, the settlements may be controversial for different reasons in different places. Israeli criticisms of the settlements and settlers, for example, often differ from those of Europeans and Americans. Israelis, understandably, tend to be more concerned about the costs they incur in building and protecting settlements, and they worry about the threat that extremist settlers pose to the IDF and even to Israeli democracy. In general, the international community's critique of Israeli settlements typically consists of three core charges: (1) settlements are illegal under international law, (2) settlements are harmful to Palestinians, and (3) settlements are "obstacles to peace" between Israel and the Palestinians. To be sure, many other criticisms and accusations have been leveled against Israeli settlements over the years, but these are by far the most common complaints. Each one is worth examining in more detail because they are at the center of the long-running international controversy over the settlements.

The charge that Israeli settlements violate international law is widely accepted in the international community. The UN, the ICJ, almost every state in the world, and the vast majority of legal experts all consider Israeli settlements to be illegal and, in fact, a war crime according to the Fourth Geneva Convention (specifically article 49, paragraph 6). The Israeli government and a small number of legal experts dispute this, arguing that the Geneva Convention is not applicable to the West Bank because Israel is not an occupying power there (since the territory had no legitimate prior sovereign) and that, even if the Geneva Convention does apply, it only prohibits forcible population transfers (like the mass deportations carried out by Nazi

Germany), not people voluntarily moving to occupied territories (like Israeli settlers).

While debate over the legality of Israeli settlements still continues to some extent (despite the legal consensus that exists), it is not nearly the greatest source of controversy surrounding Israeli settlements. If it were, then Israel's settlements on the Golan Heights would also be a focus of international activism and public criticism (Israel conquered the strategic plateau from Syria in the 1967 war, and officially annexed it in 1981, but the UN and most of the world still considers it to be occupied territory and the Israeli settlements that are there to be illegal, just like those in the West Bank). They receive hardly any popular or diplomatic attention, however, let alone the kind of uproar that erupts whenever Israel announces plans to build more housing in West Bank settlements. The main reason for this inconsistency is the fact that Israel's settlement enterprise in the West Bank dwarfs its settlement enterprise on the Golan Heights, where only 20,000 to 25,000 Israeli settlers live in thirty-four, mostly small, agricultural settlements (the fact that Syria has been engulfed in war since 2011 is another reason why Israel's occupation of the Golan and its settlements there haven't received much attention in recent years). The sheer scale of Israel's settlement enterprise in the West Bank—specifically, the size and spread of its settlements and the number of settlers—accounts for the controversy they generate, not just their illegal status under international law.

What really troubles most critics of Israel's West Bank settlements are their practical consequences for Palestinians, for the Israeli-Palestinian peace process, and for the prospects of peace. Critics contend that Israeli settlement building seriously harms Palestinians in the West Bank. Most obviously this is because settlements have often been built on land expropriated from Palestinians, in some cases taken from private Palestinian landowners. But the harmful impact of settlements on Palestinians goes well beyond the land taken for building them (and the much larger amount of land—more than 40 percent of the West Bank—exclusively reserved for their future expansion). Additional West Bank land has been taken to build an extensive network of bypass roads connecting settlements to Israel and to each other, which are generally off-limits to Palestinian drivers. Not only do settlements dispossess and displace Palestinians, according to their critics, they also make daily life more difficult for them. It is claimed, for example, that the IDF checkpoints dotted all over the West Bank that restrict Palestinians' freedom of movement and hamper their ability to engage in commerce are there primarily to protect settlers (the Israeli government and its supporters counter this claim by arguing that the checkpoints are there because of the threat of Palestinian terrorist attacks). Whether or not this is true, the IDF certainly does protect settlers from Palestinians, but it does little or nothing to protect Palestinians from settlers. Although they constitute only a small minority of settlers, extremist settlers living in the heart of the West Bank frequently employ violence and intimidation against neighboring Palestinians, sometimes under the watchful eye of Israeli soldiers (who, for one reason or another, are generally reluctant to stop them). There are countless reports of these extremist settlers, many of them armed, violently attacking Palestinians, burning their fields, and uprooting their olive trees. Some of the most extremist settlers, including members of the "hilltop youth"—young, radical settlers who were born and raised in settlements and then set up their own unauthorized "outposts"—deliberately target Palestinians as part of a strategy called "Price Tag," which is aimed at deterring the Israeli government from acting against settlements and outposts ("Price Tag" acts can range from spraying graffiti and other acts of vandalism to physically assaulting Palestinians and firebombing their homes).

The harassment and violence that ordinary Palestinians are regularly subjected to by extremist settlers is just a dramatic example of the way in which the settlements and settlers can harm Palestinians in the West Bank, especially when they live nearby. Critics of the settlements blame them for a litany of violations of Palestinian human rights. A damning report on the settlements, submitted to the UN Human Rights Council in 2013, concluded:

> The existence of the settlements has had a heavy toll on the rights of the Palestinians. Their rights to freedom of self-determination, non-discrimination, freedom of movement, equality, due process, fair trial, not to be arbitrarily detained, liberty and security of person, freedom of expression, freedom of access to places of worship, education, water, housing, adequate standard of living, property, access to natural resources and effective remedy are being violated consistently and on a daily basis.

The Israeli government and most Israelis dismiss such allegations out of hand, especially when they come from the UN Human Rights Council, which is widely regarded in Israel as biased (because it devotes a disproportionate amount of attention to Israel's alleged misdeeds and ignores other countries that occupy and settle their citizens in the territory of others, such as China and Russia) and hypocritical (since there are often far worse violators of human rights among the Human Rights Council's own members). Supporters of Israeli settlements often go further than just disparaging their critics, arguing that Palestinians actually benefit economically from their presence (since some work on the settlements and even help build them). These supporters also insist that relations between settlers and local Palestinians are much better than the international media typically portrays them to be. They point out, for instance, that settlers and Palestinians shop together and even work together in some places, but they tend to omit the fact that settlements are guarded, and generally gated, communities, which Palestinians can only enter with official permits.

Perhaps the most widely voiced criticism of Israeli settlements, and certainly the most hotly debated, is that they are impediments to making peace between Israel and the Palestinians. Even Israel's closest ally, the U.S. government, which since the Carter administration has officially refrained from calling Israeli settlements "illegal," has repeatedly criticized them as "obstacles to peace." The Obama administration frequently and publicly criticized Israeli settlement building on these grounds, provoking domestic controversy and recurrent tensions with the Netanyahu government. Early on in his presidency, in 2009, President Barack Obama even pressured a reluctant Prime Minister Netanyahu to impose a ten-month freeze on settlement expansion in the West Bank (but not in East Jerusalem) in order to restart the peace process with the Palestinians. And in December 2017, during the waning days of his presidency—as a parting protest, if nothing else—President Obama chose not to veto a UN Security Council resolution (2334) strongly condemning Israeli settlements. Shortly after coming into office in January 2017, even President Donald Trump—whose ambassador to Israel, David Friedman, is an ardent supporter and longtime patron of West Bank settlements—said that Israeli settlement expansion "may not be helpful" to advancing peace.

A number of different, but related, arguments are made for why settlements are obstacles to Israeli-Palestinian peacemaking. The first is that Israeli settlement building undermines the peace process because Palestinians perceive it as evidence that Israel is uninterested in a two-state solution and not willing to withdraw from the West Bank. Many Palestinians also oppose their leadership engaging in peace talks with Israel while it is "stealing" more and more of their land (as they see it). Settlement building, therefore, erodes support for the peace process among Palestinians, and instead it increases popular support for violent tactics against Israel, including terrorism.

The second argument put forward is that Israeli settlement expansion makes a two-state solution more difficult, if not impossible, to achieve because it makes it harder to create a contiguous, viable Palestinian state (this was the intention behind a lot of settlement construction under Likud-led governments). Put simply, the more West Bank land that Israeli settlements take up, the less there will be for a future Palestinian state, leaving it with a truncated and fragmented territory that cannot possibly prosper.

The third argument for why settlements are an impediment to peace is that no Israeli government is likely to be willing to dismantle many settlements, let alone forcefully remove some of their residents, as any possible peace agreement is likely to require it to do. Israel would probably have to evacuate as many as 100,000 settlers who now live beyond the West Bank barrier. What makes such a mass relocation a particularly daunting and fearsome challenge for any Israeli government is the presence of extremist settlers—though relatively few in number, no more than twenty thousand—who will fiercely, and perhaps violently, resist any attempt to remove them from isolated settlements deep inside the West Bank. These settlers fervently believe that Jewish religious law prohibits abandoning any part of biblical Israel that is under Jewish sovereignty. Since Jewish law takes precedence over the Israeli government's laws and decisions (as far as they are concerned), these settlers consider a government decision to evacuate Jewish settlements and withdraw from parts of Judea and Samaria (the West Bank) to be fundamentally illegitimate and immoral. It is doubtful that a future Israeli government will ever risk having a potentially bloody showdown with these extremist settlers and possible mutiny by some national-religious IDF soldiers who refuse to comply with orders to evacuate them (a growing proportion of IDF commanders and combat soldiers are settlers or have ties to the settlements).

Needless to say, Israel insists that settlements are not an obstacle to peace (according to Prime Minister Netanyahu, the real obstacle to peace is "the ongoing Palestinian refusal to recognize Israel as the state for the Jewish people in any borders"). Refuting the popular claim that settlements are spreading across the West Bank, eating up the land for a future Palestinian state, and steadily making a two-state solution harder to achieve, Israeli officials point out that, in fact, the built-up areas of the settlements (their "footprint") occupy less than 3 percent of the West Bank. Moreover, they argue that while Palestinian officials publicly denounce settlements, in peace talks they have already agreed to the idea of a land swap that would enable Israel to keep the large settlement blocs near the Green Line, where the majority of settlers live, in exchange for some portions of land within Israel. Finally, in response to the contention that Israel will never be willing to dismantle lots of settlements and evacuate many settlers, Israeli officials and pro-Israel advocates note that it has already demonstrated on two previous occasions that it was willing and able to withdraw from territory, dismantle settlements, and remove settlers: the first was in 1982, when Israel dismantled its settlements in the Sinai following its peace treaty with Egypt; and more recently, in 2005, Israel dismantled its settlements in Gaza and extracted the roughly eight thousand settlers from there, despite some stiff settler resistance (albeit largely nonviolent). Furthermore, Israeli officials and pro-Israel advocates often argue that the Gaza withdrawal not only demonstrated that settlements and settlers can be removed but also that doing this does not lessen Palestinian hostility to Israel or violence against it. On the contrary, the Israeli withdrawal from Gaza only resulted in Hamas taking over the coastal territory and using it as a base from which to launch thousands of rockets at Israeli communities nearby. Factually correct though overly simplified, this narrative is widely held by Israelis and has now become a big part of the reason why many of them do not believe that settlements are a major obstacle to peace (even if they see them as harmful).

Why did Israel withdraw from the Gaza Strip?

In retrospect, it might seem fitting that the person responsible for razing Israel's twenty-one settlements in the Gaza Strip and removing all eight thousand or so of its settlers from there was the man Israelis nicknamed "the Bulldozer," Ariel Sharon. When he became Israeli prime minister in February 2001, after trouncing Ehud Barak in the election for the premiership, nobody would have believed that Sharon of all people would completely and unconditionally withdraw Israeli settlers and soldiers from Gaza. A former general and defense minister, Sharon had a well-deserved reputation for being hawkish and hardline (for example, he was one of the architects of Israel's 1982 invasion of Lebanon, and he later opposed the Oslo Accords). He was also widely known as "the father of the settlement movement" because of the major role he played in planning and implementing the Likud Party's extensive settlement building program. Nor was it any more conceivable that Sharon would unilaterally withdraw Israel from Gaza when he was reelected in January 2003. During the election campaign, Sharon ridiculed his main challenger, Amram Mitzna, then head of the Labor Party, when Mitzna proposed such a withdrawal. Sharon even stated that, for him, the settlements in Gaza were no less important than Tel Aviv, and he warned that evacuating them would only "bring the terrorism centers closer to [Israel's] population centers."

Less than a year later, however, in a highly publicized speech in December 2003, Sharon announced his intention to carry out a unilateral withdrawal (he did not specify then what areas he intended to withdraw from). When Sharon subsequently laid out what he called his "disengagement plan," it was a stunning development in both Israeli domestic politics and the Israeli-Palestinian conflict. Sharon shocked international observers and Israelis alike, especially his right-wing supporters, including settlers who felt bitterly betrayed. Besides widespread surprise and even disbelief, Sharon's disengagement plan elicited sharply different reactions. The international community largely welcomed it, hoping that it might somehow resurrect the peace process that the Second Intifada had killed off. United States President George W. Bush publicly hailed the disengagement plan as a "bold and historic initiative that can make an important contribution to peace." The UN and EU also endorsed Sharon's disengagement plan, albeit less enthusiastically, as at least a step in the right direction toward peace. Even among those who doubted that Israel's pullout from Gaza would revive the peace process, there was hope that if it was carried out successfully it could pave the way for a unilateral withdrawal from the West Bank (Sharon's inclusion of four small West Bank settlements in his disengagement plan hinted at this possibility). Although Israel had withdrawn from occupied territory and dismantled settlements before (in the Sinai), it had never done so in the West Bank and Gaza—areas within the historical Land of Israel and hence of greater nationalist and religious significance to Israeli Jews. Dismantling and evacuating the Gaza settlements, therefore, would set an important precedent, potentially making it easier to do the same thing later in the West Bank. Indeed, some people speculated that this was actually Sharon's long-term plan, and that his ultimate intention was to withdraw from most, if not all, of the West Bank as well, with or without an agreement with the Palestinians. Others were more skeptical, if not cynical, about Sharon's motives. They saw the disengagement plan as merely a ploy by Sharon to fend off growing international and domestic pressure. And some suspected that it was really a calculated move to consolidate Israel's long-term hold on the West Bank, claiming that Sharon was only giving up Gaza in order to keep the West Bank.

Whether or not Sharon's disengagement plan was a prelude to a future withdrawal from the West Bank, the evidence suggests that his decision to unilaterally withdraw Israel from Gaza was at least partly driven by his desire to avoid more international, especially American, pressure on Israel to resume peace talks with the Palestinians. By all accounts, Sharon was increasingly concerned by the mounting international pressure on Israel to make a deal with the Palestinians that would require it to withdraw from the West Bank and Gaza and accept Palestinian statehood in those territories. In 2002 and 2003, various peace initiatives were being proposed along these lines and attracting increasing attention, most notably the Arab Peace Initiative (launched by the Crown Prince of Saudi Arabia and then unanimously approved by the members of the Arab League) and the Geneva Initiative (a draft Israeli-Palestinian peace agreement drawn up by Israel's former justice minister, Yossi Beilin, and the PA's former minister of information and culture, Yasser Abed

Rabbo). In addition to worrying about the growing support for these peace plans, Sharon was also under pressure from the Bush administration to begin implementing the steps outlined in "The Roadmap to Middle East Peace," which the United States, EU, UN, and Russia (collectively called the "Quartet") had announced with great fanfare in April 2003 as a way to end the Second Intifada, restart the peace process, and eventually resolve the Israeli-Palestinian conflict.

Although Sharon had publicly accepted a two-state solution to the conflict (after stridently opposing one for many years), he still believed that peace talks with the Palestinians were pointless, and he frequently asserted that Israel had no Palestinian partner with whom to negotiate. To avoid being forced into negotiations, and possibly pressured to make concessions he strongly opposed, Sharon seized the initiative. His disengagement plan was a way of placating and preempting pressure from the United States and the rest of the international community. The timing of Sharon's declaration in December 2003 of his intention to carry out a unilateral withdrawal, just weeks after the launching of the Geneva Initiative and only seven months after the Road Map for Peace was introduced, points to this motive. Sharon himself openly acknowledged it, telling the Knesset when he presented his disengagement plan in March 2004 that "only an Israeli plan will keep us from being dragged into dangerous initiatives like the Geneva and Saudi initiatives." Even more pointedly, Sharon's chief of staff and personal adviser, Dov Weisglass, gave an interview in October 2004 in which he described the disengagement plan as "formaldehyde" for the peace process, boasting, "The disengagement plan makes it possible for Israel to park conveniently in an interim situation that distances us as far as possible from political pressure. It legitimizes our contention that there is no negotiating with the Palestinians. There is a decision here to do the minimum possible in order to maintain our political situation."

Withdrawing from Gaza, however, was not just a concession to external pressure. Sharon also saw it as benefiting Israel because it would significantly reduce the number of Palestinians living under Israeli control and thereby help safeguard Israel's long-term future as a Jewish and democratic state. After entering office, Sharon recognized that demographic trends threatened Israel's ability to be both a Jewish state and a democracy because Palestinians would, sooner or later, outnumber Jews (in the entire area between the Mediterranean Sea and the Jordan River). Enfranchising them all would jeopardize Israel's Jewish identity, but denying them citizenship or the right to vote would be undemocratic. Thus, Sharon became convinced that Israel could not indefinitely rule over Palestinians in the West Bank and Gaza. By leaving Gaza and relinquishing its control over the 1.4 million Palestinians who lived there at the time, Israel's demographic future looked much brighter (in Sharon's eyes). For this reason, Sharon often justified the Gaza withdrawal as a demographic necessity. Demography was more important to him than geography. To ensure a long-term Jewish majority within Israel, Sharon was willing to give up the dream of a "Greater Israel"—which, unlike many of his Likud colleagues, he was never that committed to in the first place—and abandon part of the Land of Israel (Gaza), which in any case he did not regard as holy (he was secular). Sharon also thought that giving up Gaza would be good for Israel because he had become convinced during the Second Intifada that occupying Gaza was a military liability rather than an asset (this was also the IDF's assessment and the view of many Israelis). More than 200 Israeli soldiers had been killed there since the beginning of the Second Intifada. The IDF was spending tens of millions of dollars a year and stationing thousands of troops to protect the Gaza settlements and the roughly eight thousand Israeli settlers who lived in them. Withdrawing from Gaza, it was hoped, would save Israeli lives and money.

Sharon's newfound belief that occupying Gaza was a demographic and military burden for Israel was the reason why he chose to withdraw from Gaza when he encountered growing international pressure and domestic criticism (and it was also why a majority of Israelis supported his disengagement plan). This does not necessarily mean that Sharon had no intention of later withdrawing from large parts of the West Bank as well. Throughout the long and heated domestic debate over his disengagement plan, Sharon never revealed his long-term strategy or vision, if indeed he had one. He probably didn't clarify his plans for the West Bank because he would have lost some support for his disengagement plan had he done so. Sharon's deliberate ambiguity about the West Bank helped him to implement the withdrawal from Gaza, but it also fed incessant speculation about what he would do next—was it Gaza first or Gaza last?

Less than five months after Israel's withdrawal from Gaza was completed on September 12, 2005, Sharon suffered a debilitating stroke and fell into a coma (he never regained consciousness and died in January 2014), so we will never know what his ultimate intentions really were. A number of Sharon's close associates and advisers (including Ehud Olmert, his deputy and then successor as prime minister) have said that Sharon was, in fact, drafting a plan for a unilateral withdrawal from much of the West Bank. It is unlikely that Sharon would have succeeded in carrying out such a plan. For any kind of future unilateral withdrawal from the West Bank to happen, the disengagement from Gaza had to be judged a success by Israelis. But since the Gaza disengagement, most Israelis have come to regard it as an abject failure and a serious error. They overwhelmingly concur with the damning assessment made by Moshe "Bogie" Ya'alon, the IDF chief of staff who served under Sharon (and later became defense minister under Netanyahu), who stated in July 2006 that "the Disengagement was a strategic mistake of the first order. It brought about the Hamas victory. It emboldened terror groups. It has fueled the Palestinian struggle for years." In particular, the increasing number of rocket attacks from Gaza after Israel withdrew was taken by many Israelis as proof that the disengagement had undermined Israeli security, just as many of its right-wing critics had warned. Even more Israelis came to regret the disengagement from Gaza after Hamas took control there in 2007. A nightmare scenario for Israelis had apparently come true—a radical Islamist terrorist group supported by Iran was now ruling a quasi-state right on Israel's borders.

Israelis did not miss Gaza—far from it—and they had no desire to return there. But they realized, slowly and painfully, that no matter how much they wanted to rid themselves of Gaza's problems and threats, they simply could not do so. Palestinians would not let them, and the international community still held Israel at least partially responsible for what happened there (indeed, most international legal experts disagreed with Israel's assertion that its occupation of the Gaza Strip was over and that it no longer had any responsibility for the welfare of its residents). In short, Israel was not able to really "disengage" from Gaza. If anything, since Hamas came to power there, Israel's military involvement in Gaza has intensified, and its tight control over Gaza's perimeter, particularly over the passage of people and goods—which Israel has refused to relinquish because of its security concerns—has meant that, effectively, the lives and livelihoods of Gazans have become even more dependent on Israeli government decisions, much to their frustration.

While Israel's withdrawal from Gaza has been a big disappointment for Israelis, it has been an even bigger letdown for Palestinians, especially for those living in Gaza. Most Palestinians (more than 70 percent in polls) supported Sharon's disengagement plan, despite their deep distrust and dislike of Sharon. They looked forward to the end of Israel's nearly four-decades-long occupation of Gaza and the departure of its settlers. Many expected that it would bring greater freedom and prosperity to Palestinians in Gaza, and even move Palestinians in general closer to the realization of their national aspirations. Buoyed by these high expectations and convinced that Israel's exit from Gaza was a great victory for them, Palestinians jubilantly and triumphantly celebrated when Israel's settlers and soldiers finally left. But this joy was short-lived. Although Palestinians were expected to seize the opportunity of governing Gaza and building a flourishing economy there, in reality Gaza's economy was heavily dependent on Israel, so it was hit hard by its withdrawal. It led to a sharp economic downturn, with Gaza's exports declining and local unemployment rising. Living conditions in Gaza seriously deteriorated. The long-awaited end of Israel's military and civilian presence in Gaza did not bring Gazans the economic benefits many had eagerly anticipated. They were actually worse off economically. But however bad things were for Gazans after Israel withdrew in 2005, they got much worse after Hamas took over less than two years later.

How did Hamas come to power in Gaza?

The Palestinian Islamist group Hamas is officially designated to be a terrorist organization by Israel, the United States, Canada, and the EU, and most people in the West think of it as just that. This is entirely understandable since Hamas came to public attention because of its campaign of violence against Israel, often deliberately targeting Israeli civilians. Founded in 1987 when the First Intifada began (it was an offshoot of the Palestinian branch of the Egyptian Muslim Brotherhood), Hamas initially gained prominence in the early 1990s, when it began carrying out suicide bombing attacks in Israeli cities in an effort to derail the Oslo peace process (which turned out to be quite a successful strategy). Hamas became even more notorious for its use of suicide terrorism during the Second Intifada, when it launched hundreds of suicide bombing attacks against Israelis, many more than its rival Palestinian militant groups (such as Palestinian Islamic Jihad or Fatah's al-Aqsa Brigades). But while Hamas is best known, and most feared, for its use, and even glorification, of terrorism, it has never relied solely upon violence to achieve its long-term objectives—the eradication of Israel and the establishment of an Islamic society and state in all the territory of historic Palestine. Hamas has also consistently employed nonviolent tactics to build its support among Palestinians in the West Bank and Gaza and in the Palestinian diaspora. Over the years, the group has branched out into many different political, social, and cultural activities, and in the process it has become more than just a terrorist group. Hamas also became a sprawling social service and welfare organization, providing a wide range of charitable, medical, and educational services to local Palestinians (in this respect, Hamas is like other Islamist groups in the Middle East and elsewhere who have been active in offering social services that governments have been unable or unwilling to provide). Hamas has funded and operated an extensive network of soup kitchens, orphanages, medical centers, dental clinics, schools, kindergartens, youth clubs, and even sports clubs (the financing for all this came largely from the Iranian government and from private donors in Saudi Arabia and other oil-rich Gulf states, including Palestinian expatriates). In addition to its military wing (the Izz al-Din al-Qassam Brigades, founded in 1991) and its social services wing (called *Da'wa*, meaning "preaching" in Arabic), Hamas also developed a political wing and eventually formed its own political party.

By the time Israel withdrew from the Gaza Strip in 2005, therefore, Hamas was simultaneously an underground militant group and a major social and political movement. It is essential to recognize Hamas's multiple facets because it enables us to understand how it came to power in Gaza. Perceiving it as only a terrorist group, as many people do, may well lead to the assumption that

Hamas violently seized power there. Indeed, this is how Western and Israeli media tend to describe the way that Hamas took power, often referring to its "violent takeover" of Gaza. Although this is not completely inaccurate, it is somewhat misleading and certainly not the full story of how Hamas gained power.

To be sure, Hamas did employ violence to get control over Gaza. It killed, sometimes brutally, many Palestinians who were affiliated with or supported its rival Fatah, the more secular and moderate party that Yasser Arafat founded in the late 1950s and led until his death in November 2004. These killings mostly occurred during the so-called Battle of Gaza, a mini civil war between Hamas and Fatah in June 2007, which was the culmination of many smaller armed clashes beginning in the spring of 2006 and erupting intermittently until Hamas finally defeated Fatah's forces in Gaza. Hamas's "violent takeover" of the Gaza Strip, therefore, came about in the context of internecine fighting with Fatah, and it seems to have occurred more by default than by design.

It was not only bullets that brought Hamas to power, however; it was also, surprisingly, the ballot box. Hamas had boycotted elections for both the presidency and the parliament (legislative council) of the PA because these institutions were created in the framework of the Oslo Accords, which Hamas stridently rejected. In 2004, however, Hamas's political leadership pragmatically decided to participate for the first time in local elections, justifying this decision on the grounds that the Second Intifada had effectively terminated the Oslo Accords. Hamas's entry into electoral politics was driven by a desire to capitalize on the popular support it had gained during the Second Intifada. It also wanted to seize the opportunity that came with the opening up of the Palestinian political system after the death of Arafat, the charismatic chairman of the PLO and autocratic president of the PA who had dominated Palestinian politics for so long. For the first time, Hamas officially participated in Palestinian municipal elections, which were held between December 2004 and January 2005. Although Fatah received the most votes, the strong performance of Hamas's candidates demonstrated its electoral appeal, and encouraged it to compete in parliamentary elections, hoping to replace Fatah as the ruling party. In January 2006, Hamas's "Change and Reform Bloc" scored a major victory in the parliamentary elections, winning 74 out of 132 seats in the Palestinian

Legislative Council (this amounted to 56 percent of the seats, more than Hamas's share of the popular vote—which was 44 percent to Fatah's 41 percent—because Fatah diluted its vote by nominating multiple candidates in many electoral districts).

Hamas's victory in the parliamentary elections (that were fair and free) came as an unwelcome surprise to most international observers (including the George W. Bush administration in the United States, which had pressed hard for these elections to take place—against Israel's advice—as part of its effort to spread democracy across the Middle East). Even Hamas's own leadership was not expecting to win the election. But Hamas's electoral success should not have come as such a surprise. Its popularity among Palestinians had soared in the months leading up to the January 2006 elections (increasing by 55 percent in public opinion polls conducted between December 2004 to December 2005). What caused this surge in popular support for Hamas was Israel's unilateral withdrawal from Gaza in September 2005, just five months before the election. Well before Israel's "disengagement" from Gaza took place, many critics of then Israeli prime minister Ariel Sharon's plan had warned that it would embolden and empower Hamas (indeed, the very fact that Hamas did not try to violently disrupt Israel's withdrawal from Gaza suggests that it recognized that it stood to benefit from it). This is exactly what happened. The vast majority of Palestinians viewed Israel's unilateral withdrawal as a reluctant response to the Palestinian violence of the Second Intifada. As far as they were concerned, the Palestinian "armed struggle" against Israel had forced it to retreat from Gaza. This popular interpretation of the Gaza disengagement was, at best, an oversimplification—Palestinian violence was not the only factor behind Sharon's decision to disengage from Gaza—but it convinced many Palestinians of the efficacy of violence against Israel, especially compared to what was widely perceived as the futility of negotiating with Israel (after all, the peace process did not lead Israel to withdraw from the West Bank or Gaza or even evacuate any settlements). Hence, Palestinian popular support for the "armed struggle" greatly increased, as did support for Hamas, which was most closely identified with it. Hamas took credit for forcefully "expelling" Israel from Gaza, hailing it as a great victory for its "resistance" against Israel and a vindication of its violent strategy. Most Palestinians agreed, with more than three-quarters of those surveyed giving Hamas all the credit for ending Israel's thirty-eight-year-long presence in Gaza.

It was not just Israel's exit from Gaza that strengthened Hamas, but its unilateral nature that weakened the more moderate Fatah Party. Israel refused to negotiate with the Fatah-led PA over its disengagement from Gaza, leaving the PA largely a bystander to the withdrawal. Israel's refusal to negotiate weakened Fatah politically because its standing among Palestinians was based in part on its presumed ability to negotiate an end to Israeli occupation and achieve statehood for Palestinians (since Fatah, unlike Hamas, was committed to the Oslo peace process). Israeli unilateralism, therefore, deprived Fatah of one of its main advantages over Hamas (the PLO's top negotiator, Saed Erekat, had predicted this would happen in a *Washington Post* op-ed written back in April 2004 warning that Palestinian moderates, such as himself, would be undermined by the Gaza disengagement). On top of its unwillingness to negotiate its withdrawal from Gaza, Israel was also unwilling to allow Mahmoud Abbas—the newly installed PA president who succeeded Arafat as head of the PLO and Fatah—to derive political credit from it (when Israel left Gaza, for instance, it did so without any official handover or formal ceremony).

Israel's unilateral withdrawal from Gaza a few months before the parliamentary elections was not the only reason for Hamas's electoral success. It was also the result of a longer-term process of popular alienation from the Fatah-led PA and mounting public anger over its cronyism and corruption. Under Fatah, the PA was widely seen by Palestinians as being incorrigibly corrupt and hopelessly incompetent. Whereas the Palestinian public saw Fatah as rife with corruption and riven with factionalism, Hamas, by contrast, had a public image of probity and a reputation for efficiently delivering basic public services due its social welfare network. The public perception that Hamas was "clean," at least compared with Fatah, brought it many votes in the election, or, put another way, Fatah lost many votes because of its perceived corruption. In this respect, the vote for Hamas was a protest vote against Fatah, the incumbent party. In its election campaign, Hamas shrewdly appealed to the Palestinian public's desperate desire for good governance. Rather than emphasize its Islamist ideology—which most Palestinians did not share—Hamas presented itself as more honest and competent than Fatah, and Hamas's political platform focused on rooting out corruption, alleviating poverty, and promoting local development. It proposed economic, educational, housing, and healthcare programs for Palestinians instead of Hamas's long-term goals of establishing an Islamic state and eradicating the Jewish state. In many cases, therefore, Palestinians voted for Hamas despite its ideology, not because of it (exit polling showed that 60 percent of Hamas voters actually supported a two-state solution to the conflict).

Hamas, however, was not prepared to abandon its ideology, or even moderate it, in order to take power after its victory in the legislative elections. This was, in effect, what the international community demanded from Hamas as the price for its financial support and diplomatic recognition. For international aid to continue to flow to the PA, which sorely depended upon it, a Hamas-led government had to meet three conditions spelled out by the "Quartet" (comprising the United States, the UN, the EU, and Russia) in the immediate aftermath of Hamas's electoral victory: (1) recognize Israel; (2) renounce the use of violence; and (3) accept all previous agreements signed by the PLO (such as the Oslo Accords). Hamas adamantly rejected all three conditions. Instead, it tried to a form a national unity government with Fatah, but its rival refused to share power with it. This refusal was no doubt partly due to external pressure on Fatah, particularly from the United States and Israel, who opposed the formation of a unity government and instead preferred to see a Hamas government fail because, they hoped, it would be unable to govern effectively in the face of international financial sanctions and a diplomatic boycott.

Unwilling to accept the Quartet's conditions and unable to form a coalition government with Fatah, in March 2006 Hamas established its own government, appointing Ismail Haniyeh, one of its leaders based in Gaza, as prime minister. This resulted in a freeze of international aid to the PA (as had been threatened) and a suspension of Israel's transfer of Palestinian customs revenues that it collected at ports and other points of entry on behalf of the PA (this revenue, about $50 million per month, covered a large chunk of the PA's budget). It also led to a power struggle between Hamas and Fatah over control of Palestinian security forces as well as between the PA's new prime minister, Ismail Haniyeh, and President Abbas.

As this power struggle escalated, tensions increased between Fatah and Hamas, and occasionally resulted in gun battles between their members. Repeated attempts to reach a power-sharing deal were either unsuccessful or quickly collapsed, often provoking more violent skirmishes. An agreement brokered by Saudi Arabia in February 2007 (the Mecca Agreement) was the closest the two sides came to peacefully resolving their growing conflict. It led to the formation of a short-lived national unity government in March 2007. But animosity between Hamas and Fatah continued to grow, fueled in part by Hamas's suspicion that Fatah, with the encouragement and assistance of the United States and Israel, was preparing to carry out a coup against it (the Pentagon was funding and training PA security forces loyal to President Abbas and under the control of Fatah leader Mohammad Dahlan, an archenemy of Hamas). This animosity eventually culminated in the brief but bloody "Battle of Gaza" in June 2007 between Hamas forces and PA security forces affiliated with Fatah. Dozens were killed and hundreds wounded on both sides. Within a week, Hamas routed the American-trained and -armed PA security forces (some of whom deserted while others even switched sides), and militarily took complete control of Gaza.

In response to Hamas's armed takeover of Gaza, President Abbas dissolved the unity government and dismissed Prime Minister Haniyeh, appointing a technocratic government led by Salam Fayyad, a former World Bank economist, in its place. This government, based in the West Bank, was immediately embraced by the United States and EU, who lifted their crippling economic sanctions against the PA and resumed their financial assistance to it, while Israel resumed the transfer of tax and customs revenues to the PA. Gaza—where Hamas became the de facto government—was a different matter entirely. The Hamas government was boycotted by most Western governments and even shunned by many Arab regimes. Already increasingly isolated and impoverished, Gaza's plight worsened considerably after the Israeli government officially declared it to be a "hostile entity" in September 2007. This resulted in an ongoing Israeli blockade of Gaza that, along with Egypt's frequent closure of its border with Gaza in recent years, has brought the densely populated coastal enclave to the brink of a man-made humanitarian disaster.

How has Hamas's rule and Israel's blockade affected Palestinians in Gaza?

For more than a decade now, Palestinians in Gaza have been suffering the harsh consequences of living under Hamas rule and an Israeli blockade of their territory. Although it is popular, and often politically convenient, to blame either Hamas or Israel for the hardships and misery that Gazans have experienced, the truth is that both parties are responsible (as is, to a lesser extent, Egypt and the West Bank–based Palestinian Authority). Hamas and Israel have been engaged in a prolonged, intermittently violent struggle at the expense of Gaza's civilian population. The consequences for the 1.9 million Palestinians in Gaza have been dire. They have endured economic deprivation, collective confinement, political and social repression, and recurrent bouts of intense fighting between Israel and Hamas in which thousands of civilians have been killed and many more wounded, left homeless, and traumatized. Crowded into a narrow strip of land just 25 miles (40 kilometers) long and 6 miles (10 kilometers) wide, most Gazans have been unable to leave for the past decade, trapped in what is often described as the world's largest open-air prison. In fact, since the average age of its population is just 16 years old, many, if not most, of Gaza's inhabitants have never left the area, giving rise to a widespread sense of claustrophobia, frustration, and despair.

To be sure, Gaza was already becoming impoverished and isolated before Hamas took over in 2007. This was not always the case. Gaza's poverty rate was once roughly the same as that of the United States (16 percent in Gaza in 1994, compared with 14.5 percent in the United States). But as Gazans lost their jobs in Israel during the 1990s (while the Oslo peace process took place), unemployment and poverty increased. The Second Intifada made things worse as tourism ended and foreign investment dried up. Gazans were also restricted in their ability to leave the territory long before Israel largely sealed its border after Hamas's takeover. During the First Intifada, Israel began requiring Palestinians to obtain a permit to travel between Gaza and the West Bank, and during the Second Intifada it became very difficult for Palestinians in either territory to enter Israel. After Israel's withdrawal in 2005 it placed more restrictions on the movement of people and goods into and out of Gaza, and it tightened these restrictions after Hamas won the 2006 Palestinian legislative elections and then rejected the demands of the Quartet to recognize Israel, renounce violence, and respect previous Israeli-Palestinian agreements.

By the time Hamas seized sole control over Gaza in June 2007, socioeconomic conditions inside Gaza had been deteriorating for years (especially after Israel withdrew). Since then, things have become even worse as Gaza's economy has slowly collapsed. By 2015, a decade after Israel's withdrawal, Gaza's economy was, according to the World Bank, the world's worst performing economy, with the world's highest level of unemployment. Per-capita income in Gaza had fallen from $1,375 in 2005 to $970 in 2015, and the unemployment rate had risen from 30 percent to 43 percent. Unemployment has continued to increase in recent years, with more than half of Gaza's adult population now (in 2018) unemployed and over 70 percent of young people.

The economic circumstances of Palestinians in Gaza, therefore, are far worse under Hamas rule than they were under Israeli rule. To be fair, this is not only Hamas's fault. It can justifiably be blamed for allocating scarce resources toward building up its own military capabilities—Hamas has spent a lot of money acquiring arms and building an elaborate network of underground tunnels—rather than channeling them toward Gaza's residents. Hamas can also be blamed for its role in provoking three major Israeli military offensives (in 2008–2009, 2012, and 2014) that destroyed or damaged much of Gaza's infrastructure. But the biggest reason for the steep decline of Gaza's economy has been Israel's land, air, and naval blockade of the territory. In September 2007, soon after Hamas's takeover, the Israeli government declared Gaza to be a "hostile entity" and strictly limited what could come in or out of Gaza through the border crossings that Israel still controlled. With few exceptions (mostly for businesspeople and medical patients), Palestinians have been prohibited from leaving or entering Gaza, and imports and exports have been heavily restricted—though, under international pressure, Israel has gradually eased some of these restrictions since 2010.

The officially stated purpose of Israel's blockade is to prevent Hamas from importing weapons or other items that it needs to build rockets or dig what the Israeli media likes to call "terror tunnels" (the problem is that many things can have both civilian and military uses, such as concrete). Unofficially, however, the Israeli blockade is aimed not only at carefully monitoring and regulating the flow of goods and people but also at preventing Gaza from prospering and economically developing under Hamas's rule. As one Israeli official succinctly put it, the blockade is designed to make sure that there is "no prosperity, no development, [and] no humanitarian crisis" in Gaza. Similarly, a classified U.S. diplomatic cable from 2008, published by Wikileaks, stated that the aim of the blockade was to "keep the Gazan economy on the brink of collapse without quite pushing it over the edge." This is not meant to simply punish Gazans, as some of Israel's critics contend. Rather, the intention is to diminish Hamas's popular appeal among Palestinians. If living under Hamas rule entails poverty, deprivation, and isolation, then Palestinians will be less willing to support it, so the theory goes. In short, the blockade is designed to weaken Hamas politically, not only militarily. Doing so, it is hoped, will at least prevent Hamas from taking over the West Bank as well (initially some Israeli officials also hoped that the blockade might eventually lead Palestinians in Gaza to oust Hamas from power).

Israel's blockade of Gaza is part of a broader "containment" strategy that it has adopted since Hamas's takeover. Rather than try to forcefully remove Hamas from power in Gaza, or somehow replace it with the PA, Israel has pursued a more limited and, arguably, less risky and less costly strategy (to itself) to contain Hamas and prevent it from becoming more powerful (much as the United States tried to do vis-à-vis the Soviet Union for most of the Cold War). Whether Israel's containment strategy toward Hamas has succeeded so far is debatable. The Israeli blockade has made it much harder for Hamas to obtain advanced weaponry, but this has forced it to manufacture its own weapons, including missiles and drones. By depriving Hamas of much-needed revenue, the blockade has also made it harder for the group to govern Gaza, pay civil servants, and deliver basic services to its residents (and because of the international boycott of Hamas's government, a lot of foreign aid money has also been diverted away from Gaza toward the PA in the West Bank). But Hamas has still been able to maintain order and stability in Gaza, keep all the government ministries there running, keep the healthcare and education systems functioning (just about), and, with the help of funding from regional patrons such as Iran and Qatar, managed to provide essential services to Gazans.

Hamas has lost some popular support among Palestinians, and has become widely unpopular among those living in Gaza in particular, with polls regularly showing that only around 30 percent of Gazans support it. But the erosion of support for Hamas has not resulted in a resurgence of support for its main political rival, Fatah (which also has roughly 30 percent support in Gaza), or for its leader, PA President Mahmoud Abbas. Nor can Hamas's unpopularity among Gazans simply be attributed to the effects of Israel's blockade of Gaza. Its unpopularity may well have as much to do with Hamas's authoritarian governance of Gaza and its well-documented human rights violations as it does with the dismal state of Gaza's economy (for which Israel is generally blamed). Moreover, while the Israeli blockade has weakened Hamas in some respects, it has, paradoxically, strengthened it in others, allowing the group to reward its supporters with jobs, resources, and permits (and deny them to its opponents). Some observers, therefore, argue that the blockade has actually helped entrench Hamas's rule in Gaza instead of undermining it.

What Israel's blockade of Gaza has, incontrovertibly, ensured is that most Gazans have not prospered under Hamas rule. Israeli restrictions on Gaza's imports and exports have had a very damaging impact on its economy, especially on the private sector, since the vast majority of those imports and exports used to go through Israel. Until 2013, the economic and humanitarian impact of the blockade was alleviated to some degree by the willingness of Gaza's other neighbor, Egypt, to allow goods and people to pass through its border crossing with Gaza in the Sinai (Egypt's willingness to do so fluctuated under President Hosni Mubarak and his successor Mohammad Morsi, a leader of the Muslim Brotherhood—Hamas's parent organization—who was elected president following the 2011 uprising that toppled Mubarak's regime). Egypt also largely tolerated the development of a "tunnel economy" running beneath its border with Gaza. To circumvent the Israeli blockade, hundreds of sophisticated underground tunnels were dug between Egypt and Gaza, and they were used to smuggle everything from weapons to consumer goods and even cars. Gazans came to rely upon what was, quite literally, an underground economy based on smuggling. In

2009, for instance, it was estimated that 80 percent of all imports into Gaza were smuggled in through the tunnels between Gaza and Sinai. Hamas also benefited from this "tunnel economy," as it oversaw the construction and operation of the tunnels, collected revenues from them, and brought in whatever it needed. This all changed after the 2013 military coup in Egypt, which ousted President Morsi and brought to power Egypt's current president, the hardline former general Abdel Fattah el-Sisi. Under President Sisi—who views Gaza through the lens of Egyptian domestic security concerns and regards Hamas as an enemy of Egypt because of its ties with the now-banned Muslim Brotherhood and alleged support for jihadist insurgents in the Sinai region—Egypt has generally closed its border with Gaza. In 2015, the Egyptian military shut down the smuggling industry that operated below the Sinai border by blocking and flooding the tunnels. This has deprived Hamas of a major source of revenue and many Gazans of their only source of income.

Egypt's frequent closure of its border and its crackdown on smuggling have severely exacerbated the impact of Israel's blockade of Gaza. Combined, they have had a cumulatively devastating impact on Gaza's inhabitants. Living standards in Gaza have declined, roughly three-quarters of the population now depends upon humanitarian aid, more than half live in poverty, and about a fifth live in "extreme poverty." Along with rampant poverty, food insecurity and malnutrition are now widespread (especially among children), and infant and child mortality rates have increased. Due to fuel shortages, the supply of electricity has been severely limited, sometimes to only a few hours a day. Not only does this lack of electricity seriously affect the daily life of most Palestinians in Gaza, it also affects Gaza's hospitals (making it difficult to operate lifesaving equipment or store medicine), sanitation and sewage facilities (resulting in raw sewage being spewed into the sea because it cannot be treated), and water supply (making the tap water undrinkable). As humanitarian conditions in Gaza have steadily deteriorated over the past few years, the UN has repeatedly sounded the alarm. In 2015, it issued a report warning that Gaza would become uninhabitable by 2020. The next year, another UN report described the territory as "effectively unlivable," and in March 2018, the UN's humanitarian coordinator declared that "Gaza is on the brink of catastrophe." Despite these stark warnings, the international community has done little to stop the emerging humanitarian crisis in Gaza. Many countries have not even fulfilled their financial pledges to help to pay for reconstruction in Gaza following the 2014 war between Israel and Hamas. And, in 2018 the Trump administration stopped U.S. funding for UNRWA, which provides emergency food aid to around a million Palestinians in Gaza.

Many parties bear some responsibility for the dire and increasingly desperate socioeconomic and humanitarian conditions inside Gaza—primarily Israel, Egypt, and Hamas. But also responsible, though to a lesser extent, is the Fatah-dominated PA, because in the last couple of years it has cut the salaries of its civil servants in Gaza by 50 percent and imposed other punitive sanctions on Gaza in an effort by President Abbas to pressure Hamas into permitting the PA's return to Gaza and a handover of security control back to the PA. Only Hamas, however, is responsible for the authoritarian and oppressive manner in which it has governed Gaza. Under Hamas rule, Gaza has been like a one-party state. Political opposition, principally Hamas's rival Fatah, has been heavily repressed, along with independent media outlets and local nongovernmental organizations. Hamas's regime in Gaza has restricted Palestinians there from exercising their civil and political rights, and it has committed numerous human rights violations, such as abductions, arbitrary detentions, and even extrajudicial killings. In some respects, Hamas's government in Gaza is probably no worse than the PA's government in the West Bank. According to local and international human rights groups, both Palestinian governments have suppressed domestic dissent, cracked down on civil society, arbitrarily arrested people, and mistreated and even tortured detainees. And while Hamas has tried to eradicate Fatah's presence in Gaza, Fatah has tried to crush Hamas in the West Bank, imprisoning many of its members (with the help of Israel's security forces).

In terms of their methods of governance, then, Hamas and Fatah are quite alike—unaccountable, sometimes brutal, and far from democratic. The most significant practical difference between them as rulers (besides their contrasting approaches to the conflict with Israel) is that Hamas, unlike Fatah, wants to "Islamize" Palestinian society (that is, make it more Islamic). Hamas has tried to do this since it took power in Gaza, but its approach has been cautious and piecemeal. It has not sought to turn Gaza into an Islamic theocracy (like Iran or Afghanistan under the Taliban) or a caliphate (like the Islamic State briefly established in Iraq and Syria). Instead, its model, if it has one, is the illiberal Islamist government in Turkey under President Recep Tayyip Erdoğan (who has been an outspoken supporter of Hamas). Rather than Islamizing Gaza's institutions, Hamas, so far at least, has largely focused on encouraging and at times imposing more "Islamic" and conservative mores (by, for example, informally policing what women wear in public, preventing mixed-gender gatherings, and closing shops selling supposedly "un-Islamic" products). In doing so, Hamas's leadership in Gaza has balanced their commitment to the group's Islamist ideology with their desire to maintain power in Gaza and gain international legitimacy. The same balancing act between ideological imperatives and practical considerations has shaped Hamas's approach to Israel since it took power, particularly its use of force against Israel (what it calls its "armed resistance").

Why has Gaza frequently become a battlefield between Hamas and Israel over the past decade?

During the past decade, the eyes of the world have often been directed toward Gaza. This tiny coastal enclave has received a huge amount of diplomatic attention and international media coverage. The plight of its nearly two million inhabitants has stirred an outpouring of humanitarian concern, generating worldwide protests against the Israeli blockade of Gaza. For example, human rights advocates and pro-Palestinian activists have formed a "Free Gaza Movement," staging demonstrations in cities around the world, and sending a series of boats (known as the Gaza Freedom Flotilla) to challenge Israel's naval blockade (most famously the Turkish ship MV *Mavì Marmara*, on which nine Turkish activists were killed in clashes with Israeli commandos on May 31, 2010, leading Turkey to temporarily break off diplomatic relations with Israel).

Gaza has undoubtedly taken on much greater prominence in the Israeli-Palestinian conflict in recent years, surpassing the larger, more populous, and wealthier West Bank, historically the more important of the two territories. Under British rule (1917–1948), Gaza was a relatively quiet backwater, less embroiled in the growing Arab-Jewish conflict than other parts of Palestine. Then, under Egyptian rule (1949–1967), Gaza became a hotbed of Palestinian nationalism and a staging ground for guerrilla raids into Israel. But Gaza was not the locus of Palestinian national aspirations. Under Israeli rule (1967–2005), Gaza's overcrowded, poverty-stricken refugee camps became places of stiff, sometimes violent, resistance to the Israeli occupation—the First Intifada started in one of these camps in December 1987—but the West Bank was of much greater interest to Israel because of its strategic value and historic and religious significance to Jews. Gaza, by contrast, had little, if any, strategic or ideological value for Israel. Indeed, Israeli Prime Minister Yitzhak Rabin famously remarked in 1992 that he wished Gaza "would just sink into the sea," and many, if not most, Israelis probably felt the same way. Israel was only too happy to give the newly created PA administrative control over Gaza in 1994 as part of the Oslo peace process. Eleven years later in 2005, after the peace process had collapsed and the Second Intifada ended, Israel was willing to completely remove all its settlers and soldiers from Gaza without getting anything in return.

Under Hamas rule since 2007, Gaza no longer has a peripheral status in the conflict between Israel and the Palestinians. Instead, it has become the most frequent flashpoint in the conflict and the epicenter of its deadliest violence, with regular tit-for-tat skirmishes between Hamas and Israel periodically escalating into major military clashes every few years (two of them, in 2008–2009 and 2014, amounted to full-scale wars). The West Bank, most of it still under Israeli military rule, has been comparatively calm in recent years (but by no means free of violence). There has been a steep decline in Palestinian attacks against Israel coming from the West Bank—where PA security forces actively cooperate with the IDF to prevent them. Attacks against Israel from Gaza, on the other hand, have spiked since Hamas took power. These attacks come in many different forms, including firing rockets and mortars into Israel; shooting at nearby Israeli soldiers and agricultural workers; detonating improvised explosive devices along the fence separating Gaza from Israel; conducting armed raids into Israel to capture Israeli soldiers (most famously on June 25, 2006, when Corporal Gilad Shalit was abducted and then held captive for five years until he was released by Hamas in exchange for Israel freeing more than a thousand Palestinian prisoners); and, most recently, launching incendiary kites and balloons into Israel in order to set fire to Israeli farmland and crops.

By far the most common type of attack from Gaza has been the firing of rockets and mortars into Israel. This started during the Second Intifada, and it escalated after Israel's withdrawal from Gaza in 2005. After Hamas's takeover in 2007, the number of rockets and mortars fired from Gaza into Israel sharply increased, from over 800 in 2005 to more than 3,500 in 2008. Between 2008 and 2015, there were a total of more than 10,000 rockets and mortars fired from Gaza, according to figures compiled by the Israeli government. In addition to becoming more frequent, the rockets fired from Gaza also became more powerful and reached more distant targets in Israel. Until 2008, the rockets could only hit less populated areas in southern Israel in the vicinity of Gaza, but their range has increased over time, initially putting the nearby cities of Ashkelon and Beersheba within reach, and more recently all of Israel's major cities, including Tel Aviv and Jerusalem and even Haifa up in the north. These rocket attacks very rarely killed Israelis—bomb shelters, safe rooms, advanced warning systems, and Israel's Iron Dome missile defense system (deployed since 2011) all helped greatly limit civilian casualties— but the attacks terrorized Israelis and traumatized many (especially the beleaguered residents of the small city of Sderot, located less than a mile from the Gaza border, who only have fifteen seconds to scramble and seek safety when the siren sounds alerting them of incoming rockets).

To understand why Gaza has become a staging ground for so many Palestinian rocket and mortar attacks over the past dozen years, one must look at Hamas's motives for firing them (although, it should be noted, not all of the rockets and mortars were launched by Hamas). This is seldom explained in Western or Israeli media coverage, which tends to portray Hamas's violence against Israel as solely driven by a burning hatred of the Jewish state (and Jews as well, it is often claimed) and an insatiable desire to destroy it. But there is more to Hamas's violence than homicidal hatred. Rather than being a product of some kind of pathology, or just an expression of pent-up anger or despair, as some would have it, Hamas's violence is primarily instrumental. Since forming its military wing in 1991, Hamas has strategically employed violence as a means to achieve both short-term and long-term objectives.

According to Hamas's 1988 founding charter, its ultimate goal is the complete "liberation" of Palestine (whether Hamas still remains committed to this in practice is now subject to some debate). Ideologically, Hamas believes that it is fighting a defensive *jihad* (holy war) or, in more secular terms, a war of national liberation against "Zionist aggression" and colonialism. As part of its "armed resistance," Hamas uses terrorism against Israeli civilians to demoralize Israeli society and undermine its staying power over the long run. In this respect, Hamas's use of rockets is just another tactic in the long war of attrition that it has been waging against Israel. For roughly two decades, since the early 1990s, its favorite tactic was suicide bombing (pioneered by Hezbollah in neighboring Lebanon), which Hamas used to disrupt the Oslo peace process in the 1990s. It has become much harder for would-be suicide bombers to enter Israel because of the barrier in the West Bank and the fence around Gaza, so Hamas has, partly out of necessity, switched from suicide bombings to rockets and mortars as its weapons of choice (Hamas's embrace of the use of rocket attacks against Israel was also influenced by what it saw as Hezbollah's successful use of them during its 2006 war with Israel).

Hamas's rocket attacks may be indiscriminate but they are also calculated (though Hamas has occasionally miscalculated Israel's response). They have also been calibrated—increasing, decreasing, or temporarily ceasing altogether depending on how Hamas's leadership assesses the group's needs and interests at any given time. Their primary goal has been to stay in power in Gaza, whatever the cost. To this end, Hamas has used rocket attacks for a few different purposes. First and foremost, the attacks are used to pressure Israel to lift or at least ease its blockade of Gaza, particularly when conditions there deteriorate to the point at which Hamas's rule is threatened. Hamas itself claims that its rocket attacks are aimed at forcing Israel to end its blockade of Gaza, but the strategy is not quite as simple as that. Its rocket attacks have actually been intended to provoke Israeli military retaliation against Gaza, which Hamas has hoped will then draw more international attention to Gaza and lead to diplomatic pressure on Israel to make concessions or change its policies (while alleviating pressure on Hamas to make political or ideological concessions). Second, Hamas has used rocket attacks to retaliate against Israel when the IDF assassinates Hamas leaders (as it has done on a number of occasions), kills Hamas members, or takes other aggressive actions against the group. In such instances, its rocket attacks are aimed at punishing Israel, making Israel's actions more costly in an attempt to deter it from repeating them. Third, along with trying to pressure and punish Israel, Hamas has used rocket attacks to prove that it is still committed to "armed resistance" against Israel. Since taking power in Gaza, Hamas has faced competition from other Islamist militant groups—most notably, the more extreme, Iranian-funded, Islamic Jihad, the second-largest armed group in Gaza, but also from smaller jihadist groups inspired by the Islamic State and Al Qaeda. These groups have accused Hamas of being unwilling to fight Israel, of preventing them from launching rockets at Israel (which Hamas has, in fact, done), and of failing to establish what they consider to be a proper Islamic regime in Gaza (because, for instance, Hamas has not imposed Sharia law). Hamas has, therefore, sometimes fired rockets at Israel, and also allowed other militant groups to do so, to counter these potentially damaging accusations and maintain its reputation as the leading Palestinian resistance organization (and thereby retain the loyalty of its more militant members and the financial support of its foreign donors).

Israel's frequent and occasionally devastating use of force in Gaza has also been purposeful. Although domestic political considerations have surely sometimes influenced its use of force against Gaza, Israel's consistent, overriding objective has been to stop the rocket fire, and maintain or restore calm, without making any major concessions to Hamas (such as lifting its blockade of Gaza). Since Israel cannot prevent militants from launching rockets from Gaza, nor intercept and shoot down every rocket (since that is prohibitively expensive), it has tried to reduce the number of rocket attacks from Gaza through a strategy of military deterrence. Whenever rockets or mortars are fired at Israel, the IDF immediately retaliates to inflict a punishment that will deter their future use. Most of the time, it carries out what it calls "precision" airstrikes (including drone strikes) that target sites where rockets were launched from and the militants who fired them (although civilians nearby are sometimes also killed or wounded). But since this is not always possible or effective, Israel also holds Hamas responsible for all rockets fired from Gaza, regardless of who launches them, and it retaliates against Hamas targets in Gaza (such as its paramilitary training camps and weapons depots).

When small-scale, tactical airstrikes prove to be insufficient in deterring rocket attacks, or when their deterrent effect wears off and rocket attacks resume or escalate, then the IDF responds by launching a large-scale offensive against Hamas aimed at degrading the group's military capabilities, particularly its arsenal of rockets. The purpose of these major IDF operations is not simply to destroy Hamas's weapons and kill its fighters, but to inflict such severe damage that Hamas will be not only militarily weakened but also effectively deterred from launching rockets into Israel or allowing others to do so. However, since Israel fully expects Hamas to gradually rebuild its military capabilities and become more emboldened and less deterred over time, its military offensives only achieve a temporary lull in violence and buy time. When the quiet eventually ends and rocket attacks escalate again, the IDF engages in another major offensive against Hamas, and the cycle repeats itself. Hence, Israel's military strategy against Hamas has euphemistically been called "mowing the grass," because it requires the IDF to periodically conduct major operations in Gaza to keep Hamas in line, just as a gardener has to regularly mow a lawn to keep the grass from growing out of control.

For more than a decade now, Israel has been waging major offensives in Gaza largely in response to spikes in rocket attacks. These began even before Israel's 2005 withdrawal from Gaza (in 2004, the IDF carried out what it dubbed "Operation Forward Shield" and "Operation Days of Repentance"). These offensives have continued periodically, but relentlessly, since then (in 2006, "Operation Summer Rains" and "Operation Autumn Clouds"; in 2008, "Operation Warm Winter"; in 2008–2009, "Operation Cast Lead"; in 2012, "Operation Pillar of Defense"; and, most recently, in 2014, "Operation Protective Edge"). Although these IDF campaigns have similar names, common objectives, and more or less the same causes (each, of course, had its own specific chain of events that led to a spike in rocket fire from Gaza and the Israeli government decision to mount a massive retaliation), they are not all alike. They have become much more ferocious since Hamas took control of Gaza. In particular, "Operation Cast Lead" (from December 27, 2008 to January 18, 2009), and "Operation Protective Edge" (from July 8 to August

26, 2014) went on for weeks and involved an aerial assault and a ground invasion. And both offensives resulted in unprecedented destruction and loss of life, primarily on the Palestinian side. In fact, the high numbers of casualties incurred during these two "rounds" of fighting between Israel and Hamas (and other Palestinian militant groups in Gaza) means that they can be accurately described as wars. During "Operation Cast Lead"—the First Gaza War—more than 1,300 Palestinians and 23 Israelis were killed (6 of them by friendly fire). "Operation Protective Edge"—the Second Gaza War— was even deadlier and more destructive. In 50 days of fighting, including intense urban combat, more than 2,250 Palestinians were killed (the majority of them civilians), 100,000 or so had their homes severely damaged or destroyed, and an estimated 500,000—over a quarter of Gaza's population—were internally displaced. On the Israeli side, 66 soldiers and 6 civilians were killed, and hundreds of thousands of Israelis had to seek safety in bomb shelters and safe rooms as Hamas fired some 4,500 rockets and mortars into Israel (the rockets also managed to briefly shut down Israel's main airport). Most of the rockets were intercepted by Israel's Iron Dome system or landed in open areas.

In these two Gaza wars, Israel largely achieved its military objectives as it degraded Hamas's military capabilities and deterred it from launching rockets for substantial periods of time (in the 2014 war, Israel also uncovered and destroyed thirty-two cross-border tunnels that Hamas had dug from Gaza into Israel). But during these periods of relative calm, Hamas has rearmed and grown stronger militarily. It has increased and upgraded its stockpile of rockets, built armed drones, recruited more fighters, dug more tunnels, and turned its militia into a well-organized, well-armed, and battle-hardened professional army. Despite the losses it incurred during Israel's recurrent offensives against it, therefore, Hamas has become a more powerful adversary. And it remains firmly in control of Gaza, despite the deprivation and suffering of its population. The fact that Hamas still controls Gaza is actually an outcome that suits Israel. Its offensives against Hamas (in 2008–2009, 2012, and 2014) were not intended to destroy the group or dislodge it from power (although some Israeli cabinet members have advocated for these goals). Israel wanted to deter Hamas and weaken it, but not weaken it so much that Hamas would be unable to maintain control over Gaza.

Israel does not want to reoccupy and rule Gaza since this would be costly, dangerous, and domestically unpopular. So instead, ironically, Israel has reluctantly come to rely on Hamas to govern Gaza, provide some stability, and police the more radical militant groups operating there. For Israel, in short, Hamas's continued rule in Gaza is its "least bad" option.

While the two wars in Gaza may well have served Israel's short-term strategic interests, and arguably Hamas's interests as well, Gaza's civilian population paid a terrible price. In total, more than two thousand Palestinian civilians were killed in these wars (just nine Israeli civilians were killed), thousands more were wounded, and hundreds of thousands were psychologically traumatized (studies have shown that children in Gaza, who make up almost half its population, suffer from particularly high rates of post-traumatic stress disorder because of the wars they have lived through). Regardless of whose fault this is—human rights groups and the UN's Human Rights Council have accused the IDF of committing war crimes in Gaza, while Israeli officials blame Hamas for launching rockets from densely populated urban areas, storing weapons in schools, and using civilians as human shields—in the eyes of many people around the world, Israel appears to be most culpable, if for no other reason than the hugely lopsided casualty ratios in these wars. International criticism, therefore, has focused more on Israel's allegedly disproportionate use of force in its military offensives in Gaza than on Hamas's indiscriminate rocket attacks against Israel. Consequently, Israel's reputation around the world, especially in Europe, has been tarnished, rather than Hamas's (which was not good to begin with given its long history of terrorism).

At the time of writing, both Hamas and Israel (or at least its risk-averse leader, Netanyahu) seem reluctant to engage in another round of costly warfare. After a brief flare-up of intense fighting in November 2018—the heaviest fighting since the 2014 war—in which Hamas fired hundreds of rockets into southern Israel (killing one person) and the IDF responded with airstrikes on Hamas targets in Gaza (leveling Hamas's television and radio stations and military intelligence headquarters), both sides quickly pulled back from the brink of war (with the help of Egyptian and UN mediation). But the latest ceasefire, like the ones preceding it, is fragile and neither side expects it to last. Whether a more durable, long-term ceasefire can be achieved depends upon Israel and Hamas reaching an agreement, through indirect negotiations, to support the economic rehabilitation of Gaza and the reconstruction of its battered infrastructure (Hamas also demands a prisoner exchange). Unfortunately, the prospects for such an agreement—and for the cycle of violence and warfare in Gaza to finally end—are slim (albeit probably better than the prospects for a peace agreement between Israel and the PLO).

CONCLUSION

THE LONG PATH TO PEACE

Is a two-state solution still possible?

A two-state solution to the century-old conflict over Palestine has been recommended for more than eight decades. The British government was the first to propose dividing the territory into two separate states—one for Jews, the other for Palestinian Arabs—back in 1937 (in the Peel Commission's report). A decade later, in 1947, the United Nations (UN) voted in favor of partitioning Palestine (Resolution 181). But while Jews achieved statehood with the establishment of the State of Israel in 1948, Palestinians did not. Instead, many of them experienced dispossession, displacement, exile, and, for the past five decades, Israeli occupation. Consequently, the creation of a Palestinian state alongside Israel has long been regarded as the best and perhaps only way to peacefully resolve the Israeli-Palestinian conflict. For a short period in the early 1990s, hopes were raised that a two-state solution was finally within reach, but the assassination of Prime Minister Yitzhak Rabin, the collapse of the Oslo peace process, and the Second Intifada dashed these hopes. Since then, as the conflict has dragged on interminably, with periodic eruptions of large-scale violence, the prospects for a two-state solution have grown dimmer.

Nowadays, few people still believe that a two-state solution is imminent, and they are often dismissed as naïve or ignorant. What once seemed inevitable now seems implausible, at least for the foreseeable future. The broad consensus that emerged in favor of a two-state solution is eroding as doubts about its feasibility are growing.

Policymakers, diplomats, and experts warn that the window of opportunity for a two-state solution is closing. Some believe that it has already closed due to the "facts on the ground," particularly the presence of ever-expanding Israeli settlements in the West Bank and East Jerusalem that now house over 650,000 settlers.

Current political trends among Israelis and Palestinians also indicate that the two-state solution is in trouble. After gradually, and generally reluctantly, accepting the necessity of a two-state solution (but not necessarily its morality), Israelis and Palestinians are now questioning it again and increasingly giving up on it. The failure to achieve a two-state solution after many years of trying has left a majority of people on both sides of the conflict disillusioned and doubtful about its prospects, largely because they have concluded that they have "no partner" to make peace with. Both sides believe the other side does not want a two-state solution, and both are almost equally divided in their opinion about whether the solution is possible (in a poll taken in December 2017, for instance, 48 percent of Israelis thought a two-state solution was possible, and just 37 percent of Palestinians in the West Bank and Gaza). Consequently, popular support for a two-state solution has been declining in Israel, the West Bank, and Gaza in recent years (after steadily rising during the 1990s and staying mostly stable during the 2000s).

Growing pessimism about the possibility of a two-state solution is, sadly, well-founded. Although it is still technically feasible, it is highly unlikely. For a two-state solution to work—that is, to peacefully resolve the conflict—it has to be mutually agreed upon, publicly accepted, and successfully implemented. It is difficult to achieve just one of these requirements, let alone all three. There are major political and logistical challenges to overcome. They are not insurmountable if there is enough political will, but they are certainly daunting.

The first challenge is to resume peace talks since there is really no substitute for them. Although the "State of Palestine" is now officially recognized by most states in the world and, since 2012, has observer status in the UN (but not full membership), it exists more on paper than in reality. To become a reality and give Palestinians actual sovereignty, Israel has to voluntarily relinquish its direct or indirect control over most of the West Bank, East Jerusalem, and the Gaza Strip. While some hope that Israel can be coerced into doing so, whether by Palestinian violence, diplomatic pressure, or the grassroots Boycott, Divestment and Sanctions (BDS) campaign against it, the strength of Israel's economy and the power of its military means that coercion alone probably won't succeed (regardless of whether or not it is justified). Even if, as seems likely, there is mounting international pressure on Israel to end its occupation of Palestinian territories, the international community is unlikely to marshal sufficient pressure to effectively force Israel to grant Palestinians what it has so far been unwilling to give them at the negotiating table—especially if the U.S. government continues to back Israel diplomatically and financially. Moreover, international pressure on Israel could easily backfire and only encourage Israeli defensiveness and defiance, as some observers believe is already happening.

A negotiated peace agreement, therefore, remains the best means to achieve a sustainable and lasting two-state solution to the conflict. But after almost three decades of diplomacy and intermittent negotiations, neither side is currently interested in engaging in serious peace talks. The American-led peace process, which first started at the 1991 Madrid Conference, has been widely discredited and disparaged. Most Israelis and Palestinians no longer believe in it. The failure of then U.S. Secretary of State John Kerry's attempt in 2013–2014 to broker a comprehensive peace agreement, or just the outline of one, only further confirmed what many people had already concluded after the previous failures of the Camp David summit, the Taba talks, and the Olmert-Abbas talks—the peace process has reached an impasse. Despite Kerry's tireless efforts as a mediator, few people expected him to succeed, not even his boss, President Barack Obama, whose optimism in the early days of his presidency about his ability to make peace between Israel and the Palestinians soon turned into frustration when faced with the recalcitrance of Israel's right-wing prime minister, Benjamin Netanyahu. Since Kerry's peace initiative ended in acrimony and recriminations, there have been no more Israeli-Palestinian peace talks. The leaders of both sides are more concerned with avoiding blame for the lack of negotiations than they are with restarting them.

Prime Minister Netanyahu, who has been in power for the past decade (since taking office for the second time in 2009), has no interest in resuming peace talks. Deeply distrustful of the Palestinians and disdainful of their leadership, he has always been at best skeptical about the peace process (in the early 1990s, he was an outspoken critic of the Oslo Accords). Since his first term as prime minister (1996–1999), Netanyahu has been a grudging participant in peace talks. Now that they have ended, he prefers to maintain the status quo rather than restart negotiations that he regards as a distraction from dealing with the pressing security threats facing Israel, primarily from Iran. Netanyahu is also no doubt well aware that since he is only prepared to allow the Palestinians to have a less-than-sovereign state—what he calls "a state-minus"—peace talks would almost certainly fail, and he could be blamed. Netanyahu also has no political incentive to resume peace talks. He was reelected in 2015 after promising voters that he would oppose the establishment of a Palestinian state, and he is under no domestic pressure to renew peace talks, as polls show that resolving the Israeli-Palestinian conflict has become a low priority for the majority of Israelis (they are more concerned with security and the economy). In fact, Netanyahu's political survival—currently threatened by numerous charges of corruption and a looming criminal indictment—depends upon avoiding negotiations with the Palestinians. After all, most of the ministers in his right-wing cabinet, along with most Knesset members of his Likud Party, oppose a two-state solution. Any apparent effort to reach one, therefore, would destabilize his fragile governing coalition—which has a majority of just one seat in the Knesset—and jeopardize Netanyahu's premiership (and possibly even his freedom). The strong, and seemingly unconditional, support for Israel, and for Netanyahu personally, displayed by President Donald Trump and his administration also relieves Netanyahu of his past concern that avoiding peace talks with the Palestinians could damage U.S.-Israeli relations and potentially weaken American support for Israel (which previously motivated him to reluctantly participate in U.S.-sponsored peace talks during the Clinton and Obama administrations). With President Trump in the Oval Office, Netanyahu feels little, if any, American pressure to negotiate with the Palestinians or make any major concessions to them (notwithstanding Trump's avowed desire to strike the "ultimate deal" between Israel and the Palestinians). On the contrary, Trump has only emboldened Netanyahu to escalate settlement construction, to allow legislative efforts to apply Israeli sovereignty over parts of the West

Bank, and to blithely disregard whatever international criticism this arouses (mostly from Europe).

Unlike Netanyahu, Palestinian Authority (PA) President Mahmoud Abbas (who is also the chairman of the Palestinian Liberation Organization [PLO]) has been committed to negotiating a two-state solution to the conflict (although some question the sincerity of Abbas's support for a two-state solution because he did not embrace then Israeli prime minister Ehud Olmert's peace proposal in 2008). Abbas has long been a staunch advocate of the peace process, but his enthusiasm for peace talks seems to have been exhausted. Aging and unwell—he is in his mid-eighties—Abbas is now preoccupied with staying in power and sidelining potential political rivals. He, too, is under no domestic pressure to resume negotiations, as most Palestinians currently reject a two-state solution and doubt it will ever happen. Like Netanyahu, Abbas also has a political incentive to avoid negotiations because much of the PLO's senior leadership and many members of his own Fatah movement, and its rival Hamas, are all opposed to peace talks with Israel, which are widely seen by Palestinians as futile and counterproductive (many Palestinians believe that U.S.-sponsored peace talks only serve as a smokescreen for Israel's ongoing colonization of the West Bank). Even if Abbas were willing to return to the negotiating table, he has no popular mandate to negotiate a peace agreement, let alone sign one. He is well past his presidential term in office (he was elected in 2005 for a four-year term that officially expired in January 2009) and his rule has become increasingly autocratic as he has steadily lost public support—in recent polls, large majorities of Palestinians in the West Bank and Gaza want him to resign. Since Abbas no longer really represents Palestinians, he lacks both the legitimacy and the credibility to engage in peace talks with Israel.

Israeli-Palestinian peace talks, therefore, are highly unlikely to resume in the near future, if at all. At a minimum, there will have to be a change in Israeli and Palestinian leadership. But whenever this eventually happens, there is no guarantee that whoever succeeds Netanyahu and Abbas will be more receptive to serious peace talks or, for that matter, more willing to compromise during them. Netanyahu could well be replaced by another right-wing prime minister, as his Likud Party continues to attract more public support than its centrist and left-wing rivals. Abbas's successor (or successors) will probably be decided by a power struggle behind-the-scenes rather than through a presidential election. Whoever wins this succession battle may not have the stature or popular support to engage in peace talks with Israel, especially if the PA and its leadership are still widely seen by Palestinians as corrupt, authoritarian, and lacking legitimacy. Moreover, as long as Gaza is governed by Hamas and politically separated from the West Bank—which is likely to remain the case at least in the short term given the failure of repeated attempts over more than a decade to reconcile Hamas and Fatah and politically reunify Gaza and the West Bank—Abbas's successor cannot authoritatively claim to speak, or negotiate, on behalf of Palestinians.

Even if the peace process is not yet dead and could somehow be resuscitated, with new leaders in Jerusalem and Ramallah, there is no reason to expect that the outcome of future peace talks would be any different than that of past rounds of negotiations. Contrary to the common refrain that "everyone knows what a peace deal looks like," the two sides have never fully agreed on any of the core issues—the future of Jerusalem, the fate of Palestinian refugees, the delineation of borders, and security arrangements. Although the broad outlines of a comprehensive peace agreement are indeed clearer, the two sides cannot agree on any of the details. Despite significant progress in previous rounds of negotiations, there are still substantive disagreements on all the core issues. The gap between the two sides has narrowed over time on some very contentious issues—such as how to resolve the refugee issue and whether Jerusalem could be divided—but other contentious issues have arisen, particularly Israel's demand to be officially recognized as a Jewish state. It is wishful thinking to expect that the remaining gaps between the two sides on these difficult final-status issues will somehow magically disappear if serious peace talks were to ever resume.

The track record of negotiations demonstrates that it is an enormous challenge for Israelis and Palestinians to reach a comprehensive peace agreement. Both sides will have to make some significant, emotionally painful, and politically unpopular compromises. For both of them to do so will probably require some kind of third-party intervention, most likely by the United States, since Israel will not accept any other external mediator. If peace talks reach a stalemate, as is likely, the United States could present its own ideas to bridge the gaps and use its substantial leverage to pressure both sides to accept them (as President Jimmy Carter successfully did during the Egyptian-Israeli peace talks at Camp David in 1978). Both Democratic and Republican administrations have been unwilling to do this in previous rounds of Israeli-Palestinian peace talks. Since Israel enjoys strong support in Congress and among Americans in general (especially among many American Jews and evangelical Christians), no U.S. administration since the George H. W. Bush administration (1989–1993) has been willing to incur the potentially high domestic political costs entailed by pressuring Israel to make far-reaching concessions to the Palestinians in peace talks. This might change in the future if the Democrats regain control of the White House—as their base is becoming more critical of Israel and more sympathetic to the Palestinians—but while President Trump is in office his administration is unlikely to act as an "honest broker" between Israel and the Palestinians (particularly given the fact that the administration's "Middle East peace team" is the president's son-in-law, Jared Kushner, and Jason Greenblatt, who are both Orthodox Jews deeply attached to Israel). Indeed, the Trump administration's heavily "pro-Israel" orientation, especially its recognition of Jerusalem as Israel's capital and its relocation of the U.S. embassy from Tel Aviv to Jerusalem (along with President Trump's repeated assertion that he has taken the issue of Jerusalem "off the table"), has infuriated and alienated the Palestinians, and led the PA to boycott the Trump administration. Abbas has defiantly declared in a speech to the UN Security Council on February 20, 2018, that the PLO will no longer accept an American monopoly on brokering a peace agreement between Israel and the Palestinians because the United States is, in his words, a "dishonest mediator."

Reaching a peace agreement for a two-state solution is clearly a massive challenge. Successfully implementing one will be even harder. A peace deal would first have to be endorsed by Israelis and Palestinians, probably in national referendums. Public approval is by no means assured, as is clear from the history of painstakingly negotiated peace treaties that have been rejected by voters at the ballot box (in Cyprus in 2004 and Colombia in 2016). Popular support for a two-state solution has been declining in recent years, with recent polling showing that only a minority of Palestinians and Israeli Jews continue to support it (most Palestinian citizens of Israel remain supportive). There is even less public support on both sides for what it might take to actually achieve a two-state solution. In a survey taken in 2018, for instance, just 37 percent of Palestinians and 39 percent of Israeli Jews supported a two-state solution that consisted of a demilitarized Palestinian state, an Israeli withdrawal to the Green Line with equal land swaps, the resettling of 100,000 Palestinian refugees in Israel under the rubric of family reunification, and a division of Jerusalem with West Jerusalem as the capital of Israel and East Jerusalem as the capital of Palestine (with the Western Wall and the Jewish Quarter in the Old City under Israeli sovereignty, and the Muslim and Christian quarters and the Haram al-Sharif under Palestinian sovereignty). The survey did, however, find that many of those opposed to a peace agreement on these terms would change their minds and support it if given certain concessions. For instance, they might support such an agreement if it also stipulated that Palestinians recognized Israel as a Jewish state, and if Israel recognized the Nakba and the suffering of Palestinian refugees and provided them with compensation. Public opinion is not fixed, and thus it is open to persuasion. It can shift with the right incentives and in response to the political atmosphere. Thus, while Israelis and Palestinians are not likely to pressure their leaders to negotiate or compromise, they are likely to support a peace agreement for a two-state solution if these leaders somehow manage to achieve one.

While most Israelis and Palestinians could probably be persuaded to vote in favor of a peace agreement in referendums, a sizable minority (roughly a third) on both sides can be expected to reject any agreement involving a territorial compromise. On both sides, the most dogmatic of these rejectionists are religious extremists, specifically, hardline religious Zionists and Palestinian Islamists who sanctify the land, claim exclusive possession of it, and believe that their religion forbids them from ever ceding ownership over any part of it. Since the holy status of the land means that it cannot be traded away or partitioned, according to this view, any kind of two-state solution is illegitimate and unacceptable. By no means do all religious Zionists and Palestinian Islamists hold such hardline views, but those that do have already demonstrated that they are willing and able to disrupt efforts to make peace (such as when they acted as "spoilers" during the Oslo peace process). It is highly likely, therefore, that they will attempt to obstruct the implementation of a two-state solution, possibly by any means necessary, including violence.

On the Israeli side, the stiffest resistance to a two-state solution is likely to come from among the minority of ideological settlers who live beyond Israel's barrier in the West Bank. The vast majority of Israeli settlers—approximately 85 percent—are concentrated in large blocs of settlements located near the Green Line behind the Israeli side of the barrier. Since a peace agreement will probably allow Israel to annex these large settlement blocs (in exchange for an equal amount of Israeli land), the majority of settlers would not have to move (most would actually be willing to move if they had to, as long as they were financially compensated). The roughly 100,000 settlers (or approximately 27,000 families) who live in smaller, more remote settlements and outposts in the heart of the West Bank are those who will probably have to be relocated. These settlers, many of them children and grandchildren of settlers, tend to be followers of messianic religious Zionism, seeing themselves as agents of divine redemption. The most fanatical among them, typically youth, reject the authority of the Israeli state and disregard its laws. These radical settlers will surely oppose any Israeli government effort to relocate them, and they will fiercely resist, perhaps violently, any attempt to evacuate them and dismantle their settlements. Although they are relatively small in number—no more than 20,000 settlers out of a total West Bank settler population of around 430,000—their potential for violent resistance has previously intimidated Israeli governments from acting against them, and it could well deter a future government from forcibly relocating them if need be. Compounding this threat is the question of what Israeli soldiers—a growing proportion of whom are religious Zionist settlers (especially in the IDF's combat units and positions of command)—might do if they are ordered to forcefully remove settlers. Will they obey their orders or will they instead follow the rulings of some far-right rabbis that instruct religious Israeli soldiers to refuse to comply with such orders? However slim, the possibility of a mutiny in the IDF in the event of an Israeli withdrawal from most of the West Bank cannot be ruled out.

To be sure, the IDF successfully removed all of the eight thousand or so settlers from Gaza in just five days (during August 17–22,

2005). Most of the Gaza settlers adamantly refused to leave their homes and had to be forcibly evicted, and some radical West Bank settlers went to Gaza to resist the evacuation. But despite widespread fears of violent resistance, the evacuation went quite smoothly— notwithstanding the disturbing scenes of distraught settlers being dragged kicking and screaming from their homes—and not a single shot was fired. Some soldiers did refuse to participate, but there was no mutiny, let alone the civil war that some had feared. The removal of the Gaza settlers demonstrates that an evacuation can be done, but it took more than forty thousand Israeli soldiers to do it and cost the Israeli government approximately $3 billion. Israel would need to evacuate at least ten times as many settlers from the West Bank (which is an area of much greater Jewish religious significance than Gaza). Theoretically, an Israeli government has the ability to do this—although it would be extremely costly in terms of money and manpower—but whether any future government, even a center-left one, would be willing to undertake such a huge and risky operation is very much open to question.

While Israel will have to contend with the challenge of religious extremists refusing to leave their settlements deep inside the West Bank, the PA will face an even greater challenge from religious extremists, principally from hardliners within Hamas. Although Israelis and many Westerners view Hamas as an extremist terrorist group dedicated to killing Israelis and destroying the Jewish state, many experts on the movement have argued that it is not as dogmatic as it is often depicted to be, and that its views have evolved over the years and become less extreme than those presented in its 1988 founding charter (which, in an antisemitic manner, portrayed the Israeli-Palestinian conflict as part of a broader, age-old religious battle between Muslims and Jews, and called upon Muslims everywhere to wage a violent jihad to destroy the "Zionist entity" occupying sacred Islamic land). According to this view, Hamas is no longer committed to the destruction of Israel and the creation of an Islamic state in all of the territory of historic Palestine (that has supposedly become more of a utopian ideal for Hamas rather than an actual long-term goal). Although Hamas still rejects the Oslo Accords and staunchly opposes any formal recognition of Israel (on theological and ideological grounds), its leaders, despite their fiery public rhetoric, have repeatedly expressed a willingness to accept a long-term *hudna* (an Islamic term for a truce for a specific period of time) with Israel. They have even indicated they might be prepared to accept a Palestinian state in just Gaza and the West Bank, with Jerusalem as its capital, as part of a "national consensus" among Palestinians (this position was presented in the new policy document, or political manifesto, that Hamas published in 2017, after four years of internal deliberations and debate).

Even if Hamas has become more moderate—which is certainly debatable—it is still a major obstacle in the way of a two-state solution. Although it is not necessary for Hamas itself to endorse a two-state solution (after all, there are political parties in Israel, most notably Likud, that also officially oppose a two-state solution), it is essential for Hamas to abide by one. The crucial question, then, is whether Hamas will try to obstruct the implementation of a two-state peace deal? Hamas's leadership has said that the group will abide by any peace agreement that Palestinians endorse in a referendum, but since they want all Palestinians to have a vote, including those in the diaspora, this condition would be difficult if not impossible to satisfy. If a peace agreement was only approved by Palestinians in the West Bank, Gaza, and East Jerusalem, but it received overwhelming public support, then Hamas might still reluctantly respect their will if only because it would risk facing a popular backlash if it tried to torpedo such an agreement. There is, however, a limit to how far Hamas will defer to any Palestinian consensus supporting a peace agreement with Israel. If a peace agreement required Hamas to dissolve its military wing and give up its weapons (Israel will insist on this because allowing Hamas to keep its weapons poses too much of a threat to Israel, especially once Hamas gains access to the West Bank), then it is almost certain to refuse. Its leadership has unequivocally stated on many occasions that Hamas will never disarm. And even if its more moderate leaders were perhaps open to this, under certain circumstances, they would balk at disarming simply because of the internal opposition they will surely face, and the likelihood that it would create a schism within Hamas and lead to the emergence of more militant splinter groups. For its own sake, therefore, Hamas will not agree to disarm. Nor will the PA be strong enough to forcefully disarm Hamas by itself. Hamas's fighters routed the American-trained PA security forces in the "Battle of Gaza" in 2007, and its military wing has only grown bigger, stronger, and more battle-hardened since then (having fought against the IDF in two wars, in 2008–2009 and 2014). To disarm Hamas and implement a two-state solution, the PA would probably have to be assisted by a large U.S. or NATO-led peacekeeping force with a robust mandate (Israel would object to UN peacekeepers, particularly given their failure to disarm Hezbollah in southern Lebanon). This is not completely inconceivable, but like almost every other necessary condition to achieve a two-state solution, it is highly improbable. Indeed, more likely than being disarmed is that Hamas will fulfill its ambition to take over the PA in the West Bank in the post-Abbas era. If that happens, then the already remote possibility of a two-state solution will disappear entirely.

Is a one-state solution possible?

As hopes for a two-state solution recede, interest in a one-state solution has grown. The idea itself has been around for a long time. In the 1920s, when the conflict between Zionists and Palestinian nationalists was just emerging and becoming increasingly violent, the British administration in Mandate Palestine tried unsuccessfully to advance a one-state solution by proposing power-sharing arrangements between the Arab majority and the Jewish minority at the time. During the early years of the conflict, Zionists (who were then the weaker side) also proposed various one-state arrangements. A small group of prominent Jewish intellectuals (including the philosopher Martin Buber) formed a group called *Brit Shalom* ("Alliance for Peace") that advocated for a binational Jewish-Arab state. The socialist Zionist movement, *Hashomer Hatzair* ("The Young Guard"), also supported this. Even David Ben Gurion, the Labor Zionist leader who went on to become Israel's first prime minister, at one point suggested a binational, federal state as a potential solution to the conflict (this was also the recommendation of the minority of the UN committee whose majority recommended partition in 1947). None of these proposals got anywhere, however, largely because the Palestinian leadership at the time was unwilling to accept a state in which the Arab majority would have to share power with a small Jewish minority. After Israel's establishment in 1948, only a small number of Israelis on the far-left continued to support binationalism and a one-state solution to the conflict. This remains the case today.

Palestinian support for a one-state solution has ebbed and flowed over the seven decades since their defeat in the war of 1947-1949. When the PLO was founded in 1965, its original goal was a single, democratic, and secular state in all of historic Palestine. It advocated this through the 1970s and into the 1980s (two of the PLO's smaller factions, the Democratic and Popular Fronts for the Liberation of Palestine, still do). The PLO officially abandoned a one-state solution and accepted a two-state solution in 1988. Most Palestinians in the West Bank and Gaza also came to accept a two-state solution, especially after the signing of the Oslo Accords in the early 1990s raised their expectations that a Palestinian state would soon be established. But as the peace process stalled and then broke down, and Israeli settlements continued to expand, Palestinian intellectuals, academics, and activists, many of them living in the diaspora (most notably, the late Edward Said), have renewed calls for a one-state solution. For some of its Palestinian advocates, a one-state solution was always preferable to a two-state solution because they believed the latter would not deliver justice for Palestinians. A two-state solution would not enable all Palestinian refugees to realize their "right of return" or reclaim their lost land and property (since Israel would never accept this). Nor would it end discrimination against Israel's Palestinian citizens, and could make matters worse for them by reinforcing ethnic separatism. A one-state solution, on the other hand, could potentially satisfy the needs and aspirations of all Palestinians, not just those living in the West Bank and Gaza. Hence, it has long been seen by some Palestinians, and by some of their supporters, as the most just solution to the conflict. For other Palestinian proponents of a one-state solution, it is simply the only remaining solution because they have lost hope for the establishment of a viable, contiguous, and sovereign Palestinian state alongside Israel. Convinced that a two-state solution is dead—and that Israel killed it—they argue that Palestinians should give up their futile struggle for national self-determination, and strategically shift to a struggle for citizenship and equality (for the same reason, some left-wing Israeli-Jewish peace activists also advocate this).

Until recently, intellectuals and academics mostly made calls for a one-state solution to the conflict, and they were generally ignored, dismissed, or derided. This is no longer true. Nowadays, this old idea is attracting much more attention and receiving serious consideration (in fact, the PLO has even been reconsidering a one-state solution—though this may only be a tactic to pressure the Israeli government into advancing a two-state solution). Its main appeal lies in the fact that it acknowledges that there is already one state—Israel—effectively in control of the entire territory between the Mediterranean and the Jordan River. Instead of trying to change this existing "one-state reality" by creating a separate, mini-state for Palestinians, to many it seems much easier to give all Palestinians living under Israel's de facto rule (specifically, those in the West Bank, East Jerusalem, and Gaza) the same rights as Israeli citizens, particularly the right to vote in Israel's national elections. A one-state solution, in other words, could be peacefully achieved through granting citizenship, equal rights, and democratic representation to everyone living under Israeli sovereignty. A peace agreement, which has proven to be so elusive, will not be necessary in this scenario. Israelis and Palestinians will not have to divide Jerusalem, delineate borders, or deal with many other complex and thorny issues that have bedeviled negotiations for a two-state solution. They just have to accept the basic democratic principle of "one person, one vote."

To bring this about, advocates for a one-state solution suggest that Palestinians mount a peaceful civil rights campaign, modeled after the successful civil rights movement in the United States (doing so, it is often claimed, will also generate more support from the American public and make it harder, if not impossible, for the U.S. government to unconditionally back Israel). To assist this campaign and apply increasing pressure upon Israel to enfranchise its Palestinian subjects and fully democratize, allies of the Palestinians around the world are frequently encouraged to adopt the same tactics used by the Anti-Apartheid movement from the 1960s to the 1980s (boycotts, divestment, and sanctions) that helped eventually topple the apartheid regime in South Africa.

While achieving a one-state solution might sound, in theory, relatively straightforward and attainable, compared with a two-state solution—and, for some, much more desirable—in reality, it is even less feasible. It is based upon wishful thinking, rather than a sober assessment of the facts, and it draws upon a false analogy between Israel and Apartheid South Africa. The two cases are, in fact, quite different for a variety of reasons, not least because of the simple fact that blacks formed the overwhelming majority of South

Africa's population throughout nine decades of exclusive white rule, whereas there has only recently been an equal number of Jews and Palestinians living under Israel's direct or indirect control (both sides now number roughly 6.5 million in the area encompassing Israel, the West Bank, and Gaza). There is also much stronger international support for Israel's existence (particularly because of the Holocaust) than there ever was for Apartheid South Africa. Even there it took more than eighty years of struggle against apartheid to finally achieve a democratic nonracial South Africa (from the creation of the African National Congress in 1912 to the first free election in 1994), not to mention the transformational leadership of Nelson Mandela. And, despite this monumental achievement, postapartheid South Africa is still deeply racially divided (just not segregated), with persistent, massive inequality between the impoverished black majority and the affluent and privileged white minority. Equal citizenship, therefore, is no panacea.

The biggest problem with a one-state solution to the conflict between Israelis and Palestinians is that neither of them supports it. Most Israelis and Palestinians do not want to live together in a single state. In public opinion polls, large majorities on both sides consistently oppose the idea of a one-state solution in which Palestinians and Israeli Jews will have citizenship and equal rights (only a slight majority of Palestinian citizens of Israel support this). However alluring this idea sounds to many Westerners, it has little popular appeal among Palestinians and Israeli Jews because it conflicts with their national aspirations. They both want their own states in order to fulfill their collective desires for national self-determination. There is, however, growing support for a one-state solution among a younger generation of Palestinians in the West Bank and Gaza, many of whom are politically alienated from the Palestinian leadership (both Fatah and Hamas), economically and socially frustrated due to a lack of suitable employment opportunities, and disillusioned with the idea of Palestinian statehood because they expect a future Palestinian state will be corrupt and authoritarian (like the PA). Roughly a third of the Palestinian population in the West Bank and Gaza is between the ages of 15 to 29, so if this trend continues and more and more young Palestinians embrace a one-state solution, then the Palestinian public as a whole will gradually become more supportive of it.

But it is extremely unlikely that the Israeli-Jewish public will ever support a one-state solution, at least not a genuinely democratic one. A democratic one-state solution will not necessarily prevent Palestinians from exercising their right to national self-determination since they will eventually make up the majority of the population (given their higher birth rates). Israeli Jews, by contrast, will become a minority, whose rights and security will be dependent upon the will of the Palestinian majority. The millennia-long history of Jewish persecution, the century-long history of the Arab-Jewish conflict, and recent Middle Eastern history all give Israeli Jews ample reason to fear such a scenario. Indeed, for the vast majority of them, the whole point of Zionism was to give Jews a state of their own in which they could live safely and be masters of their fate. Having secured Jewish sovereignty, at great cost, Israeli Jews are not going to voluntarily give it up, and put themselves at the mercy of Palestinians whom they fear and distrust. As far as they are concerned, accepting a democratic one-state solution is tantamount to national suicide. Not only would it spell the end of Israel as a Jewish state and quickly turn them into a vulnerable minority, it would also jeopardize the material and cultural benefits they currently enjoy by virtue of their privileged status in Israel. It is inconceivable that Israeli Jews will accept this, even under intense international pressure.

Nor will any Israeli leader agree to a democratic one-state solution. The only kind of one-state outcome favored by some Israeli policymakers is one in which Israel's Jewish character is preserved by denying full citizenship and/or equal rights to Palestinians in the West Bank, or even forcing many of them to move to neighboring Arab states (Jordan, in particular). In recent years, some members of Israel's current right-wing government have been advocating various undemocratic one-state "solutions," most notably Education Minister Naftali Bennett, head of the far-right, settler-backed, Jewish Home party, who has proposed that Israel annex most of the West Bank and grant citizenship to the Palestinians living there, but bar them from voting in Israeli general elections. It goes without saying that West Bank Palestinians will never agree to live in such a "Greater Israel" in which they are permanently disenfranchised (just as Israeli Jews will never agree to live in a "Greater Palestine" under Muslim-Arab rule—as envisioned by Hamas).

To be even remotely feasible, a one-state solution has to be, at the very least, democratic, whether it takes the form of a unitary state that treats all citizens equally (regardless of their race, ethnicity, or religion), or a binational state that officially recognizes two nations, provides them with some collective rights, and enables them to share power. Both of these options are improbable, but even in the unlikely event that a single democratic state is established it is highly doubtful that this will suffice to resolve the conflict between Palestinians and Israeli Jews. It is simply wishful thinking to believe that, after a century of bitter conflict, they will suddenly overcome their enmity and be able to peacefully coexist. Their mutual hostility and distrust has accumulated over decades and become deeply rooted. It cannot be ignored, as some idealistic supporters of a one-state solution tend to do. Even peaceful Western liberal democracies have been destabilized in recent years by resurgent ethno-nationalism, and secessionist movements have threatened the integrity of multinational states like Spain and the United Kingdom. Ethnic nationalism is not waning—as many once optimistically believed it would in an age of globalization—but strengthening. So too, is religious sectarianism, which has been violently tearing apart Syria, Iraq, and Yemen (to name just the worst recent cases). These powerful social forces would make it difficult, if not impossible, to ensure a peaceful and stable one-state solution to the Israeli-Palestinian conflict. There would undoubtedly be a high risk of ethno-religious violence, and even ethnic cleansing (along the lines of what happened in Bosnia and Kosovo in the 1990s). At best, there would be constant tension between Jewish and Palestinian citizens—as there already is in Israel (where Palestinians only constitute about 20 percent of its citizens)—and a relentless contest for political power and control over the state. This competition would be exacerbated by the fact that, unless there was a major redistribution of wealth and resources, most Palestinians would be much poorer than Jews, given the huge economic gap between Israelis and Palestinians in the West Bank and Gaza (Israel's GDP per capita is around $37,000, whereas the GDP per capita of the West Bank and Gaza is under $3,000).

A one-state solution, therefore, is not a realistic prescription for resolving the Israeli-Palestinian conflict—it is a liberal utopian dream, and a dream of religious and nationalist extremists on both sides of the conflict. In practice, it won't be a solution at all. Instead, it is a recipe for political paralysis, instability, oppression, continued conflict, and potentially civil war and ethnic cleansing. Despite these dangers, a "one-state outcome," as opposed to a one-state solution, is a real possibility. Indeed, given the demise of the two-state solution and Israel's creeping de facto annexation of the West Bank (which is starting to become de jure), we are already on a slippery slope toward a one-state outcome with a Jewish minority ruling over a largely disenfranchised Palestinian majority. This situation—which is not far away—would resemble Apartheid South Africa (as Israel's former prime ministers and failed peacemakers, Barak and Olmert, have publicly warned).

If neither solution is possible, then how can the conflict be resolved or at least reduced?

Contrary to the prevailing pessimism about the possibility for peace between Israelis and Palestinians, I believe that their long and seemingly intractable conflict can peacefully end, but it will take some time. Many creative ways to resolve the conflict have been proposed in recent years as alternatives to the conventional two-state and one-state solutions. The most promising combines elements of both solutions. It envisages two sovereign states, Israel and Palestine, who are part of a "confederation" (like the member states of the European Union). This would entail joint governance in some areas (such as managing the environment and shared natural resources like water), and extensive cooperation on certain issues of mutual concern (like security and economic matters). After a transitional period, the two states would have an open border between them, providing freedom of movement for their populations that would enable people in both states to come and go (whether for work, studying, socializing, shopping, or praying at their holy sites). It also envisions a united, not divided, Jerusalem as the shared capital of both states, with its municipal affairs run by a joint Israeli-Palestinian authority representing and serving all of the city's residents, and its holy sites managed by religious authorities and international bodies to guarantee access for all.

To some extent, this confederal approach to resolving the conflict is an updated version of the two-state solution put forward in the

UN's 1947 partition plan, which proposed a Jewish state and an Arab state with an economic union between them, and placed Jerusalem (and its holy sites) under international control. But it significantly differs from the two-state solution that the peace process has long sought, and that most people have in mind, which envisages a clear separation between Israelis and Palestinians. Instead of seeking separation, a confederal approach promotes interaction and integration, but in a mutually agreed-upon and gradual fashion—unlike a one-state solution that compels the two sides to cohabit and share power. In other words, the conventional two-state solution proposes a divorce (and a division of assets) between Israelis and Palestinians, a one-state solution proposes an arranged marriage (or even a forced one), and a confederal solution suggests they cohabit and form more of a partnership between housemates. Another important distinction between this approach and the conventional two-state and one-state solutions is the delinking of citizenship and residency. In a confederation, each state would have its own citizenship policies (including laws of return), but citizens of one state could be permitted to live as residents in the other (much like citizens within the EU), with each state setting limits on the number of noncitizens granted residency. Thus, Israeli citizens would be able to live in Palestine, and Palestinian citizens could live in Israel. In both cases they would be residents, but not citizens (Palestinian citizens of Israel would keep their Israeli citizenship, but could perhaps, if they wished, have dual citizenship). Delinking citizenship and residency could help resolve two of the biggest issues that have bedeviled peace talks, and made a two-state solution so hard to achieve: the Palestinians' insistence on a "right of return" for their refugees that would allow some of them to move to Israel if they wished; and Israel's reluctance to remove large numbers of Jewish settlers from the West Bank, especially those who are most determined to stay. In a confederation, if Palestinian refugees want to live in Israel, they could do so as residents while exercising their full citizenship rights, such as voting in national elections, in Palestine. This would alleviate Israeli Jewish fears that they would be swamped by "returning" Palestinian refugees whose numbers would give them an ability to simply vote the Jewish state out of existence. Similarly, if Jewish settlers want to stay in the West Bank, they could do so as residents of a Palestinian state, as long as they are law-abiding and peaceful.

A confederal solution offers a way to overcome some major obstacles—concerning Jerusalem, Palestinian refugees, and Jewish settlers—that stand in the way of a two-state solution. But also, by proposing joint institutions to facilitate ongoing cooperation between the two states, especially concerning their security and economic development, a confederal solution is more likely to ensure that a future Palestinian state is prosperous and stable, whereas there is a serious risk that it could become a failed state if simply left to fend for itself under a conventional two-state solution. A confederal solution will also be fairer and more democratic than any likely one-state outcome. Though it may seem far-fetched, in some respects a confederal solution is actually a more realistic approach to resolving the conflict than either of the main options (i.e., two-state or one-state solutions). Unlike a two-state solution, the confederal approach accepts the unavoidable fact that Israelis and Palestinians have become too intermingled and too interdependent to completely separate from each other, however much they wish to. For example, Israelis and Palestinians share natural resources and a common ecosystem, and their economies and infrastructure are intermeshed. A confederal solution also acknowledges both parties' national, cultural, and religious attachments to the entire territory of historic Palestine/the Land of Israel and provides both with complete access to it. And, unlike a one-state solution, it accommodates the collective desires of Palestinians and Israeli Jews for national self-determination and allows them both to express their own, distinct national identities.

Of course, like any proposed solution to the conflict, a confederal solution has some serious challenges. For instance, how will a shared Jerusalem be governed effectively and efficiently, and how can security be ensured with an open border between the states and freedom of movement? While most Palestinians would probably favor an open border, security-minded Israelis would be wary given their well-founded fear of Palestinian terrorism. Many Israeli Jews would also probably oppose Palestinian refugees coming to Israel even as noncitizen residents. Palestinians, for their part, are likely to strongly object to any Jewish settlers staying in Palestine, and such settlers could be vulnerable to attack or could themselves carry out attacks. Notwithstanding these challenges, a confederal solution might work. But it needs to be fleshed-out because it is currently more of a vague vision of a future solution than a detailed blueprint. And though a confederal solution is an attractive, and reasonably credible, vision, it is still a distant prospect. Most Palestinians and Israelis know little, if anything, about it; and when asked in recent surveys, only a minority supports the idea of a confederation (in 2018, roughly one-third of Palestinians and Israeli Jews expressed support for it, including a solid majority of Palestinian citizens of Israel). A confederal solution is, however, beginning to arouse popular interest and slowly gaining traction, largely due to the efforts of local peace activists (Palestinian and Israeli, including some settlers) who have formed a new grassroots movement called "Two States, One Homeland" to advocate for it. A confederal solution to the conflict has also received some high-profile public endorsements, most notably from Israel's President Reuven "Ruby" Rivlin (who was for many years an outspoken advocate of a one-state solution), as well as from the former deputy foreign minister and minister of justice, Yossi Beilin (who was one of the architects of the Oslo Accords and a longtime proponent of a two-state solution). No prominent Palestinian politician has publicly embraced a confederal solution yet, but this can be expected if Palestinian public support for a two-state solution continues to decline and a one-state solution remains unpopular.

In order for a confederal solution—or any solution for that matter—to be acceptable to both sides, and actually succeed in bringing peace, public attitudes and perceptions on both sides need to change, and more positive connections need to develop between Israelis and Palestinians. The socio-psychological climate—currently marked by high levels of mutual hostility, fear, suspicion, and prejudice along with mutually exclusive feelings of victimhood—must dramatically improve. This can happen, but it takes time and effort. It requires long-term "peacebuilding," involving a wide range of civil society activities designed to promote communication, cooperation, and reconciliation between Israelis and Palestinians. Peacebuilding is often a prerequisite for successful peacemaking, especially in long-running conflicts, because peace is difficult, if not impossible, to achieve in an atmosphere in which two societies deeply distrust and fear each other. Peacebuilding can reduce mutual suspicion and fear by fostering greater understanding, empathy, and trust. In doing so, it can enlarge the constituency for peace on both sides of a conflict and help ensure that a peace process or peace agreement succeeds. The peace process in Northern Ireland, for example, succeeded partly because well-funded peacebuilding projects bringing members of the Protestant and Catholic communities together were taking place years before the signing of the Good Friday Agreement in 1998.

For nearly two decades now (since the outbreak of the Second Intifada), most Israelis have had little, if any, personal interaction with Palestinians in the West Bank and Gaza (and not much with Palestinian citizens of Israel), and most Palestinians there have only interacted with Israeli soldiers and settlers, often at gunpoint. This lack of normal interaction between Israelis and Palestinians has bred misperceptions and mistrust and fed fear and hostility. To change this, Palestinians and Israelis need to regularly meet—whether in person or online—interact, talk, and become better acquainted with each other. This won't immediately dispel their distrust and fear or magically ameliorate the many factors that fuel their hostility. Nor will it necessarily subvert their clashing narratives and perspectives about the conflict, which have become deeply entrenched. But more personal interaction can undoubtedly promote more understanding and less prejudice, which is essential for any kind of lasting peace between the two peoples. These interactions are already happening on a small scale through more than a hundred peacebuilding projects currently engaging Israelis and Palestinians. Many are dialogue and encounter programs, often involving women and youth, but a growing number of initiatives focus on joint activities addressing shared interests and concerns like economic development and environmental protection. Although they receive little attention and money (especially since the Trump administration stopped U.S. funding for them), such "people-to-people" projects can have a potentially transformative impact, not only on the lives of those Israelis and Palestinians who participate in them but also, ultimately, on the Israeli-Palestinian conflict itself if it is no longer widely seen in a zero-sum manner.

"Bottom-up" peacebuilding between Israelis and Palestinians is absolutely necessary, but it is not sufficient. It should be accompanied by "top-down" measures by political leaders on both sides to improve conditions on the ground in the West Bank and Gaza and to restore a sense of hope that the conflict can, in fact, peacefully end—a hope that is sorely lacking in the current environment. As the "occupying power" in the West Bank and, arguably, Gaza, and the stronger party in the conflict, Israel can unilaterally take actions to reduce the conflict and reverse its occupation instead of just trying to manage the conflict (as the current government has been doing). There are many things that Israel can do by itself to improve relations with the Palestinians, reduce friction between Jews and Palestinians in the West Bank, and ameliorate the circumstances of Palestinians in the West Bank and Gaza. Although Israel's unilateral withdrawal from Gaza in 2005 has, understandably, given unilateralism a bad reputation, it can be done in a more constructive way. For instance, in coordination with the PA, Israel could unilaterally withdraw from parts of the West Bank and evacuate remote settlements located well beyond the West Bank barrier (centrist and center-left Israeli politicians have been advocating that Israel remove some of its settlers from the West Bank while keeping a limited IDF presence there). If Israelis will not support another unilateral withdrawal, the Israeli government can still encourage the residents of such outlying settlements to gradually leave by cutting its subsidies to them and financially compensating them if they voluntarily relocate. More broadly, Israel could freeze settlement construction, at least in the West Bank, since this would help allay Palestinian (and international) concerns that Israel intends to annex the West Bank, and build trust with the Palestinians. Israel could also transfer more of the West Bank to PA control. In addition to increasing the territory under the PA's jurisdiction, Israel could even boost the PA's power and legitimacy by officially recognizing it as the government of the State of Palestine (whose final borders will be subject to negotiation).

With regard to Gaza (governed by Hamas), Israel could greatly improve the living conditions of Palestinians there by ending, or just significantly easing, its ongoing blockade, which has hurt Gaza's nearly two million residents much more than it has hurt Hamas. By allowing greater mobility of people and goods into and out of Gaza, Israel could help alleviate the poverty, misery, and despair of Gazans, which will otherwise inevitably result in more unrest and violence. This likelihood was recently demonstrated by the "Great March of Return" weekly protests that began on March 30, 2018, with thousands and at times tens of thousands of Gazans protesting at the fence with Israel, during which more than two hundred civilians (mostly unarmed) were killed and nineteen thousand injured by the Israeli army. If Israel is unwilling to open its border crossings with Gaza, it could allow Gaza to have an offshore seaport from which goods could be imported and exported and Gazans could travel abroad by ferry (even some right-wing Israeli politicians have recently recommended this proposal). Israel can also encourage international investment in Gaza, especially for projects to replace or repair its deteriorating infrastructure. Israeli officials have already sought, with the assistance of the Trump administration, international financing for desalination plants, a gas pipeline, and economic projects in Gaza, but nothing has yet materialized, despite the international community's apparent readiness to pay for a solution to Gaza's economic and humanitarian crisis.

These are just some of the measures Israel can undertake to change the current situation for the better. They should not be construed as "concessions" to the Palestinians, because they are in the interests of both sides. Maintaining the status quo in the West Bank and Gaza is not in either side's best interests, although Israelis are much more comfortable with it than Palestinians. Nowadays, many Israelis rarely even think about their conflict with the Palestinians unless there is a surge of violence, and finding a peaceful solution to the conflict no longer dominates the Israeli national agenda as it once did (in fact, it's barely on the agenda at all). But the status quo is bad not only for Palestinians but also for Israelis, because it leads to frequent outbreaks of violence, undermines Israel's international standing, and threatens Israel's future as a Jewish state. The status quo also threatens Israeli democracy, because indefinitely maintaining a military occupation that denies millions of Palestinians their civil rights, and often violates their human rights, is contrary to democratic principles and values, and fuels illiberalism, chauvinism, and racism inside Israel. The status quo, therefore, is neither morally acceptable nor politically tenable for Israel in the long run.

While the onus is on Israel's government to improve conditions for all Palestinians living under its direct or indirect control—and, at least, to begin to dismantle that control—the fractured political leadership of the Palestinians is also responsible for addressing the needs and concerns of Palestinians, at least those in the West Bank and Gaza. To do so, Fatah and Hamas must find a way to reconcile (probably by forming a unity government), and the Palestinian polity must be reunited. Their constant power struggle has split the West Bank from Gaza, divided Palestinians, and made it easier for the Israeli government to stick with the status quo. Palestinians in the West Bank and Gaza want to live under a single Palestinian government, and it is essential for any future solution to the Israeli-Palestinian conflict that such a government control its territory and all Palestinian forces within it. The PA must also hold free and fair elections, increase its accountability and transparency, and tolerate domestic dissent because Palestinians also want to live in a democracy. This, too, is necessary for any solution to the conflict to be sustainable, although in the short term a more democratic PA might not continue its security cooperation with Israel (as it is widely unpopular among Palestinians) increasing the risk of violence, which both sides need to prevent by working together. The PA, in short, should get its own house in order so that Palestinians can enjoy more freedom and prosperity—even before an overall settlement of the conflict—and so that the cause of peace can be advanced.

While I am convinced this is all possible, I am not optimistic about any of it occurring in the near future. Sadly, conflict, occupation, and violence look likely to continue, and peace seems a distant, if not disappearing, prospect.

INDEX

Dreyfus affair (1890s) in, 38–39, 40–41
emancipation of Jews (1791) in, 38–39
First Lebanon War and, 100
immigration of Jews from tsarist
    Russia to, 31–32
imperialism in the Middle East
    and, 12–13
Israel and, 77–78
Jewish population in, 35–36
Sinai War (1956) and, 64, 77–78
Sykes-Picot agreement (1916),
    26–27, 48
Syria occupied (1920) by, 54–55
Free Gaza Movement, 203
Free Officers coup (Egypt, 1952), 67–68,
    77, 91–92
Friedman, David, 182

Gaza Strip
    Arab-Israeli War (1967) and Israel's
        capture of, 1–2, 14, 81, 83, 86–87,
        90–91, 156–57
    Battle of Gaza (2007) and, 192,
        195–96, 222–23
    blockade of, 159–60, 196–97, 198–202,
        203, 206–8, 234–35
    borders of a potential Palestinian
        state and, 143
    British era of control (1917-48) in, 203–4
    Camp David Accords (1978) and,
        111, 118
    Camp David Summit (2000) and
        status of, 128–30
    civil liberties restrictions in, 86–87
    economic conditions in, 197–98,
        201–2, 203–4
    Egypt's border with, 196, 200–2
    Egypt's control (1949-67) of, 70, 77,
        156–57, 203–4
    electrified fence surrounding, 167–68
    Fatah Party and, 200, 202
    First Intifada (1987-93) and, 120, 123,
        197–98, 203–4
    Free Gaza Movement and, 203
    Gaza Flotilla and, 203
    Hamas and, 121, 145–46, 157–58, 159–
        60, 184, 189, 190, 191–92, 193–203,
        204–11, 216–17, 234–35

Hamas's Islamist rivals in, 206–7
Israel-Hamas fighting and cease-fire
    (2018) in, 210–11
Israel's disengagement (2005) from,
    145–46, 157–58, 159–60, 173–74,
    184–90, 193–94, 220–21
as "occupied territory" under
    international law, 155–59
one-state solution and, 224–25, 226
Operation Cast Lead (2008-9) in,
    64, 65–66, 159–60, 198, 204–5,
    208–10, 222–23
Operation Pillar of Defense (2012) in,
    198, 208–10
Operation Protective Edge (2014)
    in, 64, 65–66, 159–60, 198, 204–5,
    208–10, 222–23
Oslo Accords and, 115–16, 117,
    119, 124–25
Palestine Liberation Organization
    and, 119–20, 121–22
Palestinian Authority and, 115–16,
    118, 124, 160–61, 187–88, 197, 199–
    200, 202, 203–4
Palestinian Christians in, 15
Palestinian nationalism and,
    86–87, 103–4
Palestinian refugee population in,
    70–71, 138
Palestinians' lives under Hamas rule
    in, 197–202, 203, 204–5, 210
peace process and, 126–27, 130–31
permit system in, 163–64
rocket attacks on Israel launched
    from, 25–26, 184, 189, 204–11
Second Intifada and, 187–88,
    197–98, 205
settlements established by Israeli
    Jews in, 89–91, 115–16, 173–75,
    187–88, 220–21
size of, 25, 26
tunnel network and underground
    economy in, 198–99, 200–2
Gemayel, Bashir, 100
Geneva Conference (1973), 94–95, 106,
    107–8, 113–14
Geneva Convention (1949), 156,
    158, 179–80